The Cheater's Guide
to Baseball

The Cheater's Guide to Baseball

Derek Zumsteg

Houghton Mifflin Company

Boston · New York 2007

For information about permission to reproduce selections from
this book, write to Permissions, Houghton Mifflin Company,
215 Park Avenue South, New York, New York 10003.

Visit our Web site: www.houghtonmifflinbooks.com.

Library of Congress Cataloging-in-Publication Data
Zumsteg, Derek.
The cheater's guide to baseball / Derek Zumsteg.
p. cm.
Includes bibliographical references and index.
ISBN-13: 978-0-618-55113-2
ISBN-10: 0-618-55113-1
1. Baseball — Corrupt practices — United States
— History. I. Title.
GV863.A1Z86 2007 796.357—dc22 2006033837

Printed in the United States of America

Book design by Robert Overholtzer
Line drawings by Triple Play Design

MP 10 9 8 7 6 5 4 3 2 1

Text from the *Official Rules of Major League Baseball 2005,*
copyright © 2004, reprinted by permission of Triumph Books, Inc.

To JILL, of course

To MY PARENTS, for taking me
to see Gaylord Perry back in 1982.
I do remember that stuff.

Contents

help her back up. For a long period in the late nineteenth and early twentieth centuries, there was no trick so dirty that it didn't occur to someone. Whole stadiums colluded on elaborate cheating schemes. Visiting teams were lucky to win and luckier still if they could get out of town before the locals caught up to them.

The will of the players fueled the rough play. For much of baseball's history, nearly every player was on a year-to-year deal, and the slightest sign of weakness meant a cut in the next year's salary. More important, a player might more than double his salary by getting to the postseason, and each team faced each other team trying to take food off their table sixteen times a year. That kind of familiarity bred hate. The most heated team rivalries today don't compare to the kind of brutal conflicts fought on the diamond in the 1890s, when pennants were won with pitching, defense, timely hitting, and blood.

Baseball has changed as it has cleaned itself up and become more professional. Today, only the players making the league minimum might even look at the extra money they'd receive from a World Series win and think "free car." With more teams in each league, and with interleague play, most teams play each other for only three short series over the course of a season. A hard slide into second in one game is unlikely to be remembered when they next meet.

As baseball has evolved, it's become a much slower, thoughtful affair. Fans watch not only the duel between pitcher and hitter, but also the positioning of the fielders as they try to move to where they think they're most likely to be able to make a play on a batted ball. Spectators also try to anticipate what strategies might be employed by each side, from the modern substitution of pitchers to gain the best matchup to the kind of coordinated base-stealing that came out of the dead ball era. While still based on the almost unbelievable physical skills of the participants, baseball's become smarter and more sly, and it has never forgotten its roots.

Even as we watch the more gentle game played today, we can see that baseball's been fraught with cheating since its inception and that cheating has done much to shape the game we know.

Cheating would be defined by most fans as an act that is forbid-

Introduction:
Toward a philosophy of cheating

IS CHEATING WRONG? Should you even read this book? Isn't this topic so controversial and heated that you should purchase several copies of this book in case one or more suddenly combust? Or, if you're of a moralistic bent, so that you'll always have a copy to throw on the next bonfire?

You certainly should.

But this is a more serious question that deserves a longer and more considerate answer. While the realists among us may recognize that if cheating isn't your game, then baseball is not your sport, many look at cheating of any kind as distasteful, and it turns them away from the national pastime.

This is unfortunate because it overlooks some of the subtlety that makes baseball and its long, fruitful relationship with cheating so interesting. For instance:

> Everything that's called cheating is not cheating.
>
> All cheating is not morally objectionable.
>
> A particular act of cheating may not be entirely right or entirely wrong — there is a great deal of room for personal interpretation.
>
> Where a person draws the line between cheating and not cheating tells us as much about that person as whether they draw a line at all.

For much of baseball's history, baseball was war. A player would run over his own mother if she was blocking home plate — and not

den by the rules and gives a player or a team an advantage. A pitcher who spits on the ball and then throws it is cheating — it's an act specifically forbidden by the rules of baseball, and it's intended to put the hitter at a disadvantage.

However, the more general meaning of cheating is to gain through deception, whether or not that deception is legal. You can cheat someone while selling them a car by not disclosing that the transmission is two shifts away from dropping through the underbody and causing an accident, or that the radio only picks up smooth jazz stations.

Heads-up teams do all kinds of things designed to make the opposition run when they shouldn't or stay on base when they should be running. Is this really wrong?

Some people argue that any lie is an immoral act and that any time you lie to gain an advantage, you've sinned.

Those people get really bad deals on consumer electronics.

Nearly everyone recognizes that total honesty is counterproductive. I have a friend who has recently started to date a highly annoying woman; he may have married her by the time this book is in print. I wish them all the happiness in the world if that's the case — they have a great relationship and enjoy each other's company. But when he asks me what I think of her, do I catalogue her bad habits and grating mannerisms or do I focus on the positive?

Similarly, the essence of a baseball game is the confrontation between batter and pitcher. There was a time, early in baseball's history, when batters could call for the pitch they wanted and the pitchers had to give it to them. This was boring.

At its heart, between evenly matched opponents, each at-bat is a game of rock-paper-scissors. If the player looks for a particular pitch — a fastball, say — and he gets it, he has a much greater chance to get a hit. The pitcher, then, wants to throw anything except the pitch the hitter is guessing will come next. It's a game of guessing and deception. There are fastball counts and breaking-ball counts when a pitcher is behind and ahead in the count, respectively, and watching a game, you'll see pitchers mix it up, trying to get a cheap strike.

This seems like an acceptable part of the game.

What if the catcher tells the batter what's coming, just to confuse him, and lies enough to get the batter thinking too much. It would just be an extension of the existing guessing game of deception and conflict between the batter and pitcher. That's fine, too, as long as it doesn't distract the hitter while he's watching for the pitch.

So lying to the opposition is fine. It's part of the game, and they should know better. Almost every game has this element of deception to try and gain an advantage over the opponent, from football teams lining up in a pass formation only to run to basketball teams switching defensive schemes.

None of this deception is in the rules, but it's part of the mental game that makes up so much of baseball. Every at-bat is the story of a pitcher and a hitter trying to outsmart each other, and the at-bats pile up, and the stories tie into each other. Pitchers keep records of what they threw to hitters and what happened, looking for vulnerabilities and for patterns the batter might be looking for. On the other side, batters play their own games of bluffing and faking. Lou Piniella used to intentionally make an out on a pitch he knew he could hit well if the situation was meaningless, hoping that the next time the pitcher needed an out, he'd go back to that well.

Deception and outsmarting the other guy is the currency of baseball. The game between hitter and pitcher doesn't stop when the ball is put into play but moves onto the basepaths, and we move into tricks, both cheap and sophisticated, that take advantage of the other team's good nature or their ignorance of the rules. If a runner is asked to please step off the bag so the shortstop can clean it, and the runner does, should we blame the shortstop if he tags the sap for an out? Or should we instead boo the runner, who should have known better and just cost the team the game?

And what about stealing signs? Catchers signal to pitchers what pitch they want next. If a batter peeks, he can get an advantage unless he's being tricked. Coaches signal to runners whether they should steal. If the other team figures it out, the pitcher can pick the runner off, or the catcher can call for a pitch-out and gain an advantage over the other team. Unless they've been tricked. There's an unwritten rule that stealing signs is frowned on but acceptable if done by someone on the team. It might get someone a fastball upside the noggin, but it's part of the game. That it's looked down on means that it doesn't happen very often, yet some coaches are well known and valued for their ability to steal signs.

Having someone in the stands with binoculars, relaying the signals, though, is unacceptable. But there's nothing in the rules that says you can't steal signs. And they're right out there in the open. Is it cheating to help your team win by breaking one of the nebulous, unwritten rules of the game?

Of course not. When a pitcher reveals that a curve ball is coming by the way he holds his glove before he goes into the delivery, no one stops the game to offer him a helpful tip. Well, unless they think it'll rattle him enough to make it worthwhile. And they're under no obligation to do so. If the other team's signs are so obvious that you know when they're going to try and steal, anyone who notices is obligated to take advantage of the fact, or at least to save that knowledge until it can change the course of the game.

The gray areas emerge quickly. What about deceiving the umpire? Catchers try to develop a skill called "framing the pitch." It's about making a close pitch look good to an umpire so it'll be called a strike. At its most innocent, it's all about presentation and giving the umpire a good look at the ball. But in another sense, it's about doing things not necessary to the game itself in order to take advantage of the umpire's perceptions.

Or what about lying to an umpire? Pretending you were hit on a close pitch, for instance. An outfielder who catches a ball on a bounce will often try to make it look as if he caught it cleanly — even holding up his glove, ball in webbing, and trotting in confidently. Is that part of the game, or is attempting to deceive the neutral arbitrators too much?

Only when we get illegal moves that give a player or team an advantage does a consensus form that they're not just cheating but doing something that's wrong. Tampering with the field of play to alter the way the game is played is one thing, but changing it to favor the home team is accepted. Altering bats so that they're lighter than they're supposed to be, or harder, is wrong.

Some forms of cheating can make the game better. If teams steal signs, the other team is forced to develop better signs or change them more frequently. In Japan, where games have lower scores, a much greater emphasis is on team tactics. Scoring the first run is seen as a serious psychological blow to the other side, game tactics are much more prominent, and stealing signs is an accepted part of the game. It's so prevalent, teams don't change their signs when they trade someone or think they've been broken as they might do in the United States, but may rotate their signs every few innings. The Japanese emphasis on strategy may slow things down sometimes, but it introduces a new and interesting dimension to the way the game is played, and it certainly doesn't affect the integrity of the contest.

So there's good cheating, sometimes tacitly endorsed, like taking out the fielder on a double play or a catcher's blocking the plate. Bad cheating is that which, if it became prevalent, would greatly harm the integrity or even the enjoyment of the sport.

We can easily imagine deceptions, particularly those that try to deceive or otherwise impede the work of umpires, that, widely used, would turn the game into a joke. In the 1890s, many teams — especially the Orioles, who get their own chapter — would argue with umpires on any call that went against their side, and if they were particularly angry, they'd grab and shake the poor guy. Often fights broke out. Umpires were regularly bumped by players during arguments, an act that today results in long suspensions and fines. Casey Stengel once tried to incite the crowd to riot after a call went against him, and the umpires barely escaped with the help of police. No one is served by arbitrators who are forced to do their work in fear, who are corrupt, or who are selected on the basis of their favoritism.

But even fighting, gambling, drug use, and umpire intimidation, which compose the far end of the spectrum of cheating, are established parts of the game and have shaped its evolution.

I have taken for this book the broadest definition of cheating. We'll move from the benign deception of tricking the opposing team to breaking unwritten rules, such as when teams steal signs, and end up in the darkest corner of baseball cheating, those things that threaten the integrity of the game itself, deceiving the umpires, changing the field of play, tampering with equipment, and manipulating one's own biology to play better than the competition.

The greatest cheaters in baseball history worked every angle they could. They knew the rules up and down, sideways, and probably into dimensions yet to be discovered by theoretical physicists. They could argue a point of the rules with any umpire in the league. They knew where the rules could bend and where they could be broken.

They smeared a little Vaseline on a ball, heckled opposing players into misplaying fly balls, corked bats, blocked runners, stole signs, and made baseball into what it is today. Cheating has hurt baseball — indeed, game-fixing almost destroyed it — but it is stronger for having survived those trials. At the same time, the increasing sophistication of cheaters and the roguish charms of the game's outlaws have given the game a playful personality that helped it maintain its unique place in the American mind, making it a more interesting strategic game that rewards deeper study and appreciation.

Part I
Cheating for Beginners
The Underhanded but Not Illegal

Baseball is governed not only by the hundred-page official rulebook but by interpretations and an unwritten book of tradition and consideration that is the product of every game. Players aren't supposed to make other players look bad, for example, which is why stopping to watch a well-hit home run often earns the hitter a warning pitch under the chin the next time he's up, and why hitters who don't run out ground balls find that the fielders take a little longer to field and throw so that it still looks as if everyone's trying. A team that is far ahead eases back and doesn't try to score more runs so that both teams (and the umpires) can get back to their hotels in good time.

This is also where much of the most fascinating and funny cheating occurs, from a fielder betraying the trust of a runner in order to get an out to a team running wild on the basepaths because the players know the second base umpire rarely calls base-stealers out. It's gamesmanship, knowing how far the rules can be bent without breaking.

John McGraw and his 1890s Orioles

> I played against those guys when I came up with Cincinnati,
> in 1899, and let me tell you, after you'd made a trip around
> the bases against them you knew you'd been somewhere.
> They'd trip you, give you the hip, and who knows what else.
> Boy, it was rough. There was only one umpire in those days,
> see, and he couldn't be everywhere at once.
>
> — "Wahoo Sam" Crawford, in *The Glory of Their Times*

BASEBALL IN THE TWILIGHT of the nineteenth century was a rough game played by rough men. They would block each other running the basepaths, slide into bases with reckless abandon with their spikes in the air, call each other the most vile things they could think of, argue with the umpire at any provocation, and worst of all, they resorted to violence, on the field and off, in the service of their teams.

No player was better suited to his age than John McGraw, who made his debut with the Baltimore Orioles in 1891. McGraw stood just over five and a half feet tall, which was the short end of the spectrum even for middle infielders of his time. Yet he had a great reputation as a fighter — or, rather, as someone who would pick fights and refuse to stay down.

He was a mad baseball genius, which led to a host of other traits, such as the sharpest tongue (kept honed through constant use against umpires and opponents alike and a short temper paired with quick fists. Like many players of his time, however, he was able to walk off the field and conduct himself as a perfect gentleman. McGraw was a man of culture who enjoyed even his binge drinking with music: one year, when his team held spring training in Marlin, Texas, he

John McGraw in a ready stance at first, thinking about how to cuff the photographer. *National Baseball Hall of Fame*

and three other players hired a "Negro band of four pieces — guitar, trumpet, bull fiddle, and jug" to follow them around during their drinking rounds.

After McGraw joined the team, they soon came together and began to win. Managed by Ned Hanlon, they won three National League championships in a row, from 1894 through 1896, and went 90-40 and 96-53 in the two years after Hanlon's departure. They played an intense kind of baseball never seen before, a cross between genius for innovation and blood lust. McGraw absorbed everything Hanlon had to teach him and, while not the manager or even the captain, quickly became the Orioles' leader, the indisputable center of the team.

He also was one of the best hitters in baseball when he played regularly. He hit for a good average (.324 lifetime, finishing in the top ten four times), but his real talent was getting on base any way he could, by either taking walks or being hit by pitches. His career on-base percentage makes even modern statheads swoon — it was a whopping .466 (third all-time, and he led the league in that category three times, finished second in 1898 and fourth in 1893 and 1895). Getting on base was only the half of it. Once on, he was a terror on the basepaths. Smart, observant, fast, McGraw took advantage of every opportunity, without pity turning an outfielder's weak arm or a lazy fielding play into extra bases.

But McGraw's impressive statistics can't convey what a powerful figure he was and what a cheater he made. That his legend is so great despite his being a full-time player for only seven years (1893–1900, missing 1896 due to injury) is a testament to the respect he commanded and the lasting impact he had on the game.

These Orioles are the best example of what a group of smart, dedicated, competitive, and somewhat amoral players can get up to when they hang around together too long.

The plays we think of as baseball strategy today — the sacrifice bunt, the hit-and-run, the double steal, that pairing of idea and execution — were done by Ned Hanlon and his Baltimore Orioles. Hanging around together before games, after games, and when they were traveling, Hanlon, along with McGraw and the other players, would endlessly rehash plays and consider possible situations.

That Orioles team invented dozens of crazy things they could try on the basepaths, plays that frustrated opposing teams and caused their managers to howl in protest. It became a whole school of baseball thought, called "inside" or "scientific" baseball, based on trying to hit the ball where it would most help the team and executing set plays that required coordination between runners and the hitter.

At first, other teams didn't believe that the Orioles were using the hit-and-run on purpose. That changed quickly, as the Orioles rolled over all the teams they faced and their opponents scrambled to keep up. It's often said that the dead-ball era led to these innovations, and there is some truth to that: in 1896, for instance, the most home runs any team hit was 45 (the Washington Senators). On the other hand, an average team that same year scored six runs a game (the Orioles scored 7.54; second place was Philadelphia's 6.85), when a hundred years later, in 1996, the average NL offense scored only 4.68 runs a game. It wasn't that the Orioles figured out how to use signals to score runs; they were obsessed with winning and would look for any possible way to do it.

For instance, the runner at first would bluff a steal, the hitter would watch which fielder covered, and on the next pitch the runner would go and the batter would hit the ball in the gap left by the fielder covering second against the steal. Often, the runner could keep going to third, leaving men at first and third, and the Orioles could repeat the trick, scoring the man on third, leaving runners on first and second (or third) again.

The Orioles were adept at fouling off balls until the pitcher tired. They became expert bunters, going so far as to tilt the foul lines at their home park inward to help keep bunted balls fair. When their opponents caught on to that trick, they learned to beat the ball into the ground — "the Baltimore chop," as it's still known — so they could run to first before an infielder caught it or to get it to bounce over the infielders and drop into the outfield as they ran into second. The chop also made a great hit-and-run play.

The Orioles lost the 1895 Temple Cup, a postseason series between the first- and second-place finishers in the National League, to their hated rival the Cleveland Spiders. McGraw and other disappointed, dissatisfied Orioles stuck around in Baltimore, rehashing

One year of Orioles rule changes

The year 1897 brought a set of rules that had McGraw's team's finger-prints all over it. The bunt was clearly defined, and a foul bunt was ruled to be a strike. Their constant arguing over fouls helped force rule clarifications over what was and was not a foul and a rule that once an umpire had made a call (ball/strike, safe/out), he was not al-lowed to reverse it, no matter how persuasive the opposition's argu-ments or threats. The team's defensive foul play led to a rule that run-ners were entitled to take a base if they were obstructed by a fielder who didn't have the ball. While running, their habit of cutting bases when the umpire wasn't looking (running from first to third or second to home) led to a rule that runners must touch all the bases in order and touch them in reverse order if they have to return.

That was just 1897.

the series, working out how they could have done better, and in-vented the outfield cutoff throw: an outfielder, on catching a ball, throws to an infielder who's moved out toward him as the ball was hit. The infielder is then better positioned to catch a runner between bases or make a strong throw home to prevent a run being scored.

In the 1890s, the game involved a level of physical contact that would make today's fans turn white and swoon in their seat. Even the clean teams dabbled in blocking runners, occasional tripping, and constant heckling. The dirty teams, like the Reds, the Spiders, and particularly the Orioles, would take full advantage of a single umpire by running directly to third from first, holding runners forcefully at their base, using the pretense of a tag to sock a player with a ball, and running into fielders trying to make plays. Generally speaking, teams would adjust their level of play to that of their oppo-nents, with a Reds-Orioles game being the nastiest spectacle the sport could offer.

Some of McGraw's peers were even dirtier players. Tommy Tucker played first for the Boston Beaneaters, and he was by far the more physically dirty player. He spiked far more players maliciously than McGraw, trying to hurt them as badly as he could.

Over his playing career, McGraw held runners, blocked them off

> ## Great moments in the Orioles-Reds rivalry
>
> Harry Vaughn, the Reds first baseman, is blocked by McGraw as he tries to round third and go home. McGraw uses both arms to restrain Vaughn at his neck, but Vaughn escapes and scores. McGraw then spikes Vaughn in a play at first base. The two exchange words, and when McGraw walks to the dugout, Vaughn throws the ball at him and hits him squarely in the back.
>
> When Reds pitcher Frank Dwyer runs to cover first on a ground ball, McGraw punches him. Reds first baseman Jake Beckley knocks McGraw down in retaliation.
>
> Later the same year, in a similar play, McGraw again punches Dwyer while running to first, which says as much about Dwyer as it does about McGraw.
>
> The next year, McGraw takes offense at a tag by Reds catcher Heinie Peitz and kicks him in the face. Peitz punches McGraw in the eye in response and keeps at it. McGraw escapes and goes for a bat, and only police intervention keeps the two from killing each other.

the base, got in the way of runners, and did all the other things that his fellow players did, if more frequently and with more zeal. But he'd do something obviously wrong only a dozen, two dozen, times over a season. Tucker, in addition to doing everything McGraw did even more often, hip-checked runners off first base and then tagged them out. His frequent use of the trick made him notorious.

McGraw's version of Tucker's hip check was belt-grabbing. Like all fielders, McGraw would hold a runner at the base when he thought he could get away with it to keep them from advancing or scoring. McGraw said that when a runner on third waited for a fly ball to be caught so he could run home, he would reach out, grab the guy's belt, and "jerk him back just as the catch was made and prevent him from getting a quick start for the plate in an attempt to score after the catch." The player, making a late break, would get thrown out.

Pete Browning, a longtime Louisville player whose career wound down as McGraw and his team ascended, embarrassed McGraw (Browning barely played at all in 1894, when the Orioles won their first pennant). Browning needed to score and suspected McGraw would hold him, so he unbuckled his belt. When the catch was made and McGraw went for the grab, he was left holding a strap of leather as Browning scored.

Despite being outwitted, McGraw continued to use the tactic. "Other runners took to doing the same thing. McGraw, too wary to be caught again, simply bided his time. When their vigilance was relaxed he went back to his belt-grabbing, and the screaming started all over again," commented Frank Graham in *McGraw of the Giants*.

That's some smart cheating, even it happened only a few times a year.

Even compared to Tucker, McGraw was no choir boy — maybe a choir boy who snuck money from the collection plate. The difference in their reputations today comes from the difference in their personalities. Tucker was an affable, humorous man, while McGraw was a gruff jerk. Through the years McGraw's actions have been exaggerated and amplified while Tucker's seem to have been forgotten.

McGraw and Tucker, as might be imagined, didn't get along. McGraw once kicked Tucker in the head (while wearing spikes, remember), and they fought on the field repeatedly.

Too much is made of spiking by McGraw, Cobb, and others. Most spiking was accidental and noted in game stories as such. It's easy to look at today's well-choreographed slides and fielding plays and think that the only way a player could get caught in another's cleats would be if the runner had murderous intentions. But in those days, runners were spiked as well as fielders. Fielders often tried to block the runner off the base, and runners in turn had horrible form — coming in feet first, legs scissored out or one foot in the air. Minor scrapes happened all the time.

In that environment there were accusations, and some players, like McGraw, would remember someone who had cut them and wait until they could return the favor. But, reading the news stories, there's very little serious spiking, and no fights were sparked by those incidents. Stories that McGraw spiked umpires are not supported by contemporary accounts.

Innovative or not, McGraw and the Orioles played dirty as often as any other team, but they buried them at verbal abuse.

The Hall of Fame's copy of this photo of a famous Cobb spiking incident has a long note from Cobb on the back, complaining about his undeserved reputation as a dirty player: "I am trying only to reach the bag with my toe, he had a slight cut on forearm, never lost an inning of play, Cobb was a dirty spiker — look how far I am inside bag." *National Baseball Hall of Fame*

The Orioles would argue with the umpires endlessly over any call that went against them. Of all their sins, this "kicking" was the most widely condemned and is the real source of much of their nefarious reputation. The Spalding yearbooks and writers in other cities condemn McGraw at length, not for spiking or fighting, but for his language, his verbal needling of opposing players, and most of all for arguing with the umpires.

McGraw's mouth was the lair of the sharpest tongue in baseball. Once, in a spring training game — an exhibition — McGraw started a fight with a team in Savannah, Georgia. The *Sporting News* wrote only that McGraw's words were "so filthy and vile that it is impossible to even hint at."* He was warned about his penchant for mock-

---

* Hint, hint! A hundred years later, we need to know these things.

ing opposing players and speculating on their heritage in the most spicy terms. Umpires fined and ejected him for arguing, for disrespecting them, for language, for insolence, for bringing up previous disagreements.

These continual arguments proved counterproductive. The *Baltimore Sun*, an admittedly biased source, wrote in 1902 of the cumulative damage they did to his relationship with the umpires: "McGraw's one-time reputation for hot-headed action on the field was apparently used as a club with which to smash his career in the league which he did so much to form. Umpires have persistently applied the rules more strictly to him than to other men in the league. Fouls have been called strikes on him, and all a player has had to do to get home from third was to yell that McGraw held him, and the run was allowed as a matter of course; he has been nagged while batting, and when making the legitimate protests to an umpire which were justified by his position as manager, the occasion has been seized to put him out of the game."

McGraw's legacy, though complicated, is undeniable. The tales of his brutality have been greatly exaggerated over time while the tales of his short temper and talent for insults and debate have waned, but certainly he was one of the dirtiest and loudest players at a time when routine play would horrify modern fans. And as such he made the game worse — more violent, more dangerous to play. Teams kicking at every call made the job of umpires harder. Their constant profanity kept a rougher crowd coming out and the more civilized fans from visiting the park twice. It took many years before the sport was able to move away from the style of baseball McGraw played, and the presence of such players hindered that.

Still, as a player McGraw shaped the game. Certainly his teams didn't come up with every innovation, but no team turned these innovations into organized strategy like the Orioles did. They would find an opponent's weakness, a way to exploit it, and then, without conscience, humiliate that team over and over until some countermeasure was found. Their work led to the development of game tactics and overall approaches that became part of the strategies and offensive philosophy of baseball, used by every team since for over a century.

They first created much of the intellectual challenge of baseball, which makes it so nuanced and interesting: guessing what the other team might do, choosing when to play for one run, looking for ways to make the most of the tools at hand to find an advantage over the other team. If McGraw gave us several years of being one of the worst players of a bad time, he also gave baseball the tools to evolve into the cleaner, more sophisticated game that it has slowly and fitfully grown into: he revealed the possibilities for strategy and finely practiced execution that could be picked up and built on by future teams until, eventually, they could give up the punch-tag to the face in favor of a smartly run double steal. When the players moved away from the constant grousing, insults, and physical play of McGraw, they found themselves moving toward the "inside baseball" he helped pioneer.

McGraw's second life as a manager testifies to this evolution. When McGraw took over as a player-manager of the New York Giants in 1902, it wasn't long before he gave up playing regularly. He turned thirty the April before the 1903 season — becoming a full-time strategist, essentially — and took the field in only 24 more games over the next few years, usually as a defensive sub.

As a manager, McGraw created a legend that is more than the match of his playing years. "Little Napoleon" was a greater figure than any player, even any team. No one could evaluate talent with a keener eye: McGraw found players anywhere and turned them into stars. But each discovery and acquisition was raw material to be melted and reforged into a gleaming cog in McGraw's machine. Players who would not fit or broke down were discarded; the machine went on producing wins.

McGraw managed the Giants from 1902 to 1932 (though his involvement waned in later years, as did the team's fortunes). His teams won three World Series titles and claimed the National League pennant another seven times on top of that, including four years in a row (1921 to 1924). He won 2,583 games and lost 1,790 for a ridiculous .591 winning percentage. Over a modern 162-game season, that's an average of 96 wins every year for thirty years.

In this period, the game changed dramatically. It grew far less violent, but it did become rotten with gambling and game-fixing.

Then it cleaned itself up: the spitball was banned, gamblers were banished, and Babe Ruth ascended to stardom, bringing the home run and an entirely new style of play to the game. McGraw adapted readily to all of these changes, and in the end his single-minded dedication to winning also made him one of the best managers in baseball history.

More than any other single figure, McGraw illustrates the close and confused relationship between cheating and the sport. The first time he and his teammates did something legal — but which no one had thought of and no one else could quickly adopt — baseball was confronted with a set of choices: Is that legal? Do we make it illegal? What one opponent called unfair as a victim might be outlawed the next year or become a standard tactic in both leagues. Without McGraw's constant drive to win, today's game would be far poorer.

Home field advantages: Groundskeeping

> This is a game of inches . . . We try to have the
> inches go our way.
>
> — Emil Bossard, Cleveland Indians groundskeeper

IN THE TOP OF the first, the visiting team comes to the plate.

The leadoff hitter, a righty, steps into the batter's box. With his back foot he starts to dig in — but he can't: the ground doesn't budge at all, he's barely scraping at it. Uncomfortable, he sees that the first baseman is playing him deeper than normal despite his well-known prowess with the bunt. The hitter tries not to grin, and on the first pitch he drops a perfect bunt down the line and sprints to first. "Foul!" calls the ump. The hitter looks back, baffled.

He tries again on the next pitch, and again he lays down a perfect bunt toward first and it goes foul. The first base coach tells him they're fine bunts, but once they hit the line they make a dive for foul territory. He gives up. The next pitch is a fastball, a little high, and he tries to smash it, but he can't push off his back foot and winds up missing it entirely for strike three. He yells in frustration and sits down next to his manager to complain.

The next hitter punches a curve hard into the ground. The ball comes off the turf energetically and looks as if it might get through the gap between the shortstop and third base, but the home team's quick, sure-handed shortstop barely gets there to snag it in time to throw to first and make the out.

The last hitter smashes a line drive to right field. This territory's manned by Slowee Van Slugger, a fan favorite who hits home runs, has a cannon for an arm, and has had at least one knee surgery every off-season, robbing him of what little speed he once had. The batter races out and digs for second. But the ball doesn't skip to the wall, as he'd expected; it dies on the bounce and then loses speed in the grass to roll to Van Slugger, who has to take only a few steps to snag it. He makes a strong throw to nail a surprised runner at second to end the inning.

In the bottom of the second, with the home team up, the visitors take the field.

On the mound, the pitcher is baffled. He likes to set up on the extreme left side of the rubber and dig himself in a bit to push off better, and he finds he has the same problem his hitter did — there's no give, and he has to pitch without being comfortable.

To make matters worse, his landing point — where his lead foot sets down during the lineup — is uneven and even slippery, throwing off his balance. He's having trouble keeping his delivery consistent and hitting his spots.

The leadoff hitter drops a bunt down the third base line. As the pitcher and third baseman charge, it looks as if it's going foul. The two make no move to pick it up, waiting until it's foul, but when it touches the line, it rolls to a stop in fair territory. The third baseman picks up the ball, but it's too late to make a play.

He kicks at the baseline in frustration and says some things that cause the television producers to cut away from him for the protection of young lip-readers.

The second batter grounds sharply to the shortstop, the same hit as in the top half, but this shortstop isn't as quick on his first step and doesn't have the same range, so the ball skips by into the outfield for a single.

With men on first and second, the frustrated pitcher kicks at the rubber, still unable to get the toehold he wants. His attempts to smooth out his landing spot seem only to make it worse. Facing Slowee Van Slugger, he needs to hit his spots perfectly. For his first pitch, though, he wants to throw a curve low on the outside corner and try to get the hitter to hit a double-play ball to the right side. But as he comes forward, his front foot is off the mark, his body opens a little too soon, and the low outside curve hangs over the plate.

Van Slugger's eyes widen with glee as the ball comes off the pitcher's hand, and seconds later a fan in left field has a souvenir. It's 3–0 in the bottom of the first with no outs. Below the stands, the head groundskeeper spits a sunflower shell into a garbage can and smiles.

The way a field is set up can turn good pitchers into bad ones, change hits to outs, twist games into wins, and make batting champions of hitters. The dimensions of the field are set out in Rule 1.04, including the distance between the bases and the dimensions of the pitcher's mound, and so forth, but within the rules is a world of interpretation and over a hundred years of innovation. The rules say nothing about whether the field must be dry or sufficiently watered, or how high the foul lines can be built up, or if the grass must be within certain height boundaries or even uniform in composition. Even if they did, no umpire's going to take a ruler around the field before the game and check.

As a result, groundskeeping changed how the game is played. If Henry Fabian, the longtime groundskeeper of the Polo Grounds, is to be believed, he was the first to build up the pitcher's box when he was with Dallas in the Texas League during the 1890s. He did it to favor Virgil Garvin, a pitcher who threw a curve ball with such terrific break, he often bounced it in front of the plate. With Garvin boosted, his pitch was a strike more consistently, and he went on to success. But when a player left the team he gave away the secret, and soon a new term — the mound — arose to describe that protrusion in the middle of the infield. A 1903 rule change established the height of the mound at 15 inches, beginning a century of massaging mound dimensions around the rules.

The Orioles, under McGraw, were the first to really think about how to turn their park into an advantage that could win games. They would practice beating the ball straight into the ground so it would take an enormous bounce, and by the time it came down where a fielder could catch it, the batter would often have made it to first base. This is still known as "the Baltimore Chop" (and is sometimes confused with "the Butcher Boy," where the batter fakes a bunt to get the first and third basemen to charge him and then tries to take a short swing and whack the ball past one of them). The Orioles made sure that the ground was particularly hard and well suited to this tactic — to the point that you'll still hear that they paid their grounds crew to bury concrete slabs and cover them with a thin layer of dirt

Emil Bossard and his sons tamper with the mound at Cleveland's Municipal Stadium before a 1948 game. *National Baseball Hall of Fame*

to get maximum bounce, a rumor unfortunately without any good contemporary evidence.

That kind of trickery was refined to an art by Emil Bossard, who fell into the work almost by accident. In 1911, he was in St. Paul, Minnesota, working at his dad's hardware store, but also hauled lumber at the minor league ball park. After a few weeks, they asked him to help the head groundskeeper, and he took over when the groundskeeper fell ill. Bossard listened to the players' requests and complaints and experimented, and it wasn't long before his minor league fields made players swoon and other owners ask him for help with their own parks.

Yet it was twenty-five years before he got his big break. The Indians fired their groundskeeper and asked their manager, Steve O'Neill, if he could recommend someone. "The best in the business," he said, "is Emil Bossard at St. Paul."

When Bossard took over, he was the first to tailor a park to its home team: he had a genius for making the ground suit his team's fielders. When the Indians moved Vic Wertz to first base, where he had never played, Bossard and his staff softened the ground around the base to slow any balls hit to him. As the season progressed and Wertz grew comfortable, they let the ground get faster and faster until it played normally.

From year to year, the same field might have entirely different characteristics. Cleveland's was relatively soft when the team won the World Series in 1948. But by the mid-1950s it was as hard as concrete unless a ground ball pitcher was scheduled to start for the Indians, when suddenly it would soften up again to deaden the balls beaten into the dirt.

"The secret is to keep your tricks hidden," Bossard said.

It was part of his amazing preparation. The groundskeepers could have built a field suited to the peculiar talents of the Indians' fielders and, to a lesser extent, their hitters, and they would have been the best staff in the majors. But they went further than that. Assisted by his sons, Bossard paid attention to the hitters and the staff, making adjustments to the playing surface for each home game based on what they knew about the other team's tendencies and the Indians' lineup.

Bossard and his crew worked, in particular, on the areas where the ball would take its first bounce. With right-handed pull hitters, for instance, they'd try and make the infield fast close to the third base line by rolling it and watering less. By switching around, they ensured that other teams couldn't count on the cheating going one way or the other, so the visitors had to worry about the opposing team *and* the field.

At least one time, Emil's quick thinking won the team a game outright. In a 1947 game against the Red Sox, with the Indians up by four in the fourth inning, a heavy rain delayed the game for more than an hour. When it ended, the infield was dry, but the outfield

> ### Also, it rained in just that one spot
>
> Roger Bossard, the head groundskeeper for the White Sox, said, "Sometimes the dirt in front of home would be so muddy, the umpire would call my dad over and say, 'What's this?' Dad would pull his cigar from his mouth, shrug his shoulders, and say, 'My hose leaked' or 'My watering can spilled.'

was a swamp. The Red Sox wanted the game called while the Indians wanted to keep going. The umpire gave Bossard half an hour to get the field ready. His crew swarmed out, digging holes in the outfield, then bailing water out of the holes, and in less than half an hour the field was ready for play. The Indians won.

Of course, grounds crews aren't always so attentive when the score is against their team — see "Delaying the game for fun and profit," later in part I — but here we see that a great crew can also act as an effective countermeasure.

Joe DiMaggio jokingly blamed the Bossards for ending his 56-game hitting streak, saying that they'd watered down the infield until it was "a swamp" to slow down the ground balls he hit. "The Yankees hated to come here because our every defensive flaw was exploited by the Bossards the way they prepared the playing field," he said.

DiMaggio was right; even the most famous Yankee, Babe Ruth, yelled at Emil. "Give us a break," he finally barked in frustration at the man who'd turned right field into a swamp and messed with the batter's box so Ruth couldn't get set.

Did the Bossards' hard work help their teams win games? Lou Boudreau managed the Indians from 1942 through 1950, when Emil Bossard led the crew with his sons Harold and Marshall. Boudreau knew how effective Bossard's work was. "I wouldn't be surprised if he helped us win as many as ten games a year," he said. He thought their work was so valuable that when he became manager of the Kansas City Athletics in 1955, he called Harold and offered him as much money as he wanted to join him. Harold declined.

The Bossards' success in helping their team was of course copied by others.

Earl Weaver, the manager of the Orioles from 1968 to 1982, claimed that by changing the infield conditions to better suit his players, he increased the team's batting average by "more than 30 points." If you take that at face value — and given that it's Weaver, who knew his statistics and his players — this is an amazing figure. Thirty points of batting average is the difference between a middle-of-the-pack team and a league-leading offensive juggernaut.

A key advantage to the groundskeepers' behind-the-scenes work is that home teams can prepare to play on the modified field they make. If fielders have to face conditions designed to cause a batted ball to slow down, they can take grounders until they're familiar with how it plays and how to compensate for it. But a visiting fielder won't realize that particular characteristic unless good advanced scouting tells him, and he still won't have the time to master it. And if the grounds crew is as aggressive as the Bossards were, conditions might change with each series to try and expose the visitors' weaknesses.

The Indians weren't the only team to resort to excessive watering to slow things down.

Sparky Anderson, the manager of the Detroit Tigers from 1980 through 1995, said, "Ours is the slowest infield in the league and will always be kept that way because the ball goes into the stands very quick. We must prevent people from getting on by ground balls. If you hit a ground ball, our grass and dirt around home plate is going to eat that ball up. The only way you're going to beat us is if you hit that ball in the air.

"If somebody else did something like that, I would complain very strongly, but also be very proud of the team that was doing it. I'd be the first one screaming and hollering but I'd also be in my house telling my wife and kids, 'I respect that guy. He'll try anything.'"

Of course, a fast field is better for some clubs. The secret is cutting the grass as low as it will go. Different varieties of grass and grass mixes vary in how densely they will grow, their maximum height, and their tolerance for being cut extremely short. So it takes some thought and experimenting to get the right fit, but it's effective. It's also important to pack down the dirt as much as possible, using rollers or other techniques, and water it as little as possible. And of course to time those waterings to make sure the field is at its driest come game time.

On the lines

Groundskeepers frequently build up the foul lines so that bunters see more of their balls stay fair. This goes from the modest — building up the lines themselves so that it's tougher for a ball to roll up and on them — to the crazy. In Philadelphia, the crew built a third base line that was inclined to favor left-handed bunter Richie Ashburn. You could roll a ball from home to third, and it would have trailed off happily into the infield grass.

Ashburn won the 1955 batting title with an average of .355, almost a hundred points over the NL average of .259, and 19 points higher than the competition, Willie Mays and Stan Musial.

Emil Bossard used to work the foul lines, but he went to great lengths to conceal his work. He'd dig up the infield along the lines so he could sink them or blend the slope into the surrounding area and so on, refining it to get the most he could without appearing to be doing anything at all.

On the mound

Phil Niekro, talking about the ways mounds are groomed to favor one side, said, "Some mounds look higher than other ones and some are made of different material. But both pitchers have to pitch off the same mound."

That's true and misses the point. Two pitchers will most likely have different deliveries and, in particular, different landing spots where their lead foot strides forward in their delivery. Catfish Hunter experienced this as few have.

"He doesn't like the mound hard," George Toma, a grounds-keeper for the Kansas City Royals, said. "I know this because when he used to pitch here, I would dig a hole and make the slope of the mound soft so he could push off. Now when he comes here, I wet it down and make it as uncomfortable as possible."

That's not the worst that's been done to a pitcher. Casey Stengel once gave the grounds crew a tip about the opposing starter: "This feller who's pitching for the other team likes to dig a hole in front of the mound." The Yankees crew went out "with a kerosene lamp and burned it so hard it was like concrete. You couldn't dig a hole in it with a jackhammer."

There are other venues for mound trickery as well. Despite the official surveys done twice a year to ensure that mounds are within regulations, some have consistent characteristics that change the game. Dodger Stadium, for instance, is always said to have a high mound. The Bossards admitted that they built the mound up as high as 15 inches for some of their pitchers. The rubber on the mound at Fenway Park is often buried under dirt. Because there's no way for umpires to tell if the pitcher's standing in the right spot, some will cheat forward to decrease the distance between the release of the ball and the batter, even if it's just by inches. Batters stand outside their box; why shouldn't pitchers do the same if they can get away with it? Some mounds are steep, others flat. A mound can even change from series to series and game to game to suit the preference of the home team's starting pitcher.

Even though both the bullpen and field mounds are inspected, pitchers frequently complain about the difference, particularly in height, between the visitor's bullpen and the actual mound. A pitcher warms up in the visitors bullpen, and gets his stride and motion down, then find the real thing is a little wider, steeper, or softer.

The mound provides an excellent example of the dangers of co-operating with a crew. If a player, particularly a pitcher, is interested in trying to tailor the conditions to allow him the best chance to succeed, he'll find the head groundskeeper is an attentive listener. And if he's ever traded, or leaves through free agency, he'll return to the field to find his every revealed weakness exploited by his former ally.

On the boxes

Once they've stepped into the batter's box, many hitters dig their cleats into the dirt to brace their back foot and allow them to swing harder without slipping, and in order to get a few extra microseconds to look at a pitch (seriously, an inch in the box doesn't even get a full thousandth of a second additional time), it's not uncommon to see batters wipe out the back line of the batter's box and put their back foot illegally outside the box. As if the umpire's fooled. Though considering how rarely it's enforced, maybe it's effective after all, if only to give him an excuse for taking no action.

While managing the Seattle Mariners, Maury Wills asked his groundskeepers before an April 25, 1981, game to draw a batter's box that was illegally large: it extended an additional 6 inches toward the mound. Six inches is a lot, and he was trying to get away with it against Billy Martin, who was a stickler for the rules when it suited him.

Wills got fined and suspended; he tried to play it off as part of groundskeeping gamesmanship. Martin laughed, alluding to his own staff's reputation as cheaters: "They talk about the spitters, but we caught them cheating. How about that. They must think I'm the new kid on the block."

Wills's attempt annoyed AL umpire supervisor Dick Butler. "It's like moving the bases 88 feet apart," he said. "If it is a couple inches, which Wills admitted, it is just as bad as a foot."

In June 2000, the Atlanta Braves were caught remarking the catcher's box to make it wider so the catcher could set up farther in and away than he should. For the Braves, with pitchers who pounded the corners of the strike zone, the wider box helped get more strikes called. They were found out when their own television crew showed comparison footage from two games, the first, showing the catcher's box several inches larger than it should be, and the second, following the opposing manager's complaints, noticeably thinner.

Not surprisingly, the Turner Broadcasting System team was not allowed on the team's next charter flight. The Braves felt, understandably, that their TV guys should be on their side and not divulge their secrets. But the crew, also understandably, felt that it was interesting and worth showing the fans. They made up after a few days.

On the basepaths

To slow base-stealers, teams use sand, they loosen the dirt up, they water the basepaths until they're declared protected federal wetland areas (and then, presumably, surveyed for possible oil drilling) — all to try and make it harder for speedy players to get a good jump off the base.

After betting a broadcaster a dollar that a speedy White Sox team wouldn't steal a base during a visit to Cleveland ("I knew when I shook hands with Emil that I had just lost a dollar," the broadcaster said later), Emil Bossard went to work and collected his buck. "All we did," he said, as if it was no big thing, "was loosen up the soil about an inch deep so their spikes wouldn't grip. They had to stay close to the bag or get picked off."

When the ground is more slippery and harder to run on, it's also harder for a runner to take a good lead, making stealing even harder: the treacherous dirt makes it more likely the runner will slip trying to get back to the base on a pickoff move.

Maury Wills was a Dodger shortstop and feared baserunner through the 1960s. At his best, he was almost uncatchable: he stole 104 bases in 1962, breaking Ty Cobb's twentieth-century record of 96, set in 1915, and was caught only thirteen times that year. Whenever the Dodgers came to town, the host groundskeeping crew would use everything they could think of to keep him from running wild on the bases.

When Wills and the Dodgers played in San Francisco, the only thing the grounds crew didn't try was a camouflaged spiked pit between first and second. The Giants, who have never been friends with the Dodgers (except when both teams betrayed their New York fans by moving west together, but that's another story), were so determined to stop him that they watered the dirt down to the point where the umpires would stop the game and threaten a forfeit to get them to clean things up. In one game, umpire Tom Gorman stopped play for an hour and a half to let it dry. In another, the Giants grounds crew put so much sand between first and second that Wills complained, and the crew was forced to come out and remove their improvised beach.

The Dodgers, for their part, were caught cheating at home.

After Wills complained that he had a tough time stealing second, they went into action. They dug a shallow trench, six feet wide, between first and second, only a few inches deep, and filled it with hard clay. Then they covered it with your average, everyday dirt: it would look good and play fairly but offered runners great traction as they broke away from first and ran to second base.

When an umpire came to the park early to watch batting practice, he saw a bulldozer on the field. The Dodgers were rolling it over the basepaths to pack the dirt down, which of course favored Wills.

But the ump couldn't do anything. As long as the field is playable and the dimensions are correct, it's legal.

In the air

For all of the watering, gardening, and general playing in the dirt teams do, though, that isn't the only way a team can use their park to their advantage.

Opposing teams have long suspected that the Minnesota Twins use their dome's ventilation system to help the team's hitters. The Metrodome is unique: it's essentially a balloon you play in. The pressure to keep the roof inflated comes from giant fans placed around the stadium in a special corridor, and there are intake and exhaust vents throughout the stadium, far beyond the normal air conditioning you'd find in a domed park.

Dave Ericson, a Metrodome superintendent, admitted he tried to work it to the home team's advantage. In an interview with the *Star Tribune,* he said, "You'd want to be blowing all the air out and up you can."

The advantage, if there was one, was limited. In order to keep the roof inflated, the crew couldn't monkey with the flow too much. But late in the game, they had to crank the intake up when people started to leave, opening exit doors that let air escape outside, and that provided the cover they needed to turn up the fans around home and get some air currents running.

Ericson said he tried to time it so if the Twins were behind, he'd turn up the fans for the bottom of the eighth (with the home team batting), then they were kept up for the top of the ninth (visitors up) and the bottom of the ninth when it was played (home team bats again), giving the Twins two times up with wind assistance while the visitors got only one. If the score was tied, he wouldn't turn them up until the middle of the ninth.

Whether it made any difference is difficult to determine. Practical tests showed mixed results. The *Minneapolis Star Tribune* ran a series of tests at the Metrodome. Using an air cannon to fire balls consistently with the same force, they asked the operators to turn fans on and off. In the first test, with the fans blowing out, the balls gained several feet; when the fans blew toward home plate, they lost several feet. But later, in a second test, they found that the air currents made no difference at all.

As the *Star Tribune's* physicist said, "Setting [the fans] up to do something is tricky, and you could not be sure on any particular day whether you are actually doing something or not. I think there is reasonable evidence that on some days there could be an effect."

If, for example, under the best conditions running the vents might get a ball hit to the outfield 5 more feet, and at worst it's a wash, that's a significant effect. Those 5 feet could be the difference between an outfielder's standing on the warning track and looking up at a home run over the fence. That difference is enough to get players to tamper with their bats, so it's worth experimenting with, and you certainly can't blame Ericson for trying.

It's even more interesting to think about what the Twins could do. They control the stadium and can conduct far more elaborate and detailed experiments than a newspaper armed with a bunch of university students. They could better simulate batted balls and hit hundreds to left, center, and right for each adjustment they made to the system to try and determine the precise settings that offered the greatest advantage.

Air currents are just one thing the Twins could try. Increasing the air pressure to help a home-run-prone starting pitcher and then lowering it to help the team put some balls over fences against a fly ball pitcher.

Heck, they could run trials for each game, before anyone got there, looking for the kind of tiny advantages that the best grounds-keepers find in the slope of a mound. Of course, the real problem with this kind of operation is that the harder you work at it, the more potential witnesses there are who might squeal to the commissioner.

But for the crafty cheater, the possibilities seem endless. That kind of data can be gathered at any park. Many new parks feature a retractable roof, and whether that roof is open or closed has a huge effect on the hitting environment, particularly the direction and force of the wind. Broadcasters and players speculate about what it might do.

There's no reason teams should have to guess, though. They can pepper the stadium with weather stations, work with forecasters to get an exact idea of how the conditions inside are affected by local weather conditions, and be singularly well positioned to make the most of their home field's peculiarities. If you know a strong wind will be blowing out to left field, you might even consider swapping a left-handed fly-ball pitcher for a normally less effective ground-baller. Home teams may not control the weather, but they can be prepared to make the most of it.

In the future

The recent wave of new ballpark construction reopened this avenue of cheating for many clubs. When the playing field is a roll of plastic grass laid over concrete, and the infield dirt is a simple cut-out, there's not a lot the staff can do. Fortunately, only three teams (Tampa Bay, Minnesota, and Toronto, all in the American League) play on an artificial surface. These new parks, with natural turf of new and exciting grass blends, dirt infields, the whole thing with complicated underground irrigation systems built in . . . it's enough to make a creative cheater drool.

At the major league level, teams have the resources and incentive to think beyond the innovations of the Bossards — the dirt, the grass, even the lines and the basepaths. Technology can be applied in new and evil ways.

Even beyond the obvious application of irrigation systems to keep the field wet (or dry, for that matter) and ever-more-subtle trickery in the visiting clubhouse, teams could dramatically escalate the war of the home field.

Using new high-frequency technology, teams can target distracting noises right at the hitter, projecting a foul-mouthed heckler, or anything they wanted, the moment a ball comes out of a pitcher's hands. Hitters are exceptionally good at tuning out distractions, but in the end they're only human. They can be thrown off their game.

A really adventuresome team might carefully wire powerful electromagnets under the basepaths to slow down opposing players. Spikes are made of steel, so a magnet will attract them. You have to get into some seriously expensive stainless steel alloys so a magnet won't stick to them. It would take some experimentation to determine if it could be done in practice and, if so, how powerful the magnetic field would have to be to slow an opposing runner or fielder the small amount that would gain an advantage.

A good grounds crew, one that really pays attention to a team's needs and does an exceptional job tailoring the grounds to suit it, might be worth a few games a year. Advanced cheating, in crossing the line of what's legal, offers an opportunity to choose the moment you apply hidden advantages. They could be both an unprecedented chance to change the outcome of a critical play and a dramatic escalation in the war on the field.

Cracking codes and baseball's Midways:
Stealing signs

Stealing signs is part of the job. If you don't try, you're not doing your job.
— Tom Kelly, Minnesota Twins manager, 1986–2001

THERE ARE HIDDEN LINES of communication on the baseball field. A catcher and pitcher use signals to determine the next pitch, and the other players in the field may adjust their positions based on the choice. Another stream of encrypted data flows from the hitting team's manager to his coaches at first and third. They recode it and send it to the batter as well as any runners on base.

While they're all talking to their teammates, they're also listening to the other side. Breaking the other team's code grants a look into the future. A hitter who knows what the next pitch will be can become much more dangerous. A pitcher and catcher who know the runner on first will be stealing second can turn his attempt into an out and an empty base.

Both sides need to share information with their own team while keeping it from their opponent. Both sides would love to know what information the other team is sharing.

The struggle begins.

Signs came into being thanks to pitchers' cheating. Baseball's earliest rules required a pitcher to deliver a hittable pitch "high" or "low," to the batter's taste. Pitchers didn't want to throw a good pitch, of course, so they'd try to give the hitter the worst possible pitch that would still qualify. The rules changed almost every year in an attempt to keep pitchers honest, but by the 1870s, they began to recognize that the pitcher was naturally the batter's enemy and allowed the competition. Starting in 1872, pitchers could legally

Jim Leyland is telling his coaches something, or nothing. His nose may also have been itching. *AP*

throw a curve ball. Suddenly, catchers needed to know what was coming, and baseball had signals.

The battery's communication remains the center of baseball's sign language. Every pitch, catchers squat and use their fingers to call for a type and a desired location. The pitcher can refuse the catcher's request, and the catcher will either offer a different suggestion or insist. When they've agreed, the pitcher delivers and the process is repeated. In a normal nine-inning game, a catcher will call for about 140–150 pitches. A bad night will run over 180, and even a brilliant performance, like Randy Johnson's May 18, 2004, perfect game (no hits, no walks, 13 strikeouts) required 117 pitches. By contrast, in the same average game a team will have about nine baserunners they might need to give signs to. A catcher's signs are the most common, and tempting signal for another team to break.

Some hitters don't want to know what the pitcher and catcher decide to throw next. They see the ball and hit it, reacting in a fraction of a second, their amazing hand-eye coordination allowing them to approach each pitch with a perfect, uncaring ignorance. Hank

Aaron, baseball's career home run leader, wanted only to step into the batter's box, watch the pitch, and react.* Such a hitter is rare even among the best in the major league. Most batters try to guess what's coming, because it helps them watch for a pitch's location and time their swing better. These batters love to know what's coming, and they'll cheat to find out.

It starts innocently enough. The hitter can get hints without seeing the catcher's signs. If a pitcher's in love with his curve but can't get it over the plate, the catcher will call for the fastball when they have to get a strike. If the count is 3-2 and the pitcher's shaking the catcher off, it's a good bet the pitcher wants to throw the curve he's so smitten with.

A good hitter will also try to read hidden meaning in all of the things that make up a pitcher's delivery. Details like how high they hold their glove before they start their windup can be unconscious clues that tell a batter what pitch is coming. It's called "tipping pitches," and both sides look for it. Pitchers strive for a delivery that's easy, smooth, repeatable, and deceptive, so a fastball and a changeup look as close as possible until the ball comes off the pitcher's hands, and with their pitching coach they watch the tape, ensuring that there are no clues a hitter could pick up. Hitters spend time in the video room too, studying footage of the pitcher, trying to find flaws that give information away that the pitcher hasn't noticed or hasn't fixed.

The hitter can also look back for clues. Knowing where the catcher is set up tells him where the ball will go and gives him a better guess about the kind of pitch that will be coming. Some hitters wave the bat, wiggle their fingers, or open and close their grip on the bat handle to disguise their wandering eyes.

This is fairly safe. A catcher wants to give the pitcher an easy target to throw to, so he wants to set up early. He doesn't want to set up and then have to move. It's harder to catch the ball if you have to move, and it's harder on the pitcher to throw where you're going to be. Further, a catcher doesn't want to get in the umpire's way: the

---

* Once on base, though, Aaron would happily steal signs and help whoever was at bat; he was supposedly quite adept at it.

Will Clark, lip reader

During the 1989 National League Championship Series, the Giants were ahead of the Cubs, 4–3, in the fourth inning. With two outs and the bases loaded, Cubs pitcher Greg Maddux faced Giants first baseman Will Clark, who'd already homered off him in the second inning. Cubs manager Don Zimmer came out to talk to his pitcher, and Clark watched. "I was standing there, adjusting my batting glove, and I had a clear view of Maddux's face," he recalled. "I could see him say 'fastball in' to Zimmer." Clark hit a grand slam home run, and the Giants went on to win the first game, 11–3, and took the series, four games to one.

Now pitchers hold their gloves over their mouths during mound conferences. Clark's moment of insight created what is now a baseball convention. And yet he was on only 4.4 percent of the 2006 Hall of Fame ballots. It's a disgrace.

better a view of the pitch the ump gets, the more likely he'll call it a strike. A catcher might bark at a batter he sees looking back, and if the batter doesn't knock it off, he'll make a point of waiting to set up while calling for a fastball inside, but for the most part it's not worth worrying about.

If a batter can't figure out what a pitcher's throwing by a careful examination of the pitcher or sly looks at the catcher's position, he can try and watch for the sign. Usually, a catcher's signals are extremely simple. One finger means fastball, two fingers is a curve ball, and so on, varying a little depending on the pitcher's repertoire. If it works and the hitter gets sign and location, the batter is perfectly prepared.

Catchers don't put up with this. Using an arranged signal or having planned the set-up between innings, the catcher will ask for something slow and away, and the pitcher will agree but instead throw a fastball up and in. The hitter steals the sign and leans in to better swing at something on the outer half of the plate, thinking he'll wait a little bit on the slower pitch. Instead he sees a ball coming right at his ribs, and if his reflexes are good, he'll manage to get out of the way in time. Then the catcher laughs at him. This is why batters don't steal signs themselves.

Fortunately, batters can sometimes get someone else to look for them (and get plunked, too). A runner on second base can see a catcher's signs just as well as the pitcher and can tell the hitter what's coming. He can do this by offering a visual cue as he takes a lead. For instance, he could put his hands on his knees for a fastball, his hands at his side for a breaking pitch. He can also yell encouragement as the pitcher goes into his set position, with one phrase or word for a fastball, a clap for a curve, and so on.

But catchers and pitchers aren't stupid. When a runner is on second, instead of a simple "this sign means this pitch" signal, they use "rolling signs." They may use one sign to indicate which following sign is real. So, 1 finger, 2 fingers, 1 finger, 3 fingers, 1 finger could mean:

1. "fastball" (first sign repeated)
2. "curve" (first sign indicates which of the following signs are live — in this case, the next one)
3. "change-up" (second sign indicates which following sign to pay attention to — the second one)

It could be as simple as "fastball," the last sign in the sequence, or even more complicated, such as using different sign systems depending on any number of other factors, like the inning, what piece of equipment the catcher touches first, and so on.

Rolling signs make it far more difficult for a runner to figure out what's coming. The drawback is that the more complicated the system, the more likely screw-ups become. A mistake can mean a curve ball gets by an unprepared catcher and the runner advances a base. This is why the battery uses the more complicated rolling signs only when they have to.

Still, a smart runner can figure out rolling signs, especially if they get to see a lot of pitches while they're at second. When a catcher suspects they might be figuring it out, he'll walk out to the mound and say, "Look, I'm going to throw down a bunch of random signs,

The uncrackable codes

Some pitchers call their own pitches, signaling to the catcher, who then accepts or refuses the choice. These are generally veterans with weighty reputations, particularly pitchers who rely on pitch selection and location over raw speed.

Jamie Moyer, the veteran crafty left-hander for the Phillies, has used systems where it looks like the catcher's calling a pitch, but the pitch comes from how many times Moyer shakes off a sign, or how he nods.

This kind of system is almost impenetrable. If a catcher learns a whole new way of negotiating pitches that involves progressive arithmetic, what chance does anyone on the outside have of figuring it out in the course of a game?

but let's go fastball in, curve out, and if we don't have this guy out by then, we'll go fastball up and then change down."

Runners have two reasons to steal signs from the catcher: one selfish, one altruistic. They want to run on breaking pitches, which are slower and harder for the catcher to field cleanly, giving them a better chance of making it the ninety feet to the next base before the catcher's throw. Rickey Henderson, who once stole 130 bases in a season, was adept at stealing signs, but he could also read more subtle things — from a catcher's stance or how he gave the signs — that would tell him what was coming. And when that failed, he was a good guesser.

The runner can also try to help his teammate at bat. Even if he is baffled, he can still signal the batter where the catcher's setting up, which gives the hitter a location without his having to take his eyes off the pitcher and look back. And location, again, can help determine pitch type, which is almost as good as knowing what the sign was.

Sometimes a runner on first or third will be able to pick off the signs and alert the hitter. Catchers try to give their signs to the pitcher while using their legs to shield them from view, but they don't always do a good job. They might reveal their hands by opening their legs too wide or dropping their fingers too low. Then, because the catcher's not using the complicated signaling, the runner can see and tip off the batter quickly.

Some runners are known as pests. "Pete Rose worked hard at trying to get location," Steve Rogers, longtime leader of the Expos pitching staff, said. "If he saw a catcher slide outside or inside, he could relay not only location but possibly the type of pitch too. The Phillies were a damn good team when Rose was there, and my God, you didn't have to give the Big Red Machine much information back in the '70s."

Batters don't always need a runner on second to help them out. Throughout baseball's history, teams have crossed the line into cheating by using their home field advantage to set up spies that signal the batter. In 1876, the Hartford Dark Blues hung a small shack off a telegraph pole outside their park to signal batters.

The first known use of electronics came in Philadelphia in 1898, when visiting Reds shortstop Tommy Corcoran's spikes stuck in the dirt at third base. He found a buried wire, and with the groundskeeper yelling at him and players from both sides gathering around, he pulled it up. Starting at a small, concealed vault that contained a battery and other "electric apparatus," the wire ran all the way to the home team's clubhouse in the outfield, where a player would sit with binoculars and signal the pitch by setting the ground under the third base coach shaking, and the coach would in turn alert the batter.

Corcoran joked that the contraption entombed at third was either "an infernal device" or a mine laid for Philadelphia's coach. The umpire asked them to get back to the game, saying, if the clipping is to be believed, "Back to the mines, men. Think on that eventful day in July when Dewey went into Manila Bay never giving a tinker's dam for all the mines concealed therein."

It is incidents like these, by the way, that highlight how argumentation and witty repartee on the field have declined in modern baseball. When was the last time an umpire settled a dispute with a timely historical reference? But we digress.

Since then, it's been variations on the theme, a Choose Your Own Adventure of cheating: a [hired spy/scrub player/coach/low man on

Don't stare too closely

Eddie Stanky, the second baseman for the 1951 Brooklyn Dodgers, was at times too devoted to helping his teammates. "I'd get picked off first now and then, because I'd be so engrossed in studying the catcher's signs, but [manager Leo] Durocher didn't care because he knew what I was doing." This, it turns out, was just one of the sign-stealing tactics the 1951 Giants used.

the organizational totem pole] is placed [in the scoreboard/in a nearby apartment with a view of the field/in the stands/on top of the fence] and alerts the batter to the next pitch using [a mirror/the way they sat/an electronic device/opening or closing a hole in the manually operated out-of-town scoreboard], but with only one ending: you have to shut the operation down. It's almost tedious, but sometimes a variation is funny, such as when Bernie Brewer, the mascot of the Milwaukee Brewers who lived in a center field home and would slide into a mug of beer at County Stadium* after his team hit a home run, probably† stole signs. You can imagine him signaling a fastball to a batter and then, when the batter yanks the pitch into the stands, going down the slide and hustling, soaked with beer,‡ back up to his spot to try and signal again.

As Rogers Hornsby put it in his book *My War with Baseball*, "Every team with a scoreboard in center field has a spy inside at one time or another."

The most famous incident involved the 1951 New York Giants, who made one of the greatest comebacks in sports. Behind 13½ games to the Brooklyn Dodgers in August, the Giants played so well, they tied their rivals at the end of the season and forced a three-game playoff. They then won the pennant in dramatic fashion when Bobby Thomson hit the famous "Shot Heard 'Round the World" home run to and sent the Giants to the World Series.

Rumors that the Giants had been stealing signs made the rounds

---

* Moved to Miller Park, he now has a slide that goes nowhere. This is ridiculous.

† Almost certainly.

‡ He did not actually dive into a giant stein of beer. That would have been too cool.

Stupid morals, always getting in the way

If a team's stealing signs, some players won't want them, either because they don't want the distraction or because they don't want to cheat. Almost all of them will keep their mouth shut. A few, though, will demand a stop to the practice or ask for a trade to another club (where, their current team can reasonably guess, they'll spill the beans). Pitcher Al Worthington, a Giant in September of 1959, told manager Bill Rigney that he felt using binoculars crossed the line into cheating, and since as a devoted Christian he'd been telling people they didn't need "to lie or cheat in this world if you trust Jesus Christ," he couldn't abide by the practice. He wouldn't play unless they stopped.

Worthington said that Rigney agreed to stop using the system. "He did come to me and say he couldn't pitch if we stole the signs," Rigney said years later, after initially denying they'd had any system at all. "Naturally, I thought what we were doing was legitimate, but I told him we'd quit it right away if it upset him." The Giants then got beat up by the hated Dodgers and lost the pennant. The lesson here is that God doesn't reward righteousness, at least not on the field of play.

A year later, Worthington played for the White Sox and found that they too were stealing signs with binoculars, so he had a similar conversation with manager Al Lopez, then argued with executive Hank Greenberg (who, as a hitter, loved being tipped off by his runners). Greenberg, putting the sign-stealing in historical perspective, tried to convince Worthington that it wasn't a big deal. Worthington left the team, sat out the rest of the year, then returned to the White Sox minor league system. It was years before a team was willing to take a chance on bringing him in.

a few times over the next fifty years, but in 2001 Joshua Prager wrote an article in the *Wall Street Journal* based on extensive interviews with surviving Giants, who revealed they'd been stealing signs. (He expanded the article into a book, *The Echoing Green,* in 2006.)

It started with a July 19, 1951, team meeting. The Giants were second in the National League, 7½ games behind the Dodgers. In a team meeting, manager Leo Durocher asked if the players wanted to know the signs, and according to the accounts Prager collected, only half of them said they did.

The scheme didn't help their hitting. They did go a shocking 23-5 at home until they faced the Dodgers for that three-game playoff, but it was stellar pitching that won them game after game. The Giants didn't score more runs at home using the system. Despite all the furor over the revelations and overwrought hand-wringing about how the revelation tainted a title won half a century earlier, there's no evidence that it helped them win the pennant.

But take Bobby Thomson's home run. Did he have the sign? In the *Wall Street Journal* article, he's asked repeatedly. Thomson doesn't answer directly at first ("I'd have to say more no than yes") before he seems to hint that he did, then finally denies it. So he did. No matter how little it may have helped him, sign-stealing was part of the home run that made the Giants National League Champions.

Did it break any rules, though? Stealing signs on the field is accepted, if underhanded and devious, while using spotters outside the stadium, plants in the stands, or interns in the scoreboard are all considered cheating. Baseball's standard is that once you use equipment or people not actively involved with the game, you've crossed a line.

But is there a rule? There's nothing in the Official Rules that says you cannot steal signs. Signs are barely covered in the rules at all: there's a brief mention: "Pitchers shall take signs from the catcher while standing on the rubber," but that's about it. You might think that it would be covered in the Major League Rules, which is the framework for how Major League Baseball works: there's a commissioner, two leagues, and the press needs their own bathrooms so they don't have to mingle with people like me,* and so on. But it's not covered there or even mentioned in the section that defines the standards of a major league stadium.

Why, then, don't all teams do it all the time? It's covered under the commissioner's broad powers in Rule 21, Misconduct (which defines penalties for gambling and game-fixing, which we'll get to):

---

* "It is recommended that all facilities provide media restroom facilities separate from public restrooms, located with direct access to the press box."

A hypothetical conversation between the commissioner and a team stealing signs

Commissioner: I understand you're stealing signs.

Team: Uhhhhh, no I'm not.

Commish: That's not what the other team told me. They said your mascot hangs out in center field and uses those giant novelty pennants to signal the hitter in semaphore.

Team: Those tattletales! They stole signs first! They've got a guy who sneaks into the hotdog sign in left field and wiggles the bun if it's a fastball.

Commish: I understand you're upset, and we're going to investigate the other team, too. But you have to stop this.

Team: You can't make me!

Commish: Now, don't be like that. You and I both know I can if I have to, but I don't want to do that.

Team: Oooookay.

Commish: Go and give your mascot the week off, and when he comes back, I don't want to see him anywhere near the bleachers when your team's up, and no flags of any kind. Do you understand?

Team: Fine. I didn't want to steal signs anyway.

Commish: And no pouting . . .

Team (heavy sigh with eyes rolling): Fine.

(f) OTHER MISCONDUCT. Nothing herein contained shall be construed as exclusively defining or otherwise limiting acts, transactions, practices or conduct not to be in the best interests of Baseball; and any and all other acts, transactions, practices or conduct not to be in the best interests of Baseball are prohibited and shall be subject to such penalties, including permanent ineligibility, as the facts in the particular case may warrant.

Major League Baseball decided early in its history that they were willing to allow sign steals on the field but that using outside observers, cameras, or anything like that was unacceptable. The result's been decades of ad hoc enforcement.

Besides tattling, a team can take practical steps to prevent a catcher's signs from being stolen.

The easiest is for the pitcher to work faster. When a catcher's sign is stolen, even by a runner, the batter has to be alerted before the pitch is thrown or the information's useless. Watch a baseball game with a stopwatch, and you'll see just how short it is. With no runners on, the average time from the catcher flashing a sign to the pitcher starting his motion is about two seconds. That means that any system can't have too many steps. Someone in center field on the phone with someone in the dugout who shouts a clue to the batter is going to miss a lot of calls.

With slow pitchers like the Mets' Steve Trachsel (who's been booed even by home town fans for his amazingly boring mound manner), their lethargy makes them vulnerable to sign-stealing techniques that use carrier pigeons. But a fast worker like Mark Buehrle of the White Sox makes stealing signs almost impossible. Even if someone in center field could see a sign and instantly put up a giant "fastball in" message up on the scoreboard, a batter risking the glance might look back to see the pitch already on its way.

Efficient pitching is effective. Hall of Fame pitcher Whitey Ford (who did some cheating of his own) was so fast, he never worried about sign-stealing, knowing that opposing teams couldn't get a signal around to the batter in time.

Teams that suspect they're being watched can also use more complicated rolling signs constantly instead of only with a runner on second. The risk of having the pitcher throw something the catcher doesn't expect increases, but it beats hitters knowing what's coming. When the Red Sox were accused of signaling pitches from the bullpen during the 2003 season, smart or paranoid teams, like the Yankees, went to rolling signs when they had to play in Fenway Park.

While the signs between catcher and pitcher are the most commonly given and stolen, they're not the most lucrative. Knowing the pitch that's coming can give a hitter an advantage, but he still has to get the hit, and that's never easy.

The other stream of communications on the field, those of the offense, provide information that can be used to turn runners into outs.

These signals go from the manager in the dugout to his two

coaches, at first and third base. They in turn signal the hitter and any runners what to do.

For example, with a man on first, a manager calls for a hit-and-run. His third base coach goes into a long, convoluted dance as the hitter and runner watch. If everything goes well, the runner will sprint from first as the pitch is delivered. The second baseman, seeing the runner go, will run toward second base to be in position to receive a throw from the catcher. The batter tries to put the ball into play toward the hole the second baseman was covering. If he succeeds, the runner can keep going to third and the hitter gets to second.

A lot can go wrong, and the juicy bit of information there is obvious. The runner waits until the pitcher is definitely throwing home and then runs, which means he breaks late. If the hitter doesn't make contact, the catcher has an excellent chance of throwing to second in time to make an out. If the pitching team knows that the runner is going, they'll use a pitchout — an unhittable pitch thrown high and outside, putting the catcher in perfect position to make a strong throw.

Instead of having runners on first and third, the hitting team burns an out and loses a runner. Every set play that depends on coordination of action and surprise can become a horrible move if the other team takes effective countermeasures, from the hit-and-run to being freed to charge the corner infielders when you know a bunt is coming.

How does a defensive team pick off that sign? There are two ways: the cheap and the elegant.

The cheap way is to ignore the coaches with their long, complicated routines and watch the players receiving the signs. It's like poker players reading tells. "Baserunners are like thieves," Roger Craig, manager of the Giants from 1985 through 1992, said. "A lot of times, they give themselves away. It could be the way they fix their helmet, or look at second base, or if they do something different when they squat down."

Hitters sometimes resent being asked to bunt. Their manager's choice to give away the batter's chance for a hit in order to advance a

> ## It's not a mating dance
>
> There are only a few signs of any importance that a third base coach gives for the runner and hitter:
>
> - hitter, do not swing at this next pitch
> - hitter, go ahead and swing at the next pitch if you like it
> - runner, take off on this next pitch
> - runner, take off on this next pitch, and you in the batter's box, for God's sake swing and put the ball into play hard, preferably where the fielders aren't
> - runner, take off on this next pitch, and you in the batter's box, for God's sake lay down a decent bunt
>
> with variants for each runner (or all), if there's more than one on, of course.

runner can be taken as a lack of confidence, and their annoyance at having the bat taken from their hands will flash on their faces.

No matter how industrious, the moves a team can make in any situation are limited. For instance, the runner can either run to the next base on the pitch or stay and see what the hitter does. He can't sprint into the outfield and tackle the right fielder. This makes reading their reactions profitable. A slow runner who does a double-take while watching the third base coach was asked to steal. A fast runner who gets a steal sign on an unconventional count (3-0, for instance, when a fastball is likely) may have the same reaction. Knowing a play is on allows the pitching team to guess at what the play is and gain the advantage.

Decryption is the elegant means. When first used, signs were intended to be secret: if a coach adjusted his belt, the other team wasn't meant to see it as a possible sign. Now coaches go through a series of exaggerated, formal motions as everyone stares at them.

Hypothetically, a team could invent an uncrackable sign system. If the number of pitches the pitcher has thrown is a multiple of three, look for the second signal, but only on Tuesdays and Thursdays unless it's a day game, for example, it would be almost impossible to figure out. Fortunately, some players are not as gifted crani-

1. Shoulder touch: meaningless. **Belt touch:** the next sign is live.
Brush-off of the arm: steal second. **Touch nose:** meaningless.

2. Roll head around on shoulders: a real sign is coming . . . **Touch belt
buckle:** bunt. **Clap hands:** steal second. **Pull earlobe:** okay, the next sign
is the live sign. **Tap chest:** take the next pitch

SOME SAMPLE SIGN SEQUENCES

3. Hitch pants up:
repeat what I told you last pitch

4. Shake head with hands, palm up, in front of body: I don't know why we
signed you. **Rub thumb against index and middle finger:** we pay you a ton
of money. **Swing imaginary bat:** get a hit. **Point to burly dude in stands:** or
this guy I know, **run thumb across throat:** will kill you.

ally as they are athletically. If a player can't easily figure out what he's supposed to do, it doesn't matter what a golden opportunity it is. The complexity of a team's system is limited by their dumbest player.

That means that it's breakable.

The first step is to watch the signs. There's almost always information immediately available. Coaches use two signs the player must see: the "takeoff" sign, which means that whatever sign was just given is to be ignored, and the "live" sign. So the sign to steal might be a tug of the hat brim. If a tug of the brim is followed by the takeoff sign, which is usually obvious — like brushing across the team name on front of the coach's uniform — the runner stays put. These signs are usually even more exaggerated than the other ones and will look like breaks in the coach's rhythm.

Watching for the cadence of a coach's signs will quickly reveal whether a play is on or not. After that, it's a matter of figuring whether each of the many individual fidgets is meaningful.

Some players and coaches devote themselves to this work and can contribute to the team's success. Becoming one of the game's great sign-stealers requires dedication, a quick mind, and a long memory. A manager or coach might use a set of signs and change them to avoid detection, but they are creatures of habit, and an old sign may creep into use again. Coaches who learn good systems from a manager will carry them into their own managerial jobs, so you can trace the pedigree of a sign.

Some sign-stealers come to know the other team's signals better than those of their own players.

White Sox coach Joe Nossek once called an opposing coach the day after a player blew a play and needled him, asking, "Will you teach your guys the signs?" It's a case where a player's missing the sign likely saved him from being thrown out, but it also shows that sometimes the other side can identify and pick up signs better than the players who are supposed to act on them. It's also a case where Nossek, who had a tremendous reputation as a sign-stealer — to the point where opposing managers confessed they would change signs more than once a game when they faced him — saw a chance to tweak the other guy and make him even more paranoid. "Even if we don't have the signs, they think I might have them, so it works as a psychological advantage for us," Nossek said.

While most sign-stealing comes from the manager, his coaches, and bored players on the bench, the pitcher and catcher shouldn't be overlooked. It's easy to think that they're so preoccupied with their own signals, they couldn't be paying attention, but they are. "The biggest thing for me was being able to pick up a hit-and-run or steal sign," pitcher Bill Lee said. "I picked a lot of guys off just by picking up on little clues."

There's another set of signs the defensive team can try to attack: the manager to the coaches. This is why in some stadiums there's no place to hide from easy view in the visitor's dugout, forcing managers to use human shields or have other coaches or players send the signs in. Cardinals manager Tony LaRussa resorted to the team's trainer when everyone else was being watched.

Billy Martin used a microphone and a transmitter and gave his coaches earpieces to avoid the chance that his signs would be stolen. But the agitated Martin was exposed when he couldn't contain himself and took to shouting when the transmission wasn't working. (Which entirely defeated the purpose of having a "secret" transmission system.)

Sometimes a team doesn't have to work. When a player is acquired from another team, he'll be debriefed about his previous employer: Are they stealing signs from the scoreboard? What can you tell us about their sign system? Do you know if their pitchers have any flaws we might not have seen yet but are obvious to you?

If a player's willing to talk, the information they give about their system can be valuable even if the other team changes their specific signs.

Joey Amalfitano, a Cubs manager and sign-stealer, gave each player his own sign to make it harder for the other team to figure out and also compartmentalize: Getting rid of one player didn't reveal anything about the system. But facing Colorado, he gave the steal sign to a player twice, and both times the other team pitched out and nailed the player at second. Amalfitano suspected something; the player confessed that he had shared his sign with a teammate. Amalfitano looked across the diamond at the player's pal, now with the Rockies in the other dugout, sitting next to the coach who'd called for both pitch-outs.

Even when teams can find out the other side's signs, they may not use that information. As the legendary Earl Weaver wrote in the seminal *Weaver on Strategy:* "Say you find out that a runner is stealing on a 2-2 pitch. The manager calls for the pitch-out, and the runner is nabbed. Well, the guy in the other dugout isn't stupid. He'll see what happened and immediately change his signs. Stealing the steal sign might work once all year."

Weaver said that some signs were more exploitable than others and could also be used to discover if your signs had been broken. "You might get more mileage from the bunt sign, because in most situations the bunt is so obvious that no one is sure if you stole the sign or were simply guessing that there'd be a bunt. Usually you know the opposition has your bunt sign if it's clearly a bunt situation but you let your hitter swing away — and on the pitch the infielders don't move. That indicates the other team has your sign because they knew the bunt *wasn't* on."

There are other reasons sign-stealing isn't as prevalent as it could be. Many managers see it as underhanded or not worth the trouble.

In general, there's a gentlemen's agreement that teams won't try. They don't want to start an arms race. If every team starts cracking every other team's signs, all they have to come up with harder systems for their own team, and then rotate them, and it's all a pain in the butt, especially when most teams have bigger problems to worry about, such as who plays where and how the designated hitter was arrested scaling a fence at a summer debate camp for high school girls.

This is disappointing. A home team using cameras and other trickery is bad, because it means the two teams aren't playing on a level field (which they may not be anyway, but that's the chapter on groundskeeping). Sign-stealing by players, coaches, and managers is good for the game, adding a new, complex dimension.

Strategy plays a much larger role in Japanese baseball. An oversized importance is attached to scoring the first run in a game, which they believe hurts the other team's morale so much that it's difficult to overcome. Tactics like the sacrifice bunt, where the batter

How to steal signs: A fan's guide to impressing friends and annoying enemies

The trick depends on exposure, first and foremost, so it'll be easier for you to pick off the home team's signs over an eight-game home stand than it is to decipher the visiting team's signs in a few games.

That said, pay close attention to the third base coach. He'll go through a routine for each pitch. Watch. When there's a play on, he wants to make sure the runner gets the signal, so at least one signal should be slower and more exaggerated than the others.

Sit back and say, "They're going to try something." If you're wrong, pretend you said nothing. You probably picked off the "takeoff" sign. If you're right, you picked off either the specific "do this" sign or, more likely, the "live sign," which tells whoever's watching that all the other gestures are for real and should be followed.

That's valuable information. Most plays are obvious: a sacrifice bunt, a hit-and-run, a straight steal — if you go to a fair number of games, you'll know what the manager uses. Knowing the game situation, the manager's preferences, and the "live" sign, you should be able to predict the play.

Or you may have managed to decode the actual play sign ("go steal"). Congratulations! Now watch for each play when the sign's given and see if they go for it or not. If you see the play sign and nothing happens, one of the other signs in that sequence was the "take off" sign (or, more properly, "never mind"), or the "live" sign wasn't given.

If you pay close enough attention, it shouldn't take you more than a game or two to get any team's "live" and "take off" signs. A particularly obvious third base coach will give up his entire signal system to you in a game.

Go get 'em.

intentionally gets himself out in order to move the runner ahead one base, are far more frequent. There are strategy meetings on the field. Sign-stealing is so valued that teams may use several entirely different systems and rotate among them every few innings even if they don't think the other team's broken one. They're so paranoid that teams have actually issued code sheets to fielders. The sign from the dugout would be two numbers, and the fielders would have to look at the sheet to take appropriate action. It slowed the game so much, the commissioner banned its use.

Sign-stealing is slumping. There aren't as many coaches with fearsome reputations or players with eagle eyes and time to kill. But this can't last. The rewards are too high. The difference between making the playoffs and staying home for the postseason means millions of dollars to a team, and for many it can be the difference between losing money and pretending you're losing money.

Even if we assume that you can't hire or train a staff of expert codebreakers, the cost of cameras and signaling equipment drops daily, so the temptation to deploy a sophisticated sign-stealing system at a team's home park will only grow. A team could easily set up a camera with a wireless connection to broadcast a signal right back to the dugout so someone could tip the hitter off. Today's sophisticated scoreboards are far better suited to convey information than yesterday's could and don't even require a player to look away — they can put some dumb "cheer!" message up where the color background tells the hitter if a fastball is next.

Teams could record the signs of each opposing coach all game and then have their college interns tag and collate everything and deliver a complete report the next day. It wouldn't take a four-game series to produce a key to reading the other coach.

This kind of ploy is so cheap, so easy, and the rewards so high that teams will give in to temptation, and the commissioner's going to have to do a lot of time on the phones.

Arguing with umps

I've never questioned the integrity of an umpire.
Their eyesight, yes.

— Leo Durocher, manager

UMPIRES ARE A HALLOWED, honored part of the game. And they're human. They make mistakes. As much as they may strive to be impartial — and some don't strive much at all — as humans they are imperfect, and generations of players and managers have tried to take advantage of that imperfection.

Umpires tolerate a certain amount of cheating, and their tolerance affects how the game is played. Take the evolution of a double play. A player takes the ball at second, has to touch the bag for the force-out and throw to first to get the batter. Early in baseball's history, fielders would block the runners from reaching base, and runners would do what they had to to get past them or knock the ball loose. Over time, obstruction rules prevented a fielder from getting in the runner's way, which gave runners a free shot at taking out their opponent. Fielders started using the modern move, where they try to keep the bag between them and the runner as modest protection. Runners then slid late, past the bag. Fielders moved farther back and runners went with them, and today the fielder taking the throw doesn't need to tag second base at all for the out as long as he's in the vicinity — this is called the phantom tag. The runner, as compensation, is allowed to slide at the fielder even though the fielder's nowhere near second.

The result is that you can see double plays turned where the shortstop doesn't get closer than three feet to second base while the runner barrels into him. Both sides break the rules: the umpires are giving the second baseman an out he did not make, because it's tra-

When the umpires start to walk off, it's time to let the argument go. Here, Leo Durocher keeps after Jocko Conlan over the ejection of his pitcher. *AP*

dition and they want him not to get hurt, but the runner is not called out (or ejected) for attempting to interfere with the fielder and possibly injure him, because breaking up the double play is part of the hard, physical game of the late nineteenth century.

Umpires allow catchers to cheat and block the plate on a run-scoring play. They're allowed to do everything shy of building a brick wall to stop the runner, even though it is clearly an illegal obstruction. As long as they can hang on to the ball, they'll get the call. So runners are forced to try and knock them down, and this too has become a dangerous, accepted illegal play.

As runners and fielders worked over a hundred years to determine how much they can get away with, in every game the pitchers find what that night's strike zone is, how it differs from the rulebook definition, and then set about getting it changed.

Because their every action is judged by an umpire and their success depends entirely on the outcome of his decisions, pitchers try to influence an umpire more than any other player, coach, or manager. But arguing balls and strikes has always been a dangerous dance as long as baseball has had umpires behind the plate. As the *Spalding Guide* warned in 1894: "It is the height of folly on the part of a pitcher to work against the umpire by repeated appeals for judgment on strikes, as it is simply a tacit questioning either of his judgment or his impartiality. A pitcher who, by word or action, incurs the prejudice of an umpire in a match, is simply working against his own interests."

Some pitchers huff after what they think is a bad call, glare at the ump as if they can't believe a strike wasn't called, or stomp around the mound like a toddler. They might go to the rosin bag, load up their hand, and then toss the bag hard, back into the dirt. This is called "showing up the umpire" and is not to be done. It certainly doesn't make an umpire more sympathetic, and it might make him dramatically less so.

Instead, watch how some of the really brainy, polite pitchers do it. Jamie Moyer, the aging-like-wine crafty left-hander of the Phillies, for instance, works an umpire over like he's giving him a shoulder massage — arguing as if he's doing a good job of customer service. He pumps the ump for information on balls ("Too low?" Ump nods. "Okay") as he works out what he can and can't get called a strike that day, and when he wants to make a point about the pitch he just threw, he might look at the ump a little quizzically, as if it's he who misunderstood the umpire's strike zone. He might ask, entirely politely, "So . . . too high, then?" Even umpires who start out offering him no information often find themselves giving away valuable evaluations after a few innings, and by the end of the game they're inviting him to drop by their kid's birthday party in the off-season if he's in the neighborhood.

That's working an umpire.

The most explosive eruption of Mt. Piniella

Manager Lou Piniella, now with the Cubs, has had many amazing blowups with umpires, even in his later, more mellow years. Umpires ejected him from the game over fifty times in his career. He kicked dirt on home plate, threw bases, and said all kinds of unkind things. He once kicked dirt on home plate to protest John Shulock's (horrible) strike zone and, unsatisfied, went down on his knees to bury the plate in dirt with his hands. But September 18, 2002, saw the greatest eruption of Mt. Piniella ever.

It was a medley of almost everything he'd done before, and more. Piniella ran out to argue a close call at first base, tossing his hat down and screaming at umpire C. B. Bucknor. Bucknor ejected him immediately, and his smirk enraged Sweet Lou. He kicked his cap, yelled at Bucknor, got the first base coach to bring his hat back, threw it again, picked up first base, threw it down the first base line, walked to the base, and threw it again. "I think I hurt my hamstring and right shoulder," Piniella said afterward.

Some managers change styles as they age and gain experience. Casey Stengel once intimidated and abused umpires to the point of sparking riots (an incident that appears in the heckling chapter). Later in his life, he made his points frequently and forcefully but without the abuse. "If I'm going to be buggered, I don't want an amateur handling the grease pot," Stengel said.

Earl Weaver was as well known for his argumentative nature as for his long and impressive record as the manager of the Orioles. He was thrown out of almost a hundred games, including an ejection from a World Series game (a rare occurrence; umpires tend to be much more tolerant the more important the game is). Yankees owner George Steinbrenner said Weaver's style of dealing with the umpires won him eight or ten games a year. Weaver disagreed.

Weaver offers three basic rules for arguing with an umpire in his book *Weaver on Strategy:*

1. Never curse an umpire. Curse the call, say it was a bleeping bad call, but never call the umpire a name. Try not to get personal.
2. Know the rules. If you know the rules, you might win one now and then.
3. Be yourself when you're dealing with umpires.

Given Weaver's success in managing, it's wise to heed all his advice. On the other hand, he sure got thrown out of a lot of games for a guy who never cursed and was right all the time.

While Weaver often argued points of the rules, most of the time he acted as a fuse for his enraged players. He felt that he didn't mat-

Signs you're about to be ejected

You've repeated your arguments twice, and the umpire has said that
while he understands your point, the call stands.
There's dirt on the umpire's shoes (you kicked it there).
Umpires start to discuss where they're going to eat after the game.
You've just thrown something.
The umpire keeps looking at his watch, yawning.
You asked the umpire to eject you.
You just called the umpire a sharp name that ends in -cker.

ter as much as any of them, so if they got in an argument and risked
ejection, Weaver wanted to argue so well on their behalf that they
would calm down and let him handle it. As Weaver saw it, if he got
ejected and his player stayed in the game, it was worth it.

Does arguing with umpires matter? There's no clear evidence
that any approach helps a team get better calls. But while Weaver's
strategy got him tossed frequently (his 98 career ejections is the AL
record), it kept valuable players in the game. Those angry players,
who might have been ejected, did not win games, so it's fair to give
Weaver some credit.

It's more important for a manager or a player to choose the style
that most fits him personally. If he's better off as a calm, reasonable
debater, able to make lucid, intelligent arguments, that's the best
way for him to approach an umpire on a questionable decision. If
he's better at displaying anger and confusion through swearing and
arm-waving, then this is likely how he'll be most effective.

In his book, Weaver also offers a piece of advice that opens up a
whole tangent: "On the pickoff move to first base, you can sometimes cheat a little. Certain umpires will not call balks. The pitcher
can twist his shoulder halfway to the clubhouse and they won't call a
thing. You add a little 'cheat' move to a pitcher's repertoire and tell
your pitcher that he can use it when certain umpires are on first
base. It doesn't mean a balk won't be called, but you can get away
with it most of the time. I know of an umpire who has called only
one balk in his career. He told me this, and said he only called the

balk because the pitcher dropped the ball while he was on the mound, and that's an automatic balk. Furthermore, the umpire said he waited until the ball bounced twice before making the call."

Ron Luciano, who often fought with Weaver (including ejecting him from both games of a doubleheader in 1985), said, "I never called a balk in my life. I didn't understand the rule." Given their relationship, it seems unlikely that Luciano had a friendly conversation with Weaver in which he revealed this, so there were at least two umpires who didn't call balks working at the time.

Most pitchers have two pickoff moves:

1. The slow move ("Come on, get on back to the base and cut your lead, or I'll bore you to sleep with this throw over and over").
2. The fast move, used when the pitcher is actually trying to get an out ("Now that I've bored you to sleep . . . think fast!").

But some teams add a third:

3. The totally illegal balk move ("Nooot doing anything, doot doo — gotcha!").

Some teams, like the Oakland A's, do this. Their pitchers will develop one (or more) totally illegal pickoff moves and stash them away. When they really need an out, and the umpires watching them are of the breed Weaver talked to, they'll use it and get a confused baserunner out. Then the opposing manager comes out but to no avail — the A's are already walking off the field, disaster averted by well-timed, well-considered rule-breaking. If they did it more frequently, there might be protests that would result in the league's issuing a memo to umpires to crack down on it, but they're crafty enough to know that if they use it rarely, they'll continue to get away with it.

That kind of intelligence goes even further. When deciding whether to steal, smart teams think about more than the pitcher, the catcher, and the runner when they make the decision. They often consider the umpire, who has a tremendous role in whether a runner is safe. Fans have seen players who pretend they've made a tag — Derek Jeter is a master of the graceful-looking fake tag* — get the call when they make the play look good *even if they didn't make any contact with the runner*.† A 2000 study of umpire performance by Michael Wolverton of *Baseball Prospectus* found that "over a two-year period, Chuck Meriwether was about two and a half times more likely than Mike Everitt to send a would-be base-stealer back to the dugout."

Now, is this cheating? The balk personalization is, but because it breaks the rules and relies on the circumstances of enforcement to overlook it, it falls into the larger category of accepted behavior like "framing the pitch." It's tailoring actions to get the maximum advantage out of the game, and if umpires were perfect, the opportunity would disappear. And stealing bases more frequently because one ump pays close attention to the rules is exactly the same thing.

Working the umpires is part of the greater tradition of finding an advantage. Just as good managers and players will memorize the rulebook, so paying attention to those given the task of enforcing the rules is a natural and entertaining extension.

---

* Oh, how it boils my blood to see him pull this off over and over.
† Seriously, if I have to see Jeter nail another Mariner this way, my head's going to explode.

Delaying the game for fun and profit

BASEBALL IS THE ONLY major sport without a clock. You can be down 10 runs in the ninth, and you have all the time in the world to complete that inning. You don't have to rush batters up to the plate. There's no hurry-up offense. Until you make those last three outs, you're still alive.

This romantic notion of the timeless game came about only when parks could use banks of electric lights to illuminate the field at night. Major league teams once played under a curfew, and games were often called on account of darkness — which led to all kinds of chicanery as teams tried to get their games finished or called depending on the score.

For an example, on September 8, 1889, the Brooklyn Bridegrooms hosted the Boston Browns, led by their player/manager Charles Comiskey. The two teams were in a pennant race, with the Bridegrooms just one and a half games ahead of the Browns.

The Browns pestered the ump to call the game at the end of the sixth because of darkness. The ump ignored them, so the Browns took to all sorts of crazy delay tactics. They refused to throw runners out, trying so little to play the game that Bridegrooms catcher Bob Clark took two bases on a missed third strike. The team's president, Chris Von der Ahe, "sent to a grocery store for some candles, and after lighting them placed them in front of the bench occupied by his players."

Starting in the seventh, the Browns argued constantly with the umpire: every play, every call, every pitch, and every rule. They managed to drag the seventh inning out to 30 minutes. A full game played that slowly — without commercial breaks or any pitching changes — would take about four and a half hours — over twice as long as a typical one.

With the umpire still refusing to call the game and probably rightly annoyed, Comiskey pulled his players while he still led, 4–2. The umpire waited for five minutes and declared the game a forfeit to Brooklyn. Had they continued to play, the Browns probably would have won, though accounts differ on how serious the Brooklyn threat was when his team left the field.

The *Brooklyn Eagle* was appalled: "Not in the history of professional ball playing in this city has the game received such a blow to its continued favor with the best patrons of the national game as was given it yesterday at Washington Park at the hands of the St. Louis Club players and the club's president, the latter of whom sat on the bench and aided and abetted Captain Comiskey and his gang in their ball playing tricks on the field and in their bold and impudent exhibition of the bulldozing work through which they have gained so many of their victories this season. Hundreds were present yesterday who, on witnessing the disgraceful conduct of the visiting team in the closing part of the contest, declared that if that was professional ball playing they would have nothing to do with it."

The Browns were fined $1,500, which in 1899 . . . huzzah!

Casey Stengel, managing the Brooklyn Dodgers from 1934 to 1936, once wanted a game in which his team was leading called on account of darkness, as heavy rain clouds made it increasingly hard to see. The umpires denied him, so he signaled to his bullpen for a relief pitcher using a flashlight and was thrown out of the game. In other games, Stengel made his point by approaching the mound with an umbrella and a lantern, as if afraid he'd lose his way in the storm.

While lights have made playing for darkness obsolete and modern cities no longer have curfews or blue laws that deter Sunday games, the weather remains. At every park without a retractable roof, a situation arises in which one team wants to drag things out while the other wants to have it called so it goes into the books.

This is almost always playing for (or against) the rainout, and it's one of the greatest flaws in the modern rulebook. No game counts

Casey Stengel practices his theatrics during a rain delay at Yankee Stadium.

— or even officially exists — until five innings have been completed (four and a half if the home team's winning, because it doesn't matter if they get that last half inning). A game that's called because of weather before five innings isn't suspended — it's canceled. The statistics don't count; it's as if it never happened. The team that's behind gets a fresh start if the game is rescheduled.

Further, a set of bizarre rules operates around partially complete games after five innings have been played:

> If the game is called while an inning is in progress and before it is completed, the game becomes a SUSPENDED game in each of the following situations: (1) The visiting team has scored one or more runs to tie the score and the home team has not scored; (2) The visiting team has scored one or more runs to take the lead and the home team has not tied the score or retaken the lead.

If you're the home team, and you're up by one run in the top of the eighth inning, and the other team's loaded the bases and their best hitter is up, you have every reason to play for rain. Under the rules, if a downpour causes the game to end, that's it: you win by one run. If they tie or take the lead, it'll turn into a suspended game, and you'll be forced to continue from that point (and probably lose).

August 1, 1972: Brewers-Tigers. Rain started in the fourth. The Tigers, who trailed, began to slow the game down, hoping that it would have to be halted before it became official. It was crazy: a Tigers outfielder refused to catch a fly ball. The Detroit pitcher made repeated throws to first even though the runner took no lead. The Brewers players even begged to be tagged out, trying to end the game, and the Tigers refused. The umps called the game after an appalling six innings and immediately recommended that the two managers, Del Crandall (Brewers) and Billy Martin (Tigers), be fined for turning the game into a farce.

In 1978, the Orioles were playing in Memorial Stadium and leading the visiting Yankees by three runs. In the seventh, the Yankees scored five runs — but it started to rain, and there was a delay. The grounds crew, of course, was in no hurry. They brought out the tarp, pouring the water already on it into left field. Then they slowly pulled it out to cover the infield. The field lost; the umps called the game. Because the inning wasn't completed, the score reverted to the last completed inning, and Orioles won, 3–0, after trailing, 5–3.

One case, though, had the opposite result. In 1941, the Washington Senators were leading Boston, 6–3, in the eighth inning when the head umpire stopped the game. The grounds crew, though, didn't come out to cover the field. They didn't come out at all. The

Recognizing delay tactics before you fall asleep

Given the glacial pace of today's game, where using eleven or more pitchers is all too common, you might not notice delay-of-game tactics in use.

Here's what to look for: if the weather's obviously bad, particularly if the game's suffered more than one significant delay already and if it's getting late, the umpires want to get the game over with as much as anyone.

The leading team desperately wants to get far enough into the game that it's official when the umpires call it, so they'll be trying to get themselves out, swinging at any pitch.

Meanwhile, the trailing team will try and slow the game down, hoping the umpires will call it off and force the whole game to be played from scratch. It can make the game almost unwatchable. You'll see frequent, pointless pitcher-catcher conferences so transparently time-wasting that the home plate umpire nearly follows the catcher to the mound to tell them to hurry up. The pitcher will take as long as he can to get ready to throw again — pausing in the rain to load his hand up with rosin, walking the circumference of the mound, kicking at the rubber, checking his spikes — all of which is just as boring as it sounds. Add frequent throws to first when the runner isn't taking a lead, and soon the game'll be called out of frustration.

If they're at bat, they'll do the Mike Hargrove routine. If you ever have a chance to see one of the Human Rain Delay games on ESPN Classic, I highly recommend skipping it. Hargrove didn't step out of the box and adjust his batting gloves between pitches. He would walk down the third base line, take a few practice swings, go into the dugout for a drink of water, come back up, tie his shoes again, spend some quality time with his family, give an interview to the local paper, and finally step back into the batter's box. Then he'd call time again. When your normally eager hitters start acting like that, they're playing for the rainout.

Fortunately, a team so rarely runs into a situation that calls for these game-killing tactics that you'll see them only a few times a year even if your team has an open stadium and plays somewhere, like the Northeast, that sees a lot of rainouts over the course of a season.

Senators claimed they couldn't be found. It kept raining, and forty minutes later the umps called the game because the infield wasn't playable. The Senators won, 6–3, in part because of their disappearing crew. But that wasn't the end of it.

The Red Sox, who'd had a man on with no one out when play was halted, protested to the league, and AL President Will Harridge ruled that the Senators, by failing to cover the field in a timely fashion, had acted negligently. He awarded a victory by forfeit to the Red Sox. The moral of the story is that lazy and shiftless work is rewarded while no work is heavily punished.

It's hard to believe that baseball, with many years of tweaking its rules, still has a section that encourages teams to act so badly. But baseball has been slow to revise the rules around called games, and even today there's still an incentive for one team to drag a game out so that all the events on the field become meaningless. That the rules wipe events on the field away is crazy: a player who hits four home runs in a game that's rained out would see that accomplishment disappear.

Baseball could prevent these situations by suspending every game and require that it be replayed from the point of suspension. Unfortunately, there's great resistance to this. In accommodating the fans at the game, teams would have to open their doors again and allow them back at some later date for free. Considering the number of people required to open the gates and police a stadium, that's a significant cost.

There are scheduling problems, too. Teams could play a doubleheader if any games remained in that series, squeezing a couple of innings in before or after a later game. If that was impossible, they could reschedule them for an off day or at the end of the season if they could potentially change the results of a pennant race or determine a playoff berth.

No team long eliminated from the postseason wants to fly across the country to play four innings to see if the other team gets in or not. In that situation, there's the potential for an even greater farce: a game originally played by the starting roster completed by whatever eager young September call-ups are willing to make the flight to impress management with their can-do spirit and a few players willing to take any chance to delay their arrival at home, where they'll have to resume parenting duties.

Baseball will have to deal with this problem eventually. It makes no sense that a pitcher can throw a no-hitter through four innings and have his excellence wiped from the books because the game's called off. Or a player in pursuit of a record have his chase hampered, as Roger Maris did when he hit a home run in a rained-out game in his 61–home run season.

Until that happens, though, intentionally delaying the game will continue to be an important if rarely used strategy for smart teams who want to exploit the rules to their own benefit. Subverting the pace of the game is smart, if not sporting, gamesmanship, even as it undermines the nature of the game in the service of winning.

The exotic bird of cheating: The hidden ball trick

A RUNNER STEPS OFF the base to take his lead, watching the pitcher fiddle with his glove behind the mound. A fielder slaps him on the side with his glove and the ump yells "Out!" "No," the runner says, closing his eyes, feeling the world drop out from beneath him. The inning's over, the rally dead, his double wasted. "Congratulations, kid," the umpire says quietly. "You're in the history books."

The hidden ball trick is the height of legal duplicity and the baseball aficionado's favorite bit of skulduggery. It's a beautiful rare flower of cheating, occurring once a season if we're lucky. It requires skill and guile. One player becomes the clever hero and the other the country bumpkin, easily duped, standing on the field of play freshly shorn in front of thousands of fans, and that shame is only the prelude to being a highlight on every local and national sports wrap-up that day, at least a paragraph on every sports page.

It's cost games and jobs. It's been done in the World Series — back in 1907, when in the second game Detroit second baseman Germany Schaefer and third baseman Bill Coughlin got Jimmy Slagle in the first inning.

It's been worked in one form or another as long as the game's been played, but it continues to delight and amaze. It was used in the first year of Major League Baseball (seven documented times in the National League in 1876). Bill Deane has compiled a list of hidden ball tricks for Retrosheet, a nonprofit organization working to make detailed game accounts available for every game played. So far he's got three hundred and acknowledges there may hundreds more, particularly from baseball's early history, that await discovery. Today, every few months someone makes a good try at it, and about once a year someone pulls it off.

Keep an eye out. It's a great moment to see live, even if it doesn't work.

A great example of the trick's changing the outcome of a game is when Braves second baseman Jeff Treadway pulled it off on August 11, 1989. Treadway tagged Padres outfielder Marvell Wynne out at second in the ninth inning of a close game by faking the toss to the pitcher Joe Boever and telling Boever to "stay off the rubber." Wynne, who apparently didn't see that no ball was thrown and didn't pay attention to Treadway's instruction to his pitcher, was the last runner the Padres managed to get on base, and the Braves won, 6–5.

How to make a hidden ball trick like Grandma's

Ingredients:
A smart fielder, who must have the ball in his possession
An observant pitcher in on the trick
An umpire that's paying attention
A gullible, inattentive, or dim baserunner

Optional but extremely helpful:
First and third base coaches' inattention.

Directions:
Play must still be live.
Pitcher has to stay off the mound or be called for a balk.
Make eye contact with the umpire or otherwise signal him to pay attention.
Through patience, trickery, or charisma, get the runner to step off the bag.
In the event your runner is unwilling to leave the base or calls for time, throw out the batch and try again later.

Serves one.
Serving suggestions: There are several ways you can legally conceal the ball. You can palm it, though it's hard to do that and keep the runner from seeing it in your hand. You can keep it in your glove, which works much better; with some practice you can let the glove hang down while keeping the ball secure. Some players have pulled it off by putting the ball in their armpit, which allows them to (awkwardly) show off both empty hands and put the runner at ease.

How to get the runner to step off the base is where the art comes in. The standard method is to pretend to hand the ball off to the pitcher or pretend to throw it back.

In a more *bang-bang* play, the fielder or third baseman pretends that a throw got past him into the outfield or into foul territory, and as the runner starts for the next base, he's quickly tagged out.

The hidden ball trick was once far more common, before the cursed balk rules came into play. This is rule 8.05, which includes this joykiller:

(i) The pitcher, without having the ball, stands on or astride the pitcher's plate or while off the plate, he feints a pitch

Because of that, the pitcher really doesn't want to even get near the rubber or he risks having the balk called, and then the runner advances instead of being tagged out, and that's no help to anyone.

Before that was the rule, it was a lot easier to pull off the trick, because the pitcher could act as though he was ready to deliver and then the fielder could tag the runner. Today, however, as long as the runner doesn't take a lead until the pitcher is in position, the trick cannot be played. Only the laziness of runners allows this still to occur.

Further, the hidden ball trick requires the fielder to break the bonds of fraternity with his players and, sometimes, risk a friendship. When Twins second baseman Steve Lombardozzi overcame any guilt about using it in 1986, tagging out catcher — and friend — Mike Stanley, he said, "I'm not going to tell you how I wound up with the ball, but I thought about not using the trick because Mike is such a good friend of mine. He and my brother roomed together in college, and I knew he would be embarrassed. But what are friends for?"

Few players manage the hidden ball trick more than once in their career, but some excel. Red Sox second baseman Marty Barrett managed it twice in three weeks against the California Angels, when on July 7 and on July 21 of 1985 he conned first Bobby Grinch and then Doug DeCines.

The next repeat player was Matt Williams, a third baseman who started his career with the Giants, playing on the outstanding 1987–1989 teams and the somewhat legendary 1993 team that won 103 games only to finish second and miss the playoffs (a team also featuring noted sign-stealer Will Clark and noted future steroid user Barry Bonds). In his seventeen-year career, he made five All-Star teams, won four Gold Gloves at his position, and is remembered by many fans for pursuing the single-season home run record in 1994, at the peak of his career, only to see the season ended early by the strike. He played on three World Series teams and got a ring in 2001.

What people don't know is that Williams was one of the best modern practitioners of the hidden ball trick, and he did it by talking the runners off the bag.

On June 28, 1994, Williams picked off the Dodgers' Rafael Bournigal in the sixth inning. "He asked me to step off the bag so he could clean it," Bournigal said. And Bournigal obliged. "You have no friends in this business."

Three years later, in the first inning of a September 19 game, Williams walked up to pitcher Brian Anderson, faked a throw into his glove, and walked back to third, where he first managed to show the ball to the umpire and then tagged Jed Hansen. Better still, Williams's "cleaning the bag" routine worked at least one other time, when Williams tagged Colorado Rockies shortstop Neifi Perez in 1998, but Williams was foiled when his pitcher was called for a balk.

Clean the bag. Really. Did he regularly clean off the bag to make his story more plausible, waiting for the once-every-few-years chance to make a fool of another player? How gullible were those baserunners? How persuasive must Williams have been? How innocent his smile?

The best active player engaging in this kind of shenanigans is third baseman Mike Lowell. He got Montreal Expos catcher Brian Schneider in 2004 and pulled the trick less than a year later. While with the Florida Marlins, in the eighth inning of an August 10, 2005, game, Lowell successfully fooled Diamondback Luis Terrero at third. At the time, two men were on and the Diamondbacks were behind only 6–5, with the tying run on third and the go-ahead run on first. Left fielder Miguel Cabrera fielded the single that advanced Terrero to third in to Lowell, who kept it.

Doug Jones, the Marlins pitcher, stalled once he realized Lowell was trying it again. He recalled: "I'm like walking around, talking to [Marlins catcher Matt] Treanor, trying to go through things because you've only got 10 or 15 seconds to sell it."

Terrero took a few steps off the base; Lowell swiped him with the tag; umpire Ed Rapuano, who'd been paying close (but not too close) attention, called Terrero out immediately; and the crowd roared in appreciation. With Terrero retired, Craig Counsell struck out to end the inning and the comeback threat. The Marlins went on to win, 10–5.

This is why you watch games carefully — you never know when you're going to be delighted by this kind of inspired underhandedness.

Billy Martin, a cheater's cheater

> **Winning is everything.**
> — Billy Martin

NO MODERN MANAGER approaches Billy Martin when it comes to cheating. No manager since John McGraw, Ned Hanlon, and their contemporaries a century earlier were so willing to dedicate themselves to using the rules to their advantage when it suited them and to breaking them to gain an edge on their opponents.

Like McGraw, Martin would win any way he could until he would force his own firing. So he would go somewhere else, cook up more dirty tricks, get fired, get hired, and repeat the cycle until, eventually, even the Yankees wouldn't bring him back. But the weaknesses that cost him job after job and eventually his life were also what made him one of the finest managers modern baseball has ever seen. There may have been smarter, more innovative managers. Others have gotten as much or more from their teams. There are certainly managers better at sustaining success. But no manager since has been so willing to cross the line between gamesmanship and cheating.

Martin's tactics ran the gamut from training his players to run recklessly and in unexpected situations and ordering beanballs to intimidate opposing hitters, all the way to the clearly out-of-bounds areas of cultivating a staff of spitballers and stealing signs using stadium trickery.

From the moment his hometown Oakland Oaks, a minor league team, offered him a contract in 1946, Martin was an exceptionally aggressive player. At every level he would play, pester, or push his way into playing time and a promotion. When the Yankees hired

Stengel in 1951, he made Martin's obsessive dream of becoming a major-leaguer reality.

As a second baseman, Martin played for eleven seasons, six with the Yankees. His defense was sharp and smart. Like Stengal, Martin thought through every possible event until he could take a busted play and salvage something just as good out of it.

Of course, sometimes things got rough. Martin was nominated as the Yankees' team enforcer in 1952 and charged with taking on fights for the good of the tribe. He took to his job with zeal, as on July 12, when he went after St. Louis catcher Clint Courtney. Courtney was disliked for using his spikes against opponents, which Martin knew from his experience in the minor leagues. Martin took his revenge: "Courtney was coming down to second. Instead of tagging him, I wound up and hit him right between the eyes with the ball." The blow knocked Courtney's cap off and broke his glasses. Courtney went after Martin, throwing a left, but Martin punched him in the jaw repeatedly before an ump could get there (and be knocked down by the players). Courtney was ejected, but Martin was allowed to stay in the game, ostensibly because he'd only been defending himself, but also because his retaliation for Courtney's spiking was within bounds and open fighting was not. Courtney was fined and suspended for three days; Martin escaped punishment from the league. The Yankees won, 5–4, in extra innings over a Browns team without their best catcher. He could fight, but he could also provoke opponents into actions that would cause them to be ejected.

Martin cultivated his reputation as a fighter in much the same way Ty Cobb and John McGraw had before him. Few players were as eager to start or unwilling to end a fight, and Martin was so driven to win that he found ways to turn his talent for beating other people senseless into an advantage on the field through intimidation, provocation, and, when called for, direct application.

In a 1960 game while he was with the Reds, Martin thought a pitch at his head from Cubs pitcher Jim Brewer was intended to hit him, so on the next pitch he tried to huck his bat at Brewer, missing toward first. He walked out to get it, exchanged words with Brewer on his way out, and then, as he reached to get the bat, he instead came up to sucker-punch the pitcher in the left side of his jaw. In the ensuing pushing and shoving between the two teams, his teammate Cal McLish got kicked, and he punched Brewer repeatedly in the right side of his face, breaking his cheekbone and costing him the season. Brewer sued Martin, but Martin wouldn't finger McLish or admit he wasn't responsible for the injury. It took nine years to settle the lawsuit.

There were many other fights to come. Fueled by his frequent and frequently uncontrolled drinking, Martin brawled with all kinds of people. Marshmallow salesmen. Tiger fans, while managing the Tigers. His team's traveling secretary. Sportswriters. A guy in a hotel bar. And they all started it, according to Martin. Rushed him in the bathroom! Provoked him in a hotel lobby! Tried to continue a fight that had started on the team charter!

"I'm no fighter," Martin wrote in an article that ran in the April 26, 1961, *Sporting News* after the Brewer brawl. "I never started a fight in my life. But I've never walked away from one when someone jumped me."

The mercury that ran in his blood also drove him to find other ways to fight his opponents, real or imagined. And he worked every advantage he could. Every other hitter stands in the batter's box, waiting for the pitch, but Martin would walk forward or take two quick steps during the pitcher's windup in order to take a swing at breaking pitches before they really dropped but mostly to distract the pitcher, who has to do many things exactly right to get the ball to the catcher's glove. That distraction's been credited for hits like a home run off Preacher Roe in Game 2 of the 1953 World Series.

Martin was also good at guessing what the other team's signs meant. And when he couldn't do that, he could guess what the other team was going to do without decoding the signals, which made it look as though he was getting the signs anyway. Trying to face Martin was maddening for opponents: he simply could not be outthought or outfought, and while there were many players who were more talented, the effort he put into the game made it hard to outplay him.

One of the best examples came in the 1952 World Series between Martin's New York Yankees and the Brooklyn Dodgers. Martin was playing second, and in the fifth inning his team was ahead, 1–0, but

the Dodgers had players on second and third with their pitcher, Joe
Black, at bat.

As Gil McDougald, the Yankees utility man who played with Martin, put it: "Andy Pafko was the runner on third for Brooklyn. A run
would tie the game. Charley Dressen was doing a crazy dance in the
coaching box and nobody had a clue to the sign. Three years earlier,
in the minors, Billy had played under Dressen. He remembered the
squeeze-play sign they had used then was hidden in the dance. But
Dressen had made some changes. The sign was different now. At
the last second, Billy glanced at Joe Black, the hitter. From Black's
bug-eyed look, he was sure the squeeze was on. He hollered a warning to our pitcher."

The Yankees threw a pitchout high and outside, where it was
ideal for the catcher to tag the stealing Pafko. The rally was snuffed,
the Yankees went on to win, 2–0, and win the Series, four games to
three.

"I've always figured that was a $70,000 yell," McDougald said —
the difference between a team's share for winning or losing the
World Series.

Martin's playing career ended in 1961, after eleven seasons, and
he took any job he could in baseball, studying and working. Finally,
in 1969 Minnesota gave him the chance to manage. There, he argued with the umpires so frequently and viciously that while the
ghost of John McGraw might have approved, others were not
amused. But as he did throughout his career, Martin would maintain that he always got the calls. Later, Yankee starter Dock Ellis
would say, "I saw Billy win five games the year I was there. He won
five fucking games just intimidating the umpires. Where they owed
him a call. Even if the ball was down the cock, they called it a ball,
and on the next pitch our hitter would hit a home run, and we'd win
the game."

The Twins found success, even as the team's owner turned against
Martin for his independent streak, his personal conduct, and his
constant agitation for player moves, both in public and private.
When Martin got into a fight with one of his pitchers in a bar, Minnesota fired him. It was the first of many such terminations.

After his season in Minnesota, he got another chance a year later, taking over Detroit in 1971. The Tigers improved dramatically and won a division title in 1972. But in 1973, after the league suspended him for ordering his pitchers to throw spitballs in a game where they were opposed by Gaylord Perry, the legendary spitballer, the Tigers couldn't take it anymore and fired Martin.

In what became a Martin hallmark, he argued that what his pitchers did was legal on technical grounds: "The pitches they threw were legal. They were off the mound and you can go to your mouth off the mound. What [Perry] was doing was against the rules."

"It was an accumulation of things," general manager Jim Campbell said. "There comes a point where what's right is right and what's wrong is wrong." Wrong wasn't the use of the spitball; it was the public admission that he'd ordered his pitchers to throw the pitch, which brought embarrassing controversy to the team and required his firing.

In a sentiment that was repeated through Martin's career, the person who brought the ax down said, "I have no complaint about the job he did on the field. From foul line to foul line, he did a darn good job."

The game in which Martin snapped, ordering his pitchers to throw as many spitballs as they could and then openly, defiantly, admitting it, was part of his long feud with Gaylord Perry. "If he was throwing legitimate fastballs, we'd be hitting them," Martin said after Perry shut out his Tigers that year. Martin badgered umpires to undress Perry on the mound and in 1972 threatened to bring a trained hound dog to the park to sniff out where Perry was hiding his grease. Martin would even drag Perry into accusations against other teams. In September 1973, after taking over the Rangers, Martin said, "The Angels dominate the league when it comes to guys who throw funny pitches. Bill Singer throws a greaser, Aurelio Monteagude throws a spitter and Nolan Ryan throws a steamer. All they would need is Gaylord Perry. That would make it complete." (Who knows what he was accusing Nolan Ryan of.)

Martin wasn't out of a job for long. Texas Rangers owner Bob Short fired current manager Whitey Herzog when he heard that Detroit let Martin go, so he could hire Martin to manage his team.

The Rangers improved to finish second in 1974. Then, in 1975, the team brought in Gaylord Perry, the object of Martin's venom and spite for years. But Martin bubbled with glee. "I feel like we've just traded our way right back into contention in the West Division," he said. And now that the greatest cheater in modern baseball was on his team, Martin was quick to defend Perry's integrity: "I realize now how wrong I was. I'd like to get on the record immediately as saying Gaylord Perry does nothing illegal."

But that match between great cheaters did not last long. Martin was fired only a month later, and again his unemployment was short-lived: the New York Yankees, the team his heart belonged to, hired him almost immediately. He managed the 1976 team to an American League Championship and two World Series victories in a row.

Martin knew the rulebook as well as anyone else and used it as a weapon. With his Yankees playing the Kansas City Royals, the Yankees were down, 2–1, when the Royals moved designated hitter Hal McRae to the outfield to cover for an injury. McRae took eight throws, several after second base umpire Lou DiMuro tried to stop him at the limit of five tosses. Martin, with his frightening vision of everything happening on the field, noticed and demanded McRae's ejection. When the umpires did not remove McRae, Martin protested. Had McRae later made a difference in the game, Martin's formal protest meant that the league would have reviewed the decision and considered replaying the game from the eighth inning.

He'd also use the rules as a psychological weapon. If the opposing pitcher, like Oil Can Boyd, wore gold chains and Martin thought it would tick him off, Martin would protest to the umpires, citing the appropriate uniform rules. It might spark a feud that lasted for years, but Martin didn't care as long as it won him a temporary advantage.

Even at the pinnacle of baseball success, though, he clashed over and over again with owner George Steinbrenner. They argued about players: if Martin liked a player, like Chicken Stanley, but Steinbrenner didn't like him, Steinbrenner would threaten to get rid of the player unless Martin benched him. Steinbrenner started rumors that Billy's job was in jeopardy to make sure Martin never felt

Billy Martin's temper gets the best of him in 1979, after he was ejected by umpire Dallas Parks. *AP*

too comfortable. During spring training, Steinbrenner sometimes bugged Martin every day about his lineups or criticized his decisions during a game.

A long and bizarre relationship began in 1975. Steinbrenner repeatedly fired Martin only to forgive him. Martin had five different stints with the Yankees, and sometimes the breakups and reconciliations made little sense: he resigned in July 1978 after making an unwise comment about star Reggie Jackson and Steinbrenner ("One's a born liar, the other's convicted") that referred to the owner's conviction for illegal contributions to Richard Nixon's reelection campaign. Only a month later, the team announced that Martin would return to manage the Yankees in 1980; he returned early, in June of the 1979 season, only to be fired again in October for getting into a fight with a random businessman who crossed his path in Minnesota. Martin's unorthodox game tactics and his fondness for being on the wrong side of baseball law were about the only things that weren't cause for his terminations.

He went to Oakland again for the 1980 season. The team he took over once again improved dramatically. It was with Oakland that Martin invented the style of play that became synonymous with his name: "Billy Ball." Given a team with a strong starting rotation and few good players, he whipped his squad into playing like modern Ty Cobbs, focused with almost reckless abandon on the basepaths. His players would steal, run the double steal, even use the almost never seen triple steal. They stole home. They'd play McGraw-style scientific baseball, too, using the hit-and-run and bunting to their best advantage. Martin sometimes liked to end his rallies with a sacrifice bunt to score one last runner, especially if he thought it would be the run that broke the opposition's spirit. There was another factor, too — Martin made it appear that he, and only he, controlled when his team would score and when it would relent. If that sacrifice spared the pitcher, it was Martin's mercy and not the pitcher's skill that had ended the inning.

Defending against Martin's teams was frustrating and unsettling. They would try anything, often seemingly at random, so that sometimes surprise was as great an advantage as good planning or execution by the players.

In Oakland, once again he had pitching coach Art Fowler, who followed Martin for much of his career, teach his staff the finer points of the spitball. Sportswriter Thomas Boswell named "spitballs by the gross" as one of the key elements of Billy Ball. Martin loved to have them use it on two-strike counts and pushed them to throw it to get the outs he craved.

After he was fired by the A's after the 1982 season, when the team slumped to a 68–94 record, he went back to the Yankees for 1983.

That season, the first of his second stint with the Yankees, gave us Martin's most famous moment, the one that gets capital letters: the Pine Tar Incident. During a July 24 game with the Royals, Graig

Nettles (who appears in the bat-tampering chapter for the superball incident) noticed that Royals slugger George Brett had applied pine tar far up the handle of his bat beyond what's allowed in rule 1.10(b): "The bat handle, for not more than 18 inches from the end, may be covered or treated with any material or substance to improve the grip. Any such material or substance, which extends past the 18-inch limitation, shall cause the bat to be removed from the game."

But Billy Martin, the great master of gamesmanship, did nothing, saving the information for when it would be more useful.

When Brett hit a home run in the ninth inning with U L Washington on base, putting the Royals ahead, 5–4, Martin decided it was time and challenged the bat. The umps measured Brett's bat, found that it had pine tar several inches above where it was allowed, and ruled Brett out for using an illegal bat, thereby invalidating his home run. Brett went temporarily insane with rage and charged from the dugout, and that's the archival footage they show — the great hitter being restrained as he tries to get at the umpires. Gaylord Perry (yes, the spitball pitcher) attempted to grab Brett's bat in the chaos and stroll off with it, but he was stopped (and ejected).

The decision was appealed, and the ruling on the field was changed. The league found that while the umpires had acted correctly based on the rules as written, the intent of the rule was not to penalize a hitter in that situation. The home run was allowed to stand. The game was replayed from the point of the now-reversed call on August 18, almost a month later.

When the game resumed, Martin didn't give up his fight over the call — he had his players throw to first and then third base and appeal that Brett hadn't touched them while rounding the bases of the home run. This was a brilliant tactic: not only had weeks passed since Brett had rounded the bases, but the August 18 game was refereed by new umpires.

But the original umpires, knowing Martin all too well, had already thought of this and signed affidavits (which they'd given to the new umpires), stating that they'd seen Brett touch each base as he made the circuit. Martin's appeals were denied.

Martin didn't just work the umps; he often tried to use the press to make his case. For instance, in May 1973, Billy Martin got *New York Daily News* columnist Dick Young to run his complaints about organists:

> "I'm going to call [AL President] Joe Cronin to complain about the organ playing that's going on around our league, especially Oakland," Martin said. "They don't play music. They let out a blast of noise. I don't mind it when there's no action and they want to get the crowd to chant go, go, go, or whatever the hell it is. But I think when our pitcher is ready to pitch, the organ should cut out that crap."

Then he moved into trying to figure out how to retaliate or turn it to his advantage:

> "I told one of the umpires that if the guy didn't stop it, I was going up to his booth and break his knuckles. If I don't get any satisfaction from the league, I'm going out and get one of those windhorns, and when their pitcher is about to throw the ball, I'll let go with a blast. In fact, I'll fill my dugout with those horns. If they can play the organ, I should be able to do that."

But in 1988 Martin's arguments with the umpires went too far. On May 30, facing the A's, shortstop Walt Weiss hit a short line drive that was caught by Yankee second baseman Bobby Meacham. Meacham tossed the ball to the shortstop rather than throwing to first in hopes of getting the batter, indicating that it didn't even occur to him he might not have made a clean catch. But second base umpire Rick Reed ruled it had been a trap — the ball had hit the ground before Weiss's glove — and Martin argued, as he always did, with great vigor. Crew chief Dale Scott refused to overrule the call, and Billy started to swear at Scott; he would not be calmed down and was ejected. Then Martin kicked dirt on Scott's feet, then grabbed some dirt from the infield and threw it at Scott's chest.

The league did almost nothing: Martin was fined $1,000 and suspended for only three games. The umpires, shocked at such leniency, decided they had had enough of Martin's act and they would take matters into their own hands. They declared that Martin would be ejected from any game any time he went to dispute a call or even question one. Martin, in turn, threatened to sue the umpires, but

Billy Martin's all-time all-horrible team

    P: Benito Mussolini
    1B: Curtis LeMay
    2B: Kim Il Sung
    SS: Genghis Khan
    3B: Joseph Stalin
    RF: Mao Zedong
    CF: Emperor Hirohito
    LF: Adolf Hitler
    C: Pol Pot

See the notes at the end for more on this.

This team would win more games than you might think, looking at them on paper. First, a team of dead zombie players led by a zombie Billy Martin would be amazingly scary and win by forfeit a lot. Moreover, who would dare win a game against those guys? Can you imagine how they'd retaliate?

Commissioner Peter Ueberroth brokered a peace, and the umpires relented when Martin issued an apology.

But Billy, still boiling angry, told a friend repeatedly to find a mob hitman to whack Dale Scott over the incident. His friend refused, and fortunately Martin's murderous rage waned after a few days.

The humiliation by the umpires was the low point, at least publicly, in the season that ended his managerial career.

And that was Martin. He offered teams a strange bargain: if you hired him, your team would get better but would pay a high price for that success. Martin was certain to get into incidents off the field, either with women, which could be kept quiet, or fighting, which often could not be hushed up.

He'd pester the front office to go bring in anyone, no matter their reputation, personality, or rap sheet, if he thought they could help his team, and he'd press the issue until they gave in or had the office locks changed.

He could find hidden talent in barren farm systems or other teams, but he didn't care at all about their histories or personalities. "If I had Benito Mussolini and Hitler and Hirohito on my team,"

Billy Ball's record of success

	Took over	Previous record	First year turnaround	Last season	Accomplishments
Minnesota	1969	79-83	97-65	1969	Won division
Detroit	1971	79-83	91-71	1973	Won division in 1972
Texas	1973 (last 23 games)	57-105 (1973)	84-76	1975	Manager of the Year, 1974
New York	1975 (last 56 games)	83-77 (1975)	97-62	1978	3 division titles, 2 World Series wins, Manager of the Year, 1976
Oakland	1980	54-108	83-79	1982	AL Champions 1981, Manager of the Year, 1980 and 1981
New York	1983	79-83	91-71	1983	
New York	1985 (last 145 games)	87-75	97-64	1985	

(omitted: 95 games managed in 1979, 60 games managed in 1988, both for the Yankees)

Martin said in 1983, "and they could execute the double steal and hit sacrifice fly balls, they'd be in my lineup. And they were pretty terrible people." He would force his players to become better, no matter what it took, or he'd break them. Some players would respond, either to his encouragement or his scorn, and play above any reasonable expectation. But others would not, and they were cast off to other teams or they hung around, unhappy and underperforming, and waited for him to be forced out.

But through it all, Martin would win. Even his rival Earl Weaver, one of the best managers in modern baseball, admired his success. "Billy Martin's teams don't have any particular style," Weaver said. "That's why he's so good. Look at the teams he's had in Minnesota, Detroit, Texas, New York, and Oakland. The first thing you notice is that no two of them are alike."

Billy Martin is now remembered as much for his off-field exploits as his years as a player and manager. The drinking, the fighting, his problems with women, the sad joke of his relationship with the Yankees, have all overshadowed what he accomplished on the field. The things that kept him from being normal made him a great manager.

He owed his success and his failures to a legendary temper that drove him. His obvious intelligence won him games and his team pennants, but it wasn't enough to keep him out of trouble. His knowledge of the rulebook and gamesmanship is admirable, but his competitive drive washed out all moral sense: he was just as willing to intimidate an umpire and order intentional beanings as he was to encourage his pitchers to throw spitters with two strikes. He is both the greatest cheating manager and a cautionary example: without perspective and thought, it's easy to go from the hard-nosed to the scary and unconscionable.

His dedication to winning turned teams around, and his zeal burned out players and teams and forced his stays to be short. He was the best manager no one could stand. His record speaks clearly to his success in turning teams into winners. His death reminds us of the cost his dedication exacted.

Heckling, fan participation, and riots

> I could never play in New York. The first time I came into a game there, I got into the bullpen car and they told me to lock the doors.
>
> — Mike Flanagan, Baltimore Orioles pitcher

FAN PARTICIPATION IN GAMES has a long and glorious history, always reflecting the character of the game on the field. In the early days of baseball, the game itself was a lot more rough, sure, but it was also more intimate, played in smaller, wooden neighborhood stadiums, and its fans were as rough, dirty, and quick to resort to violence as its players.

Now, the new, baseball-only parks bring us back to the closeness of the past. They have front rows so close and rails so low that anyone with a ton of money to drop on season tickets can reach out and touch a ball as they roll past, like the good old days, when stadiums would put their overflow crowds behind ropes in the outfield and along the foul lines. The best of the new parks, like Camden Yards and PNC Park, offer the fan great sightlines and bring them close to the action in the same way the classic small neighborhood parks, like Fenway Park and Wrigley Field, do.

The players in the on-deck circle are sometimes only twenty, thirty feet from the crowd, and in some parks, like Seattle, only a chain-link fence keeps the unwashed hordes from the bullpen; no opposing pitcher can warm up without some choice commentary on his readiness, general ability, and parentage.

There was little deterrent for the fans back in the 1890s. Unless a hated visiting player like McGraw or Cobb was in town, bringing with them a forecast of increased violence, security might consist of a couple of police officers. Generally, fans could wander around and do as they pleased.

Our team's in the World Series for the first time in 84 years! Let's taunt the Yankee fans! *AP*

There also wasn't the kind of economic barrier between players and fans as we know it today. For much of baseball's history, players and umpires were not paid much more than a regular Joe. They frequented the same bars and restaurants the fans enjoyed. They traveled on the same trains — imagine today's superstars flying coach, much less taking Amtrak from New York to Boston. But baseball wasn't considered a serious profession the way it is today. It was something a person might do for a few years before settling down into more respectable work, like farming or machine politics. It was not the province of million-dollar salaries and press conferences.

With the lower barriers both physical and social, fans were free to argue with and on behalf of their players, even in the middle of a game. In 1885, a Philadelphia crowd went after an umpire for a call at second base so vehemently that he ordered a police officer to throw out a particularly noxious fan from right field. "The crowd then became very unruly, and, hissing and shouting at the umpire, they jumped the fence and crowded around him." The umpire got his man tossed, and the crowd was cleared from the field.

Today, those people would be beaten and tear-gassed back into the stands, and the team would use video camera footage and ticket sales records to build a comprehensive list of suspects to hand over to the police for later prosecution.

In the 1890s, baseball worked to clean itself up, and the tide of violence, foul language, and general barbarism receded as the sport slowly became more respectable and less tied to beer sales and gambling. The audience changed as well. Fans no longer charged umpires or tried to set fire to the visiting team's carriages. They no longer threw things onto the field and took swings at opposing players who came too close to the stands. They largely restrained themselves to verbal abuse, and heckling became a baseball tradition that persists today.

Like every other form of rude, underhanded, and disruptive behavior, baseball's waged a long war with it. From the umpire who in 1885 almost incited a riot by ejecting a fan, baseball's struggled to strike a balance between letting the fans enjoy themselves and enforcing civility.

The first person recognized for his contributions to his team by heckling was Patsy O'Toole. In the 1920s and 1930s, O'Toole heckled in Detroit from behind the visiting team dugout. He used only the weapons of volume and repetition: his insult was an endless booming "You're a faker! You're a faker! You're a faker!" while his compliment was the "You're a good guy!" also repeated infinitely.

The found poetry of Patsy O'Toole

O'Toole supposedly would walk up and down the aisles chanting this ditty:

Boy oh boy oh boy
Keep cool with O'Toole
Keep cool with O'Toole
(repeat forever)

Imagine the loudest person you've ever known working a total of eight syllables continuously for nine innings, and you'll have a vague idea of what it was like to sit in the same stadium as O'Toole.

He was so disruptive and so funny that the Tigers and the Detroit sportswriters loved him ("As the No. 1 clarion crier of Detroit, Patsy O'Toole . . .") and lamented the illnesses and surgeries that robbed him of his voice. In 1933, he was a guest of Clark Griffith (owner of the Washington Senators) for the World Series and annoyed President Roosevelt to the point that he had O'Toole moved to the other side of the field. (FDR, who in March of that year had said, "The only thing we have to fear is fear itself," got a heckler tossed from his section at a World Series game.)

But O'Toole was only one member of the rowdy crowds in those decades. Fans came to games dressed in the team colors, set off firecrackers, and bought up seats to better display a sign with a player's name on it.

Sometimes they banded into booster clubs, like the Royal Rooters, the most famous example. Originally Red Sox fans who came together in the 1903 World Series, the Rooters traveled with and rooted for their team during the Sox's last sustained run of greatness, when they won four World Series titles from 1912 to 1918. Centered around a tavern owner, they would have a couple of pints and then go see the game, even if it was sold out. They simply busted their way in so they could sing "Tessie," from the musical *Silver Slippers*, to (hopefully) fire up their team and distract the opposing players. They broke up (so to speak) after 1918, and the Red Sox didn't return to the World Series until 2004, when the Dropkick

Murphys recorded a new version of "Tessie" that got played during the season.

Players pretend they don't hear hecklers, whether their tormentor is a solo fan or a well-organized group. But as long as the heckler is close enough and loud enough, they do. Imagine seeing a friend only twenty, thirty yards away and trying to get his attention. Of course you could do it. If you attend enough games, you'll see a player crack up over an especially colorful jest, sometimes even if it's directed at him.

One of the most-booed players in baseball was then-Oakland A's catcher A. J. Pierzynski after he started a brawl with Cubs catcher Michael Barrett. He said, "The standard line is just 'You suck.' You just get tired of hearing 'You suck' over and over again. Say something good, say something funny, say something I can go back in the dugout and say, 'Hey, this guy told me this.' The standard line of, 'You got punched,' that's stupid too. Come up with something original and make it funny."

Some players will even heckle back. Rickey Henderson, after being booed continually by a friend of mine from behind the visiting team's dugout, hit a home run, and as he walked back, he caught his eye, booed him back, and ducked into the dugout, grinning.

Most players just stare, though. Some may give a fan the finger or bark something choice back. If they're having a really bad time, they might have you tossed. If they can't hear, though, or it doesn't matter, why react at all?

Some players will admit they're affected. In 1912, the Hall of Fame pitcher Christy Mathewson talked about the effect of heckling on him: "It takes a long time for a pitcher to be able to develop sufficient poise to be able to steady himself against the 'Take him out' cry. They pulled that howl on me several times early one season, and, as I hadn't heard it applied to myself for quite a number of years, it sure did put a hinge in my arm, and I did have to be taken out every time the demand was hurled out by the gang, for I was perfectly incompetent to go ahead and work."

"People in the stands are as much a part of professional baseball as the players on the field," Joe DiMaggio said. "Sometimes they sandpaper an outfielder down to a thin finish. No man in his right mind enjoys being called 'bum,' 'punk,' 'palooka,' or worse, or having his personal affairs described to a park full of people by a voice that could call close-order drill for a whole army corps."

In 1945, a war veteran who enjoyed attending Brooklyn Dodgers games and heckling the team at last got to Dodgers manager Leo Durocher on June 9. John Christian said, "I called Durocher a crook, I called him a bum." A special policeman came by to take Christian from the grandstands, and Durocher met him under the seats. Then things get hazy: Durocher, in his subsequent trial for second-degree assault, said that he told the guy he wasn't going to put up with "my boys being called thieves and crooks and charged with throwing games." Then either Durocher beat the heckler up, fracturing his jaw (Christian), or tried to beat the heckler up but didn't get anywhere (witness), or Christian ran off and slipped in a puddle (Durocher).

Whichever version you pick, Christian did manage to annoy the Dodgers players and manager enough during games to cause them to do something foolish. This got him a nice payday (over six grand from the team), and Durocher spent nearly a year fighting the charges (it took almost six hours to select a jury because it was so hard to find fans not loyal to the Dodgers). While Christian's actions caused only an extended distraction — Durocher didn't lose the original game, though it was close, and Durocher miraculously escaped a league suspension — there was an excellent chance that provoking Durocher would have deprived the Giants of their successful manager and put them at a disadvantage for a while. That's worth trying, though whether it's worth having Durocher break your jaw is up to you.

In 1961, the fans in Milwaukee booed their Braves so seriously that the *Sporting News* ran an unusual headline: "Home Fans' Jeering Can Rattle Club in Own Park." They were not alone; the paper noted that other National League clubs endured abuse as well: "The Braves, always accustomed to adulation in Milwaukee, have been hearing jeers and hoots this year. Manager Solly Hemus of the Cardinals has been under constant fire from St. Louis fans. Boos have been heard for a long time in Philadelphia, and they have not lessened this season. Willie Mays of the Giants has been under attack

Lou Durocher, thin skinned and sharp tongued

As a player, Leo Durocher was a premier bench jockey, able to rattle his opponents and get Ty Cobb to chase him around the field in a rage.

In 1928, he saved a game with his tongue. Bob "Fats" Fothergill walked to the plate to bat for the Tigers with two outs in the ninth but a chance to win the game. Fothergill's official weight was over 200 pounds and during one spring training his manager was happy to see him slim down to about 250. He looked like someone who would deliver (and drain) beer kegs instead of a quality hitter. Durocher wanted to get into the playoffs and saw an opportunity in Fothergill's large form.

Durocher, playing second, called time and told the umpire there was a man batting out of turn. Puzzled, Bill Dinneen looked at his lineup card and said, "What's the matter with you? Fothergill is the hitter."

"Fothergill!" Durocher replied. "Ohhhhh, that's different. It's only Fothergill! From where I was standing, it looked like there were two men up there."

Play resumed, a reddened and agitated Fothergill struck out, then dropped his bat and chased Durocher around the field.

from San Francisco fans." One Braves veteran said, "The players are pros. Boos are part of the game." But the *Sporting News* noted, "Observers not attached to clubs, however, felt that this did have an effect on the play of some athletes."

If players can't hear hecklers — which they would like us to believe — why do they sometimes lose their temper and go into the stands? It's not as if they're offended by a loud-mouthed fan's sense of fashion. Many incidents in baseball history put a lie to the claim that taunts don't reach the field.

In a New York Yankees game in 1912, the visiting Tigers were being heckled by fans behind their bench. The incident produced an outstanding example of sportswriting in the *New York Times:*

Everything was very pleasant at the Detroit-Yankee game on the
Hilltop yesterday until Ty Cobb Johnnykilbaned a spectator right

A quick glossary

Johnnykilbaned: Johnny Kilbane was a famous featherweight boxer.
Claret: a red wine from Bordeaux. Here, blood.
Welsbach: I believe this is Carl Auer von Welsbach, who worked on
  a bunch of mantles, the streetlights of the late 1800s. Here, his eye-
  brow.
Silk O'Loughlin: the umpire.

on the place where he talks, started the claret, and stopped the flow of profane and vulgar words. Cobb led with a left jab and countered with a right kick to Mr. Spectator's left Welsbach, which made his peeper look as if some one had drawn a curtain over it. Silk O'Loughlin, without a license from the boxing commission, refereed the go. He gave the decision to Cobb and then put him out of the ring. The spectator went to a lawyer's office to make out his will.

What did the hecklers say to get Johnnykilbaned? "What they have been saying to the Georgia Peach has no place in a family newspaper or even one that circulates in barber shops only," the *Times* reported.

The object of Cobb's wrath was Claude Lucker, a former pressman who lost a hand and three fingers on his other to an accident — and he may not have even been the right heckler. Still worse, when Cobb went after him, horrified onlookers shouted, "Don't kick him, he has no hands." Cobb replied, "I don't care if he has no feet."

As a result, May 18, 1912, saw one of the worst games ever played. In Philadelphia, Cobb's teammates refused to take the field when they learned that Cobb had been suspended for fighting Lucker. They told manager Hughie Jennings that they wouldn't play without Cobb and wouldn't be talked out of it. To avoid a forfeit, Jennings went to nearby St. Joseph's College and signed a bunch of kids. That team lost to the Athletics, 24–2. Aloysius Travers, the pitcher for the day, threw a complete game in eight innings, allowing 26 hits and 7 walks (he even struck out a man).

By getting Cobb to beat him up, that heckler cost the Tigers a win. But what a price to pay.

A struggling Babe Ruth went into the stands on May 25, 1922. After he was called out on a play at second, he threw dirt at the umpire, who tossed him. The home crowd got all over Ruth, who doffed his cap in mock appreciation on his way to the bench. Two "Pullman conductors" continued the assault, calling him a bum (presumably well spiced with other adjectives and embellishments suited to the occasion), and Ruth's temper flared. He stood, turned, and charged the stands in pursuit of his quickly fleeing tormentors. Restrained by the crowd, he offered some choice words on the bravery of the men and then left the field for the clubhouse.

The next great escalation started in the new millennium, as teammates charged the stands together in response to provocations.

Wrigley Field was the scene of one of the craziest brawls in modern history in May of 2000, when the Los Angeles Dodgers went into the stands en masse when a fan stole backup catcher Chad Kreuter's hat. Kreuter leaped into the stands after the thief, followed by some teammates. They were stopped by other Cubs fans, and the fighting began. As Kreuter got bogged down fighting, more Dodgers poured into the stands, and more fans came forward to meet them. It took ten minutes for order to be restored. Sixteen players and three coaches were suspended as a result, and several fans were arrested. It's a testament to the spirit of the stands that, confronted with surging, well-conditioned professional athletes, the sea did not part but swallowed the players up. Right or wrong, how many sections in how many stadiums can say honestly that they wouldn't have fled?

In September of 2004, Craig Bueno went to see the Texas Rangers play Oakland at Oakland's Network Associates Coliseum. He passed the time by ragging on the Rangers bullpen until, when the Rangers tied the game, he yelled, "So which one of you losers is going to blow this thing tonight?" Pitcher Doug Brocail charged him, and the other Ranger relievers joined Brocail. Frankie Francisco threw a plastic chair at Craig, who ducked, allowing it to smash into his wife, Jennifer Bueno (you have to take that hit, dude, come on

Opposite page:
In the ugliest team-fan conflict in decades, the Dodgers attack the Wrigley Field crowd to retrieve a stolen hat and find the crowd poor hosts. *AP*

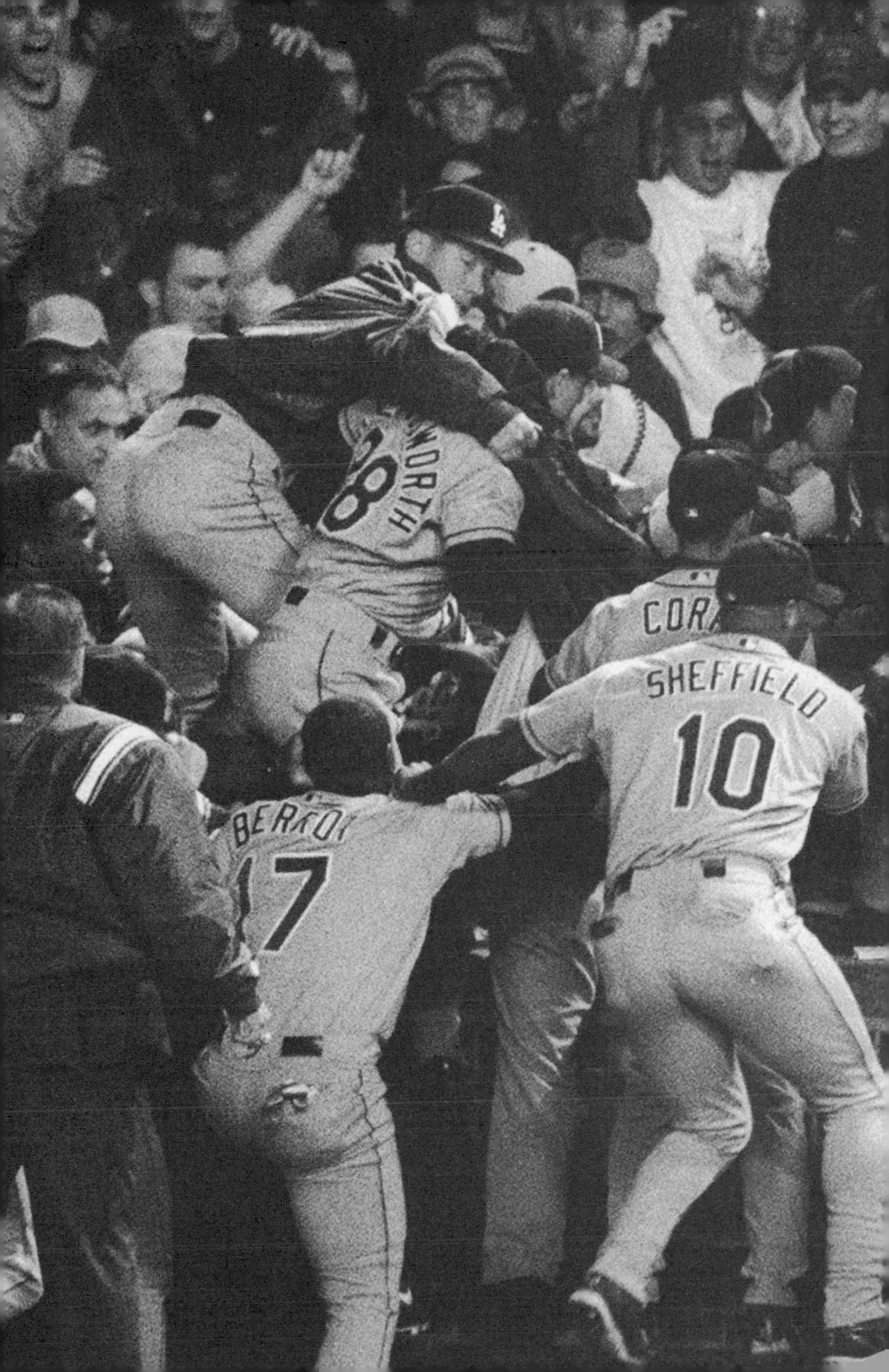
CORA
SHEFFIELD
10
17

now), breaking her nose. Police arrested Francisco on a charge of aggravated battery, and baseball suspended him for the rest of the season.

Great Places for Heckling

WRIGLEY FIELD BLEACHERS

Wrigley Field opened in 1914 and hosted its first Cubs game in 1916. Since then, the outfield fans — the "bleacher bums" — have acquired a singular reputation as the creators of one of the harshest environments for visiting players, where they are enveloped in a near-constant cloud of attacks on their professional skills and personal failings. A changing but loyal group of happy fans put up with scarce tickets and variable pricing through the team and horrible prices through scalpers in order to see their bums play in one of the best venues in all of sports, and they're as much part of the atmosphere as the ivy on the outfield walls.

Tony Gwynn said that it was his favorite place to get heckled, and the best he got there — in his first game — was "Fee fi fo fum, Tony Gwynn's a fucking bum." They also attacked Gwynn's weight, though humorously, with: "Get the cheeseburgers out of your pocket."

Blue Jays outfielder Vernon Wells was disappointed: "All I kept hearing was 'Wells, you suck. You suck.' I was looking forward to something different. I hear 'you suck' at home sometimes." Presumably, he meant Toronto's home stadium, not his house.

Wrigley's bleacher bums are hard not just on the visiting teams. They'll turn on their own when it's deserved. In recent years, every reliever who's gone through a tough stretch, whether he's talented, like LaTroy Hawkins, or not, like Mike Remlinger, got booed, and they made Sammy Sosa's 2005 miserable as they jeered the declining slugger out of town.

YANKEE STADIUM BLEACHERS

Everybody hates the Yankees, and the Yankee fans have a lot to do with that. They turn up at every road game with pinstripes and pro-

Best Rant Ever

The greatest example of how crazy the bums could drive someone came in 1983, when Cubs manager Lee Elia exploded in a press conference over the treatment of his slow-starting team.

"F*** those f***ing fans who come out here and say they're Cub fans that are supposed to be behind you ripping every f***ing thing you do. I'll tell you one f***ing thing, I hope we get f***ing hotter than shit, just to stuff it up them 3,000 f***ing people that show up every f***ing day, because if they're the real Chicago f***ing fans, they can kiss my f***ing ass right downtown — and print it! [. . .]

"They're really, really behind you around here . . . my f***ing ass. What the f*** am I supposed to do, go out there and let my f***ing players get destroyed every day and be quiet about it? For the f***ing nickel-dime people who turn up? The motherf***ers don't even work. That's why they're out at the f***ing game. They oughta go out and get a f***ing job and find out what it's like to go out and earn a f***ing living. Eighty-five percent of the f***ing world is working. The other fifteen percent come out here. A f***ing playground for the c***s***ers. Rip them motherf***ers. Rip them f***ing c***s***ers like the f***ing players. We got guys busting their f***ing ass, and them f***ing people boo.

"Alright, they don't show because we're 5 and 14 . . . and unfortunately, that's the criteria of them dumb 15 motherf***ing percent that come out to day baseball. The other 85 percent are earning a living."

fanity. At some low-attendance parks, they'll outnumber the poor home town fans to the point that it feels like a home game for the Yankees. And they can do this with a small but devoted crowd. At Yankee Stadium, though, there are more, they're even louder and rowdier, and the bleachers are the home of the most rabid of them all.

Not surprisingly, the bleachers at the Bronx Zoo have a reputation for hooligan conduct worthy of the Baltimore crowds of old. They're not known for particularly sophisticated taunting, but they are so loud and so vicious that players have been known to complain incredulously about how vile the fans were about their sister — even when they didn't have a sister. They have a frightening ability to pick up a taunt and quickly turn it into a chant. After Red Sox pitcher Pedro Martinez took a beating at the hands of the Yankees, he talked of his frustration, saying, "I tip my hat and call the Yankees my daddy." "Who's your daddy?" instantly became a cheer that shook the surrounding blocks.

If visiting players think they have it bad, fans who try to follow their players face an even more daunting task. Try and cheer for the visiting team in the bleachers. You'll be frisked in a brisk and forceful manner that may embarrass you. They won't serve alcohol in the bleachers, but there's still a heavy police presence. If you chance on an officer who's not entirely jaded, he'll advise you to turn around immediately to preserve your health. You'll realize as you look around that you're trapped: people in the bleacher seats don't get up to leave and walk around the stadium. There'll be no reseating for you, no escape. Then you'll be noticed. If you're from out of town and wearing another team's hat, it's likely to get snatched, and a full jersey means it's 50-50 whether you get a courtesy call home before you're never seen again.

But — how cool are the bleachers? The fans lead a chant during every game: they yell each Yankee's name in turn, loudly and insistently, until the player acknowledges them.

They've been known to heckle other seating sections ("You paid ten, we paid three — ass-hoooles! Ass-hoooles!" "Box seats suck!" and so on). That's like eating your own young: it's appalling, but you have to respect the enthusiasm.

FENWAY

At Fenway, home of the Red Sox, the fans are particularly good at heckling Yankees, willing to break out into a "Yankees suck!" chant at any time. Playing the Yankees? Absolutely. Bored while beating up on the Royals? Sure, why not. Wedding? Bar mitzvah? Uncle's funeral? Go for it. You're as likely to see as many Yankees Suck shirts as Red Sox garb at the country's oldest ballpark.

Their obsessive fixation–inferiority complex with the Yankees aside, Red Sox crowds are known for being ridiculously smart, which shows when they try and crack the opposing players. When they're not being crass and making homosexual jokes, they can be impressive in their speed and creativity of response.

Fenway's finest heckling is generally reserved for Yankee play- ers, and perhaps the most amusing example was when Jason Giambi came to Fenway in 2004, after his long use of performance- enhancing drugs became public knowledge. The fans chanted, "You use [pause] steroids," over and over. It's the pause that gets me. Where else do you get comedy timing in a crowd?

The Fenway crowd's also known for being hard on their own players. Even stars will hear it if they make a bonehead play, and the scrubs who just aren't any good — they'll get an earful every time they step out of the dugout. Fortunately, the Red Sox don't have many of those guys these days.

But it gets a little ridiculous. In 1950, Ted Williams was booed soundly after he made a series of misplays in the field over the course of a doubleheader, and he came out of the dugout to give the finger to the fans: once to center, once to left, once to right. The taunting continued, and the Red Sox put out a release that said Wil- liams was sorry and apologized for his acts, though as far as anyone knows, Williams neither apologized nor felt sorry.

Can a boisterous crowd be a disadvantage? We know that oppos- ing players find it hard to be heckled when they're on a road trip, but is the effect just as bad when they find their home field is no refuge?

Fenway's history of little patience for the shortcomings of even the home nine raises an interesting question about the effectiveness of heckling.

A Philadelphia A's rookie said in 1947, when the team had sunk to the bottom of their division, "I'll be glad when we get on the road. Maybe we can win some games."

Players who see that fans at Wrigley, for example, or Philadelphia will start booing a player when he shows a sign of weakness might be more reluctant to sign on there compared to a park known for supporting its players. St. Louis, for instance, is known for applaud- ing outstanding plays even by the other team and being extremely supportive of their own players, to the point where it's seen as a de- sirable destination for free agents. If heckling your own players means that the team has to spend more money to build a team, or even if it makes the city less attractive compared to other suitors, that's a significant disadvantage for your own team. If you're willing to heckle your own team, you should understand that in some small way, their lack of success may be your fault.

Is heckling wrong? Heck, no. What happens if everyone's a heckler? Wouldn't the game actually be more interesting if the crowds sang original fight songs to support their team and tear down the visitors? If you've seen Japanese baseball or World Cup soccer, where thousands of fans chant together, you've heard how impressive it is. In person, it'll give you goose bumps and make you grin stupidly for hours after the game's over. That's worth the effort.

Increasing the quality and quantity of heckling helps to make the game more interesting, helps to make home field advantage almost tangible, and gets fans more involved. Constructive fan participation, even if it makes the visitors uncomfortable, is a healthy part of the game and should be encouraged.

How do we get to that noble goal of having every park shout creative insults in tandem, serenade visiting players with bawdy limericks, and take up the fun and rewarding profession of heckling?

Heckling's available to any fan within earshot, depending on his volume and the number of cooperating friends. For a smaller segment of fans, having seats closer to the fences and fences closer to the action means that you can again affect the outcome of a game directly. But these fans have done a laughable job. Baffled and greedy, they reach for a souvenir that'll get them thrown out, even if it hurts the team, but they won't go for a foul ball if there's a visiting player after it, allowing him to catch it and end a home team rally. This is inexcusable. Fans shouldn't be smart enough to earn a good income, spend it on season tickets, and flounder about affecting games without some forethought. Where's their sense of loyalty to their team? Do you want to see the home nine win or not? Unite, fans, and help our teams to victory!

Let's consider three important situations in which fans often do the wrong thing, hurting their team:

> Should a fan let a player catch a ball, fair or foul, if you can get in his way, catch it yourself, or otherwise make a nuisance of yourself?

(text continues on page 100)

You could start yelling at people randomly, but you wouldn't be reading this fine book if you were that kind of person. You should start by learning the "rooting rules" of Pete Adelis, the Iron Lung of Shibe Park, "whose body is almost as large as his voice," as published in the *Sporting News.* Adelis once asked third base coach Al Simmons from the stands: "Can you hear me down there?" and Simmons shouted back: "Can we hear you? Do you think we're deaf?" The A's treasured Adelis, crediting him with wins by disturbing opposing hitters and particularly pitchers so that they'd play badly. The Yankees were so impressed with his effectiveness they once flew him to New York, all expenses paid, so he could go after the Indians for them. While Adelis may not be shouting at players anymore, we should still listen to him.

Adelis advises:

1. No profanity.
2. Nothing purely personal.
3. Keep pouring it on.
4. Know your players.
5. Don't be shouted down.
6. Take it as well as give it.
7. Give the old-timer a chance — he was a rookie once.

Wise words from one of the best.

No profanity keeps down the chance you'll get ejected.

Purely personal — well, work on things they're sensitive about. Ty Cobb got fighting mad when called a miser, but he would go crazy and start beating people up if they questioned the purity of his racial heritage. Albert Belle hated being called "Joey" after he'd stopped playing under that name, so fans rode him about it for years.

Which raises another important point: players fueled by anger are bad targets. They're much better about channeling their rage into actual performance, and that's exactly what you don't want. Occasionally, heckling the angry player has provoked a direct reaction — usually not a pretty one. In 1991, when Belle threw a ball at a heckler working him over about his fight with alcoholism, he not only pegged the guy in the chest but the crowd applauded. Of course, that was early in Belle's career of violence against fans, photographers, reporters, and kids, before that act grew worn and tiresome.

It's important, as Adelis says, to know your players, so you can pick the object of your heckling wisely. If you're trying to be funny, generally you're fine. You likely already know which players have no sense of humor and present brawl risks. But if you're trying to seriously rattle a player, it's worth considering what could happen if he decides to go after you.

Good: 300-pound slugger with bad knees. Might not get the 30 feet to the stands, much less make it over the rail, and then he'll be out of breath and panting while you're crossing a county line.

Bad: fast no-hit outfielder. Sure, he can't put a bat to a ball. But your head is a substantially larger target, and there's a good chance he'll cover the distance between you before you know it — and certainly much faster than the security guards can get there to protect you.

Knowing your players is also what separates the heckler from the loudmouth. It's where humor and originality come from. Players have heard they suck for years. It's not going to get their attention. You've got to work on new material. Their recent fielding woes. Their anger about not being selected for the All-Star team. The fact that they've made a throwing error, booted a grounder, and gone 0-fer at the plate, making them a complete player. Wonder how anyone could get released from the Devil Rays. Recent marital problems are probably out unless you want to get tossed or beat up, but that the kind of thing is specific and personal. Weight gags if they're big, kid jokes if they're small ("Hey Eckstein, I'm going to take your lunch money!"). Name jokes can work if you're creative, but it's almost certain a player has heard any play on his name so often that it's background noise.

You can't play on their fears if you don't know them, and that's especially effective for marginal players. Know the name of the farm team. If you're heckling in the minors, it's especially helpful to know where they were drafted from ("You'd better get a hit or they're going to put you back in Armour High School, you bum!"). Know who they're competing with for playing time or who they replaced, and chant that guy's name. Many players are afraid they'll end up playing in Japan and might find Japanese taunts particularly disturbing.

Japanese taunts for American fans:

Anata wa baka desu yo: you're an idiot.
Anata wa jouzanai yo: you have no skills.
Pantsu marro mieh: your panties are showing.

Don't be shouted down by other fans. You've got to keep at it. Desperate fans who couldn't get Adelis to quiet down any other way would resort to sending him hot dogs and drinks. "I fooled 'em,"

Adelis said. "I yelled between bites." And he was one of the greatest hecklers of his time. If you want to be effective, you must show that kind of dedication (and may your dedication also be rewarded with a free meal).

Taking it as well as giving it is important. Be prepared to have players return the favor. They may see if they, like Roosevelt, can have you thrown out or moved. But they may react with the low (hand gestures and crotch-grabbing), or they may come right back at you with a topper. Lou Piniella once told a fan: "We're missing one of our players. You better go check your wife." Rickey Henderson ran the gamut: he gave out a lot of obscene gestures, but he'd also laugh at a good heckle or return the favor if he was in a joking mood.

There are two schools to being shown up. One is to never acknowledge failure. Hit a home run? Every dog yadda-yadda. Get right back on that horse.

If you're in it more for the fun and the sport, though, the civilized thing to do is take a moment and applaud your opponent. And then get back on the horse and try harder.

Adelis advises us to give old-timers a chance. He was particular about not going after the true, undisputed great players of the time — he'd take a break on Ted Williams, for instance, and then go after future Hall of Famer Phil Rizzuto. There's value in this: saving your voice for more mortal targets makes sense, and it differentiates you as a heckler who appreciates the history of the game, which may get you a little slack with ushers and other fans.

Above all else, if at all possible, you should use the power of cooperation. If you can get a whole bunch of people in on the gig, it's more effective (or just funnier). Like when they announce the Devil Rays lineup and after every hitter is introduced you yell "Who?" that's a joke. With enough people, it's high comedy. More hecklers also mean more inspiration, as the perfect crack for a moment might not occur to one person, but with many, one will be inspired. This is part of why stadiums with a tradition of heckling are so much tougher to play in than a normal one: if a player blows a play, the crowd will ride them relentlessly. Make a wild pitch in a warmup, the whole stadium jumps on the pitcher and won't let up. That kind of massed pressure can break even a hardened player's concentration.

Most important, there's safety in numbers. The more people involved, the harder it is to throw any one of you out. And if this book teaches you anything, it's that it's important not to get caught.

The rule, 3.16:

> If spectator interference clearly prevents a fielder from catching a
> fly ball, the umpire shall declare the batter out. . . . No interference
> shall be allowed when a fielder reaches over a fence, railing, rope or
> into a stand to catch a ball. He does so at his own risk. However,
> should a spectator reach out on the playing field side and plainly
> prevent the fielder from catching the ball, then the batsman should
> be called out for the spectator's interference.

If it's a home team fielder going into the stands after a ball, clear
the way. If it's an opposing fielder, you need to catch that ball yourself or at least knock it down and out of his reach. Getting in the fielder's way isn't just allowed, it's your obligation as an intelligent fan.
And don't be afraid to knock it out of his glove if he does manage to
catch it. If he can't control it, it's not a catch. Really.

If it's a visiting player trying to make a play on a fair ball, like a
long fly ball to the warning track or any play where the stands go all
the way to the line, it's still worth trying. If you can deflect the ball or
otherwise prevent the play, the worst thing that happens is that it's
still an out (well, and you get tossed from the game, but that's what
taking one for the team is all about). If the ump misses the call — if
it's deep in the outfield, you've got a better chance of this happening
than you might suspect — and the ball drops for a double, you've
done a great service for the home team.

Smart fans can attempt an even more sophisticated trick to fake
out the umpires themselves. In 2002 Charles Gipson, playing right
field for the Mariners, went into the stands after a foul ball that
dropped next to him as he fell. The fans managed to catch him and
the ball, put the ball in his glove, and shove him back onto the field
in almost a moment. Gipson held up his glove for the umpire, who
(unfortunately for the purpose of this anecdote) had hustled all the
way over there to be close enough to see the trick. He ruled no catch.
That shouldn't discourage fans in the future, though; with only
slightly different circumstances, it would have won their team an
out.

Should a fan reach over and try to catch a borderline home run?

This can affect the outcome of a game. The most famous incident of fan interference happened in the 1996 American League Championship Series, when Jeffrey Maier reached over the right field fence and caught a ball that looked as if it would have been caught by fielder Tony Tarasco. Right field umpire Rich Garcia (six umpires work the playoffs, with an additional ump down each foul line) ruled it a home run. With that home run, the Yankees tied the Orioles and went on to win the game in extra innings on their way to the World Series.

The rule on this kind of interference is clear:

> When there is spectator interference with any thrown or batted ball, the ball shall be dead at the moment of interference and the umpire shall impose such penalties as in his opinion will nullify the act of interference.

If a fan catches a ball that would not otherwise have been a home run, it's going to be the umpire's judgment, but almost certainly a double, and anyone who is already on base advances two bases. If it was going to be a home run, the umpire rules it a home run and everyone scores. And if the fielder is right there and it was going to be an out, it is the same as in 3.16 — it's an out.

If it's barely going to be a home run, you have to catch it and make the ump's call easier. Everyone's seen blown calls when a home run barely clears and the umpires rule that it was off the top of the fence and thus a rulebook double.* Don't let that happen — make that ball disappear with no ricochet to argue over. It's important to sell it well — if there's a big yellow line below which a ball is still in play, you should avoid putting your glove between the yellow line and the umpire — he might see that dipping leather and think the ball was going to bounce off the wall and come back into play.

What about an even closer situation, where a fielder's going back on a ball and could reach out and snag it? You must. If you catch it

---

* Balls that bounce on the field of play and over the fence for a double are not ground rule doubles. Look it up.

when it's over the fence, even if the fielder has a play on it, it's the same thing as going for a foul: they've got no right to the ball anymore. That ball can't be ruled an out. If you catch it while it's still in play and the fielder's there in time to make the out, you've turned a clear play into a judgment call. If the ump rules correctly that the fielder would have caught it, it's an out, and there's no difference to the game's outcome. If the ump rules incorrectly that the fielder wasn't going to make a play, the ball turns into a double or, even better, a home run, all runners score, and fireworks go off (where applicable).

If you pay attention to the game, you should always know what the best action will be.

Should a fan on the line reach out and snag a fair ball scooting by them?

This is common in parks where the stands are close to the foul lines beyond first and third. A fair ball can pass inside first base and then pull right, skipping through foul territory but still a fair ball and in play. You see morons reach over and snag those balls all the time, not understanding the ball is fair, much less what the game situation is and how their actions will affect the game. These people should have their season tickets revoked — they're clearly not ready for the responsibility.

When a fan touches the ball, play is called dead. So if the home team is at bat, you generally don't want to touch it. This leaves open the possibility that the fielder might botch the play or the ball will hit the wall and skip into the outfield. Either one allows the batter to get an extra base, and that's good for you. When the visiting team hits one, it's a judgment call. It's worth it if stopping play ensures that the runners can't advance.

When in doubt — don't touch it. If you're not willing to spend the effort to know what effect your actions might have or if you're not willing to risk ejection to help your team — don't touch it. Let the baseball gods sort it out.

Is this cheating? Not in this book. Like heckling, it's all good sport. The home player should have an advantage in the cooperation of his fans when pursuing a foul ball at home, and the visiting team should be granted no such courtesy. As for reaching out onto the field and snagging a ball, well, there wouldn't be this many rules to define what should happen. From the overflow crowds that would be put in the outfield and roped off, allowing the hometown boys to chase a ball while standing fast for the visiting team, to the game-changing home run–making catch of some New York kid, fans are as much a part of the game as the dimensions of a park.

Once you've decided to reach out onto the field, other possibilities are going to tempt you. Like putting things on the field.

Just as in nursery school, no throwing. The players have seen everything from garbage to fireworks; whatever it is, it's been tossed on the field at least once. Players who wander too near the stands are frequently doused in beer, which (per ounce) is likely more expensive than a good celebratory champagne, and that's so commonplace it hardly gets mentioned.

When the fans in St. Louis threw lemons at Dizzy Dean, he was disappointed: "I was crying because there were no grapefruit, oranges and apples like the Detroit fans threw at Joe Medwick in the last game of the world's series. It was an affront to my pride. I rate just as many kinds of fruit as any guy on this here ball club."

When you're entirely drunk, it might seem funny to wing ginger snaps at Brady Anderson in center field. But while other fans might tolerate belligerent heckling, even the most vicious heckler, who makes things personal — the kind of person who incite players to throw chairs into the stands — draws the line at throwing things at players.

Mel Ott told about what happened to him in one game:

> The fans were on me all day, principally because Hub [Carl Hubbell] was outpitching Diz [Dizzy Dean], and also because I was the nearest Giant player to them.
>
> The Cards not only didn't get a ground-rule double, but not one of them hit a fly to our outfielders until about the sixth, when I caught a soft fly in right. Just as I caught this ball I was hit in the middle of the back with a pop bottle.
>
> I got rid of the ball and looked around, there was almost a riot among the fans parked behind me. They found the guy who threw the bottle and worked him over, and for the rest of the game everything they yelled at me was friendly and encouraging.

Nobody wants to get his butt kicked in the stands. And no fan of baseball wants to see a game decided by a player being injured so cheaply.

This goes for throwing things on the field in general. It's why teams can't give away nice things. For instance, on August 10, 1995, when Dodger fans got a free baseball, they started to throw them on the field in the ninth inning when their team trailed, 2–1, and the umpire called the game. No comeback, nothing; and now no one gets baseballs. Or bats.* All we get are rally towels,† a lanyard for the laminated ID cards 90 percent of the population has to carry, calendars — things that don't hurl well.

The Dodger forfeit, though shameful, leads us to another lesson of heckling and fan participation: the more people involved with expanding the home field advantage, the more powerful it becomes.

Back in the 1890s, entire stadiums were said to be in on the tricks. Baltimore fans in John McGraw's day, to go along with their team's reputation for rough and occasionally dirty play, were said to have secreted doctored balls in the stands so that when a foul was hit, they could return the trick ball to their team. They snuck mirrors in to blind opposing batters. A fielder who went into (or even near) any crowd in baseball to catch a ball would be lucky to escape intact, much less with the ball.

Now, of course, many of those fans bet on their team to win, so they had an extra incentive to look for opportunities, but there's no reason that sufficiently committed modern fans shouldn't be able to think like that.

And if they weren't successful and the home team lost despite their best efforts, the fans didn't give up. A visiting team would follow a victory with a harrowing escape to their hotel, weighted down by a supply of produce generously donated by the local fans.

---

* Don't forget the team logo Lawn Dart Day.
† Handkerchiefs.

When fan participation goes too far

Sadly, the fans who have done their part to help their team have often gone too far. Fan violence is as much a part of cheating and baseball's history as the sign-stealer and the hidden ball trick. Fans taunting Ty Cobb about his penny-pinching or the possibility that the racist might himself have African parentage is an amusing exploitation of his weaknesses. Heckling visitors on the street is part of creating a hostile environment, in which they can't feel comfortable. But fans of late have often turned violent in ways that are petty, stupid, and misdirected.

Take for instance the shirtless, brainless father-son yahoo tandem who jumped Royals first base coach Tom Gamboa back in 2002 at Comiskey Park in Chicago and got colossally stomped by the players, who ran to help the coach. Or John Murray, the fan who tried to go after Cubs reliever (and martial arts expert) Randy Myers in 1995 after Myers allowed a home run. Myers dropped his glove, knocked the guy down with a forearm, then held him to the ground until help arrived. Or Berley Visgar, who ran from right field to jump on the back of Houston outfielder Bill Spiers in Milwaukee in 1999, surprising Spiers and getting in a few moments of wrestling before Spiers's teammates got there to give him a licking.

What were these people thinking? Did Jerry Springer refuse to book them?* Going on the field risks a forfeit: if the team can't provide adequate security, the umps can call the game. If you're going to try to do something like this, if you're going to drink your courage up, at least have the presence of mind to try and make a difference. If you can taunt a short-tempered reliever into charging the stands and coming after you — hey, maybe they get suspended, hurting their team, or they break their pitching hand on your jawbone — and that could be the difference in the game.

As badly as one besotted fan can act, the amplifying effects of the crowd don't just make heckling funnier or cheering louder — in the

---

* I'm surprised, now that I think about it, that Springer hasn't managed to milk a show out of these people.

right circumstances, the home crowd becomes the Mob, uncontrollable and dangerous.

Sometimes this ugly transformation happens at the urging of a manager: future Hall of Fame manager Casey Stengel was ejected from a Toledo game in 1927 for arguing with the first base umpire over a close call. Stengel then appealed to the authority of the fans, giving an oratory that was, unfortunately, not recorded for posterity. We know it was effective, though, because an angry mob of fans charged the field. The umpire got away after only a few got their blows in. The game eventually resumed, and Stengel was suspended indefinitely.

That, at least, has style. Generally, fan riots aren't driven by selfless attention to the standings or the team's fortunes. They're driven, almost entirely, by beer.

Take the infamous ten-cent beer riot in Cleveland.

In 1974, the Indians and Rangers brawled in Texas during a cheap beer night. The Cleveland media convinced the Indians management that they should hold one too, and management gave in. The next week, on June 4, the Indians held Ten-Cent Beer Night. Today, that'd be like fifty-cent beer night, and you could buy them six at a time. Imagine, a beer for fifty cents at the park. It's pandemonium — people would pay to get into the cheapest seats just to start drinking, fans not interested in baseball at all!

That's exactly what happened: 25,134 people showed up. The most recent Tuesday night game the team had played, on May 14, drew only 7,155. Some would later protest that it was only a small minority of fans who got totally, ragingly drunk and started acting like yahoos — but a small minority of 25,000 is a lot of people.

Even though the security force was twice its normal size, it seemed powerless. Fans ran out onto the field early, clothed, and then they'd take off their clothes, moon other fans — whatever occurred to their beer-stewed brains. They threw hot dogs, smoke bombs, tennis balls,* beer cups, beer cans, beer bottles (I'm a little surprised they didn't manage to get a keg onto the field). They ran out to shake hands with Texas right fielder Jeff Burroughs. But there was no

---

* Who brings a tennis ball to a baseball game?

Umpire Joe Brinkman holds on to a busted-up fan during the Ten-Cent Beer Night brawl. *AP*

crackdown by security, no call to the police to please come down and bring everyone who can swing a baton. The Indians didn't even cut off beer sales or make warning announcements to the crowd.

In the ninth inning, a fan jumped onto the field out of the right field stands and went after Jeff Burroughs. The two exchanged blows, and other fans came onto the field to attack the Ranger. "They grabbed at my glove, took my glove," Burroughs said.

In the Texas dugout, manager Billy Martin picked up a bat, said,

"Let's get 'em, boys," and led a charge to rescue his player. Seeing the Rangers run to the outfield, the Indians came out too. "I'll say one thing," Martin said later. "That fan we got a hold of out there got the hell kicked out of him."

But Martin's arrival only made things worse. The crowd swarmed onto the field for a chance at the Rangers. Martin claimed later that he saw "knives, and chairs, and other things." And in this case it doesn't seem like another of Martin's pretexts for a brawl — the fans tore seats out and threw them, hitting Indians pitcher Tom Hilgendorf and umpire Nestor Chylak in the head.

"We could have gotten killed out there," Chylak said. "I'm sure the only other place you would see something like this happen would be in a zoo."

"The Yankee fans are angels compared to what we saw out there tonight," Indians pitcher Steve Kline said, a statement never to be repeated.

It took a riot squad to break up the fight. Once the players escaped from the field with the help of security and police, a bloodied Chylak ordered the game forfeited. For all of the chaos, no player or umpire was seriously injured. Seven fans were treated, and police arrested only five people for disorderly conduct. Five people!

Later, the Indians blamed the umpires for not controlling the crowd better by calling out the cops earlier, but even the Indians' own security chief said, "They were drunk all over the place. We would have needed 25,000 cops to handle it."

The worst part is that the actions of the fans cost their team a chance at a win. The Indians had just tied the game and had runners on. It wasn't a hopeless cause by any means, and the melee turned what could have been a win into a shameful loss.

It seems that every year something happens that causes baseball writers all over the country to march to their keyboards with a head of steam and file stories about the new low that fan-player relations have reached and how it wasn't this way back in the old days. That's standard-issue nostalgia. Remember that in the actual bad old days, fans in Cleveland swarmed the field and hit umpires over the head with chairs. It's going to take a lot to top that.

Even if it could be harnessed and targeted, fan rioting isn't a good

Provocation for profit

Players could take better advantage of intoxicated fans. It's the home team's responsibility to keep the crowd under control, so if that visiting bench player can get the crowd riled enough and the umpires call a forfeit, it's a win for the visitors, and they get out of the pitching match of the day.

For a visiting team, it doesn't take much to turn a crowd against them. The story-hungry modern media's happy to assist. Pick a well-spoken bench player and have him call into the local sports radio stations and spout off about how the town smells, that the women and children are ugly, and then compare it unfavorably to the next town over — whatever else they can think of. All the papers will jump on it, too, because nothing fills column inches like whipping up a controversy — and then it's on.

A few gestures as he takes the field, a little bit of egging on, and things get thrown. Then the player can start to throw stuff back, challenge fans to come down and fight him — if enough of them come on the field and the police can't handle it, the umpires will be forced to call the game.

idea. Take the generalist example from the first chapter: if everyone engaged in that kind of cheating, would baseball be better or worse off?

Clearly, it would be a disaster. If a fan could smuggle in the transmission from a 1984 Pontiac Fiero and then take out the left fielder with it, and every other fan followed suit, it'd only be a couple of games before everyone would be watching Triple-A talent from their jail cells. No one wants that. And the same thing applies to using mirrors to blind the opposition. That's just wrong.

Full-scale riots? I'm sure the novelty would wear off after the first week, and then there'd be the consequences: no one would be able to buy beer, and fans would have to endure European soccer–style security, with angry police and their irritable dogs in every aisle, moats between the stands and the field, and razor wire on the railings.

Part II
The Illegal but Cute

Illegal actions and tactics, like the spitball, are common throughout baseball's history. How the rules try to address these long-standing, often winked-at traditions change the way the game's been played, sometimes, as with the banning of spitballs, quite dramatically.

They are also quite funny.

It's not how you swing the bat, it's what you've stuffed inside

> I owe my success to expansion pitching, a short right-field fence, and my hollow bats.
>
> — Norm Cash, Detroit Tigers first baseman

THE BAT IS ONE of baseball's constants, simple and unchanging since the 1890s, when the powers-that-be shed some of the sport's cricket heritage by requiring that a bat must be entirely round. Today, bats must be made of wood (and only wood), they have to be round throughout, no part can be more than 2¾ inches in diameter, and they can't be longer than 42 inches. For players, though, bats are much more than their dimensions.

Players knock on them and swear they can hear whether there are hits left or not. On the road, they pay more attention to the treatment their bats receive than to how their luggage or spouses fare, and they jealously guard their favorites. Many hitters can consistently judge if a bat is fractionally off its stated weight. Hall of Famer Al Simmons once kept returning batches of bats to the manufacturer as unsatisfactory. Eventually they gave up and sent him the original batch again. "These are fine," Simmons wrote. "Why couldn't you have made them like this in the first place?"

The best hitters will go through new bats like a stock car crew sifts through auto parts, looking for the one that's got the exact characteristics they want. Every piece of wood is unique, and some pieces have a better grain (the alignment and texture of the wood fibers) or are slightly harder than another. There's a great deal of density variation even within a particular species, to the point where the general distinction between ash and maple, for instance, only hints at whether a particular ash bat is better than a particular maple bat.

Different species of wood have different characteristics. Mariner superstar outfielder Ichiro Suzuki's game bats are made of ash, for instance, a change for him undertaken after much study and consideration. "I used the tamo wood when I played in Japan," he said, "and when I came here I used both to compare them, and I found that with this climate, the ash is more durable than the tamo."

Players might even experiment with rarer strains of hardwoods, looking for ones that might play even better than maple, today's favorite. Exotic woods aren't used because they crack badly in the drying process, but if a way could be found around that, the first players who put 5 percent more energy into a ball will have a great advantage: a fly ball hit 330 feet into a corner for an easy fly out becomes a home run at 345. It's that kind of advantage that's driven players to do all kinds of crazy things.

Suzuki isn't just picky about the wood of his bats. He may be the most protective of his bats of all overprotective players. He is so serious about keeping his bats from gaining or losing moisture after delivery that he has a special humidor for them and even travels with a portable sealed case that holds several bats for road trips. Bat makers go through a long and elaborate process to season their wood before the bats are shipped, so they leave the factory in ideal condition, and only Ichiro so protects them.

He may seem overzealous, but he's remarkably smart. A study by the University of Massachusetts–Lowell in 2002 found that Ichiro was right to be paranoid about the moisture content of his bats. When adjusting for the added weight, they found "the bat with a 10.9 percent moisture content to have as much as 1 percent increase in performance over the drier bat with a 6.7 percent moisture content." One percent is worth pursuing in a game like baseball, where success in hitting is determined in hundredths of seconds and fractions of an inch.

It's not a new idea. In 1937, the World Champion New York Yankees weren't hitting well when their trainer, Doc Painter, had an idea. Especially in damp spring weather, left lying on the ground, the bats might pick up moisture. To make them drier, and thus lighter and harder, they went into the oven the team used to dry out uniforms, and the Yankees started hitting again. Drying them as the

Yankees did can make bats lighter and harder, but baking them also makes them brittle, with a tendency to chip and split.

Once a hitter's found the best bat made from his favorite wood and (hopefully) is protecting it from drying out or soaking, that's only the start, and he turns to the rulebook for further suggestions. Fortunately, it reads like directions on a treasure map.

> **Rule 6.06:** A batter is out for illegal action when . . . d) He uses or attempts to use a bat that, in the umpire's judgment, has been altered or tampered with in such a way to improve the distance factor or cause an unusual reaction on the baseball. This includes, bats that are filled, flat surfaced, nailed, hollowed, grooved or covered with a substance such as paraffin, wax, etc. No advancement on the bases will be allowed and any out or outs made during a play shall stand. In addition to being called out, the player shall be ejected from the game and may be subject to additional penalties as determined by his League President.

It starts simply enough. "Boning" a bat is a long baseball tradition and legal in moderation. Players rub the surface of the bat with something hard to compress the outer layer to make the surface harder. It's called boning because, shockingly, players originally used a bone, but later switched to Coca-Cola bottles. As long as it doesn't alter the dimensions of the bat beyond the legal or create a flat hitting face, it's okay.

Innocent boning, though, is the gateway to grooving. Players carve indentations, with the grain, along the surface of the bat. The hope is that the grooves will put backspin on the ball, which will keep it aloft longer. The potential gains are tremendous — up to 10 percent more distance — but in practice it doesn't help that much. For one, grooving the bat isn't going to put much spin on the ball compared with the much more important question of how the bat hits the ball, and while a grooved surface does dig into the ball and put spin on it, the ball deforms into those cracks and has a harder time coming off it in the collision — exactly what you don't want.

Grooving is also easy to notice, and players get caught at it. In 1975, Bill Buckner had a game-winning hit turned into an out when home plate umpire Doug Harvey picked up the bat and noticed three long, narrow cuts in the bat's surface.

"Think of the number of times you've seen an umpire pick up a hitter's bat after he has thrown it down," Harvey said. "If a bat has been corked, I think it couldn't be done without leaving some telltale sign, ring, or some type of marking at the barrel end." Indeed, if you pay close attention, you'll see that a good umpire will frequently pick up a bat, particularly after a home run, and give it a quick once-over. Grooving is immediately noticeable to the touch.

A catcher who spots a hitter using a grooved bat shouldn't call the umpire's attention to it immediately but instead copy Billy Martin and wait for a chance to make the most of it.

For example, if the person grooving the bat is a .250 hitter, with an illegal, grooved bat he might hit .300. That's a dramatic improvement, but he's still going to get a hit only once a game, on average. If a catcher can wait until the batter gets a hit and have it recalled because of a grooved bat, it's a great opportunity. The team gets the hit back, the hitter is ejected, and the next guy is in the hole. For instance, on July 21, 1975, catcher Ted Simmons hit a home run in the fourth inning of a game against the Padres and was called out under rule 6.08 for using a grooved bat. The Cardinals ended up winning, but it's another example of how a smart player, seeing another one cheat, can use that information to advantage.

In the same way that boning leads to grooving, pine tar leads to all kinds of mischief. Pine tar's a dark brown, extremely sticky liquid that players use on bat handles for a better grip. You'll also see it smeared on their batting helmets and uniforms, so they can easily get a little more on their batting gloves while they're at bat. Because it's readily available and commonly used, it's not so hard — though illegal — to get some on the barrel of the bat, hoping the bat will hold on to the ball a little better and help give it backspin in the same way grooving does.

But pine tar is not the only thing that can be used. Other crazy substances players have doused, rubbed into, or otherwise treated their bats with include:

- Corn oil
- Motor oil
- Linseed oil

- Pickle brine
- Resin (applied by hand, melted, and baked)
- Tobacco "juice"

Soaking the bat with any substance is almost always intended to make the bat harder, like baking it to dry it out. But motor oil? There's no way that's helpful.

The rules also call out "paraffin, wax, *and the others.*" Paraffin and wax may have once been used to smooth the bat and impart less spin, though it's unclear how that would help.

But all of these things — the coating, the grooving, the boning — only touch or deform the surface of the bat. To get to the most famous, debated, and rumored-to-be-widespread form of cheating, we need to move inside the bat.

Corking is relatively recent. We don't know who was the first to cork a bat, but we do know that the conditions that make it worth doing have existed for only the last fifty years or so.

Early hitters used bats that were far larger and heavier than those used today. Everyone believed that the best way to smash a ball was to put a huge chunk of timber on it, and corking wouldn't have helped. But today, when bat speed is so important that an ounce or two of wood can be the difference between being able to hit against the toughest pitchers and staying in the minors, weight is king.

Alfonso Soriano, a left fielder for the Washington Nationals, is known for swinging the heaviest bat on his team: it's a 35-inch 33-ounce bat. Babe Ruth went through many different sizes and weights of bats in his career, but they were all much larger than that. The Louisville Slugger model he used (the R43) ran from 35 to 36 inches and 36 to 47 ounces; mostly he was at 36 inches and 42 ounces. That's a heavy bat.

But Ruth was a large man. Since his time, bats have become much smaller and lighter, with thinner handles, larger barrels, and the cup taken out of the end to shave that last ounce. Hack Wilson, a contemporary of Ruth's, is said to have started the trend toward lighter bats. By the time Hank Aaron pursued Ruth's record, his bat was almost a full 10 ounces lighter than Ruth's.

Why did bats become lighter? Viewed strictly in terms of how far a ball is hit, the tradeoff between bat speed and weight would seem to be neutral. A lighter bat goes faster but with less weight, while a heavier bat is slower but has much more mass behind it. It's like choosing between being hit by a motorcycle doing 120 and a car doing 60. The force of the collision's going to be the same, so both bats should hit the ball the same distance.

Improved pitching has forced this evolution, making speed the most important quality of a swing. For all of the carping about how pitching's been diluted, the pitching today is the best in the sport's history. From the ace of the rotation to the last guy in the bullpen, pitchers throw everything much faster, with much more effective breaking pitches, than their forerunners did. There are entire pitches, like the forkball, that didn't exist when hitters came up to the plate swinging small trees. Babe Ruth's eyes would pop and his knees would buckle the first time he saw a split-fingered fastball thrown by today's pitchers. Better conditioning and specialization produce closers throwing a hundred miles an hour in the ninth, while the old-school pitchers throwing complete games rarely worked at full effort, reserving their best pitches to get out of jams.

Today, hitters stand as far back in the box as possible to give themselves a few hundredths of a second longer to see a pitch. Even the smallest weight saving in the bat allows them to wait a bit longer before swinging, giving them a better look at the pitch and where it's going before they swing. When pitchers throw a hundred miles an hour, those slivers of seconds make all the difference in whether a hitter can even make contact, much less put a ball into play.

Corking helps bat speed in two ways. First and most obviously, it makes the bat lighter. A player used to swinging a 32-ounce bat will almost certainly swing a 31-ounce bat faster. Second, corking takes weight from the end of the bat and moves the center of gravity in. Now, why that results in a faster swing requires a fairly long and quite confusing discussion on angular momentum. The short version is that it's true, and you can test it for yourself if you want. Swing a sledgehammer with, say, an 8-pound head, as you would when destroying a wall. Then turn it around and swing it holding the weight in your hand. It is much easier. Trust me, when the

CROSS-SECTION OF A CORKED BAT

Many people think that corking requires the entire bat to be hollowed out. In fact, the hole in the bat is only a few inches deep.

physics of this became particularly vexing, I just went down to The Home Depot to try it. (Surprisingly, I wasn't thrown out — they were quite helpful. Thanks, Home Depot!)

This helps to explain why many hitters who use corked bats describe the advantage arising from quickness. Given two bats, both 32 ounces, one with the weight closer to the hands, it will be easier to swing that bat, and the hitter will be able to put more energy into the hit — even though the bats are the same weight.

Beyond whatever gains a player may realize from possibly increasing his bat speed, he may also hit better from the increased control and placement he has with a lighter bat, which is easier to control during the swing. Better contact makes for more line drives, and line drives are far more likely to drop for hits.

Players who admit that they used corked bats swear that they

A recipe for corking a bat

1 wood bat
1 drill press
1 bandsaw
2 cups bat filling (cork or superballs, whole or ground, Pop Tarts, whatever)
superglue
concealer: dark wood stain, tobacco "juice"

Step 1. Using the bandsaw, slice off the end of the bat, about a quarter or half inch in from the start of the barrel.

Step 2. Using the drill press, drill a hole in the center of the bat from the barrel end. The hole should be from 6 inches deep and half an inch in diameter and work up to 8 inches deep, three quarters of an inch in diameter, according to taste. Discard wood shavings.

Step 3. Pack bat filling into hole.

Step 4. Glue the cap of the bat barrel back on, matching the wood grain as much as possible.

Step 5. Conceal the inevitable slight irregularity using concealer until it's difficult to pick out the grain at all.

Repeat the process, varying the filling and the size of the hole, until you've created a suitable instrument.

If you're used to swinging a 34-ounce bat, you may be whipping that bat around as fast as you can, and if you want the advantage of having a longer bat without the additional weight, you'll be seeing how best to drill out a few ounces from a longer, 36-ounce bat.

help. Earl Weaver, a modest player but one of the smartest baseball heads to manage a team, wrote: "A corked bat is bound to make a player a better hitter. I know, because I used one."

Detroit Tigers first baseman Norm Cash, who won a batting title in 1961, was caught red-handed going beyond corking in 1970, when umpire Jake O'Donnell threw out one of his bats. "It had a place for a cork on one end. It was also flat on one side and bats must be round," O'Donnell said. Two cheats at once . . . That's advanced cheating, kids. Don't try that at home.

Cash used ground-up cork to fill his holes. After his playing career was over, he even showed *Sports Illustrated* how he'd done it. Other players have used all kinds of crazy stuff:

- cork, solid and ground
- superballs, whole and ground up
- a tube of mercury, the shifting weight of which supposedly helps with power*

All of them are probably equally useless in doing anything but making the bat lighter. The collision between bat and ball takes place so quickly that it doesn't matter if it's foam or high-test rubber.

Yet there are many scientific-sounding but hollow explanations for why corking should work. The cork acts as a springboard. The cork affects the harmonics of the collision. Cork improves the bat's biorhythms.†

Another reason seems plausible: denser bats. As Tigers catcher Bill Freehan said after Graig Nettles was caught corking against his team in 1974, "You get better wood in a heavy bat than a light one. So you order, say, a 36-ounce bat, drill a hole 5 or 6 inches deep in the end, and fill it with cork. Then you've got a bat that weighs, say, 32 ounces, but you've got the good wood of a heavier bat."

This is an interesting theory. If you wish to have a bat of a certain length, you then have a choice of wood. You want a bat that's dense and hard. But density costs weight, which restricts how fast you can whip the bat around. Corking may help by allowing a hitter to have a bat that's 34 inches long, made of a very dense and hard wood so that the impact gives the ball more energy, with a much lighter weight than a solid hunk of that same wood.

So we have a couple of good reasons that bat corking might work, and a few more that, depending on your degree of gullibility, are plausible. What to do? We can't take the word of players who admitted using corked bats and said it helped them. If a player tries a

---

* This story, oddly, told by Graig Nettles.
† Okay, I made that one up.

Norm Cash with his bats in spring training, 1962. Some of them may well
have been corked. *Corbis*

corked bat and it doesn't work, he would stop and probably refrain from talking about it, so the player who thinks a corked bat works likely tried it, found success, and kept going. We need science.

But science demands data, and all the available data tell us that corking doesn't help.*

How come? One reason corked bats fail to produce is that while moving the weight in on the hands makes the bat easier to swing, it dampens the collision. Ideally, when the bat strikes the ball, you want to have all the weight of the bat in exactly that spot to transfer as much force as possible in that instant of contact. Corking, while making the bat lighter and moving the center of gravity, removes weight from that critical spot.

However, it's one thing to set a bat up in a swinging machine that exerts the same amount of force every time and use it to hit balls pitched from a machine at the same speed every time, but a game situation, with a real hitter facing a real pitcher, makes practice much different than theory.

Another reason that corking works for some hitters and not others is that they're using all kinds of different ways of doing it. From how large and deep to drill the hole to what it should be filled with, there are general guidelines but no clear agreement.

Compare it to, say, spitballs: experimenting pitchers can easily throw dozens of spitters while they discuss the subject with others, watching the effect that each change in grip, delivery, or amount of moisture has on the ball.

But with corking, there's no consensus on how wide or deep to drill for the best results. A woodworker in Cleveland drilling out bats for the team doesn't start with the shared knowledge of every hitter since baseball began, and he doesn't have the time or resources to produce generations of experimental models. After all, that's how one might get caught.

So, because there's no blueprint and no quality control, one player might do it well and have success while another botches it and gets nowhere. Amos Otis, a star outfielder for the Royals, fessed up to

---

* I'd like to thank my Latin teachers for making me a stickler about using "data" as a plural of "datum."

using a doctored bat during his career, and his comments are revealing: "I had enough cork and superballs in there to blow away anything. I had a very close friend who made the bats for me. He'd drill a hole down the barrel and stuff some superballs and cork in it. Then he put some sawdust back into the hole, sandpapered it down, and added a little pine tar over the top of it. The bat looked brand new."

Otis didn't go to a manufacturer and experiment; he and a buddy cut bats open, stuffed cork and whatever else was lying on the workbench down them, and sealed it back up so it looked good. Otis, by the way, was a five-time All-Star player who finished in the top ten of MVP voting four times and was a top-ten batting average finisher four times.

The most important reason a corked bat might help is the simplest: if a hitter believes that a corked bat makes them better, that confidence, not the bat, can produce results. Baseball's a mental game, and things like that matter. If corking a bat is a wash from the physics side but encourages a batter to hang in against tough pitchers until they get a pitch to hit, that's a big plus.

The only person to take a scientific approach to constructing an illegal bat seems to have been on the other side of the law from the hitters. Robert K. Adair, who wrote the excellent *Physics of Baseball*, was hired in 1987 by then-AL President Bart Giamatti as a sort of consulting physicist for baseball. Adair said, "I tried to invent a bat that really would do a lot of good. The idea was to make the ball go better and not be immediately obvious to the umpire, and I didn't succeed. But I wouldn't guarantee some cleverer fellow than me won't think up something."

Adair's a smart guy, and I don't doubt that he gave it a good try, but that sounds like a challenge. The problem, as with all forms of cheating, is that there's a huge difference between the motivation of the cheater and that of the enforcer. To Adair, creating a bat was an interesting intellectual problem. A hitter looking for an edge is looking at the possibility of a contract worth millions. As with steroids, where almost unlimited money drives chemists to stay ahead of detection, money and motivation create opportunity where none seems to exist.

How prevalent is corking, even though its success is difficult to measure and likely nominal at best? The players' usual answer is the unhelpful "a lot of guys." On the other side, the rationale is that it's not so widespread because it takes a lot of trouble. But this doesn't make sense: today's players are unlikely to be doing the corking themselves in their hotel rooms. They could find people to do it (or have someone else find someone), work out payment, and then they'd only have to worry about getting caught during a game.

That so few players are caught corking their bats is a good argument that it's uncommon. Hollowing out bats offers two ways to be detected. Because the bat has to be cut open and drilled out, there's a hole that has to be concealed or capped; both are easy to spot on close inspection, and the cap can come off to reveal a cross section to the suddenly curious umpire.

But more often they're exposed because corking comes with an ugly side effect. It makes bats far more vulnerable to cracking. Instead of being a thick, solid piece of wood absorbing the shock, it's a much smaller volume of wood, no matter what the filling is, made of more than one material held together with glue. Predictably, it breaks much easier. A hitter's corked bats won't last nearly as long, and if a corked bat comes apart on the field, there's no defense: the evidence is laid out before the umpire, letting him skip right to the enforcement stage.

In 1981 California Angel outfielder Dan Ford had a whole run of close calls. Against Oakland, on April 29, Ford hit a home run. Suspicious, catcher Jeff Heath picked the bat up and started to look it over. Ford, arriving at home plate, made a grab for the bat, inciting a brawl. Then, in May, visiting Baltimore Orioles catcher Rick Dempsey, suspicious, asked home plate umpire Jerry Nuedecker to investigate. Nuedecker produced a pocket knife and began poking at the barrel but didn't discover anything. Angel manager Jim Fregosi said, "No wonder the [unknown obscenity] couldn't find anything wrong. The way he was holding the bat, he had his hand right over the crack."

Then the end of his bat broke off in a game on September 4, revealing a cork-filled hole, and Ford was finally ejected. The umpires submitted the evidence to league president Lee MacPhail. "I have nothing in the Hall of Fame," Ford joked, "but three of my bats are in MacPhail's office."

One of the most famous and memorable incidents of being caught cheating, we're told, happened entirely by accident. On September 7, 1974, the Yankees were playing the Tigers. Graig Nettles hit a solo home run in the second inning to give his team a 1–0 lead. In his next at-bat, in the fifth inning, Nettles got to first on a single to left field when his bat broke, the head flying off. The Tigers catcher, Bill Freehan, scrambled out from behind the plate to pick up the super-balls that flew from the uncapped bat, and the gig was up. Nettles was called out and ejected, but the home run he hit earlier in the game stayed on the books and turned out to be the winning run in a game that finished 1–0.

Making the story even more amusing, Nettles maintained that he was as shocked as anyone. "It was the first time I used that bat," he said. "A Yankee fan in Chicago gave it to me the last time we were there and said it would bring me luck. There's no brand name on it or anything. Maybe the guy made it himself. It's been in the bat rack, and I picked it up by mistake because it looks like the bat I've been using the last few days."

This is clearly a lie. We're supposed to believe that given a bat from a random fan in a hostile city, Nettles stuck it in with his game bats — which hitters normally guard with caution bordering on paranoia — then hauled it around with those game bats for a trip back home (a three-game series against Milwaukee), all never no-ticing that this fan's bat — which Nettles himself thought looked weird — was still mixed in there, ready to be accidentally used.

That's not the strangest incident with a corked bat, though. On July 5, 1994, White Sox manager Gene Lamont went to the um-pires and asked that Indians slugger Albert Belle's bat be inspected (which he's allowed to do as a manager of the opposing team). The umpires complied, placing the bat in Dave Phillips's locker in the umpires' dressing room.

Indians starter Jason Grimsley then went on a mission: to break into the umpires' room and replace the corked bat. He climbed into the ceiling above his manager's desk by taking down a tile. Like a tunnel rat, carrying a flashlight and the replacement bat, he wiggled off. He went over the visitor's clubhouse, peeked out at the grounds-keepers, and finally found his way to the umpires' locker room. Grimsley dropped down and swapped Albert Belle's bat for one of Paul Sorrento's, with his name on it and everything. Then he escaped with Belle's bat.

The umpires, returning to their locker room, did not take long to discover what had happened. The different names and models may have given it away.

This seemingly dumb detail may been desperation more than poor forethought. Omar Vizquel alleged in his (terrible) autobiography, *Omar!*, that they'd have replaced it with a legal bat of Belle's, but "the problem, of course, was that all of Albert's bats were corked."

That seems unlikely at first. It would indicate a lack of preparation on Belle's part — wouldn't you want at least one legal bat if the umps were suspicious and watched you closely, for instance? And you can also imagine that the team, throwing together this bad plan, might have given Grimsley the wrong bat in their haste.

But the more you consider it, the more sense Omar makes. The team came up with a fairly complicated plan. Perhaps they really thought there was a chance they could convince the umpires that that was the bat Belle had taken up. It's not uncommon for players to use each other's bats, particularly if they find another make more to their liking. Or, better yet, there was a chance, however slim, that that the umpires wouldn't notice and Belle would be acquitted, or that if the evidence was obviously missing, no finding would be made on the corking accusation.

One thing we can be sure of, though — Paul Sorrento wasn't using corked bats. There is no way that question didn't get asked before Grimsley was sent into the crawl space, pushing the replacement bat in front of him.

The umpires, of course, had already seen the Belle bat and knew something was wrong. They confronted the Indians, who handed over (again) Belle's bat. At that point, why not return a different, un-corked one? You're already in deep trouble, but the umpires don't know if the bat they took from Belle was corked or not and probably have no way of picking it out of a lineup. If there was an uncorked Belle bat, you could still give it to the umpires unless, as Vizquel alleged, no Albert Belle bat would have served.

The most recent high-profile incident embarrassed one of the game's most popular figures. In 2003, Sammy Sosa was a superstar, beloved by the fans. His 1998 competition with Mark McGwire to win the home run title and break Roger Maris's single-season mark was widely credited as saving baseball and restoring public interest and love for the sport after the damage of 1994's strike and cancelled playoffs.

But on June 3, Sosa was ejected in the first inning of a game against the Tampa Bay Devil Rays when his bat shattered as he hit a single. The umpires quickly examined the bat, and crew chief Tim McClelland spotted something wrong. (McClelland was coincidentally the umpire who took the home run from George Brett in the famous Pine Tar Incident and was on the crew present when Albert Belle's bat was taken and then stolen.)

They tossed Sosa. His bats were confiscated and inspected, but no other corked bat was found. He claimed that he kept only one corked bat that he used in batting practice to put on a show for the fans.

Sosa's story is a little more believable than some of the others. For one thing, when the bat broke, he didn't react at all. Some players immediately start to try and conceal the evidence by picking up the pieces and taking them back to the dugout before the umpire can get a good look at them, rather than go to first base on their broken-bat single. Most just wince or looked shocked and then compose themselves and run to first, waiting to be called out when the home plate ump catches on. But Sosa did none of those things, which does seem to indicate that he didn't realize what had just happened.

It doesn't seem worth it to cheat. That will change.

The future of cheating with bats

The difference between the best and worst batters at a position might be 100 points of batting average and a dozen home runs.

Cubs slugger Sammy Sosa experiences the drawback of corking a bat when it comes apart in the first inning of a June 3, 2003, game. *AP*

That's sixty hits over the course of a year and a few good hits carrying over a fence.

The difference in compensation, though, is easily $10 million a year.

Sixty hits, $10 million. That's too small a margin and too lucrative a reward for more cheating not to happen.

Microabrasions on the bat could make it move quicker through

Doctoring bats for amateur players

Unless you're a professional baseball player, you're almost certainly going to be using aluminum bats. There's nothing you can do to improve them. Any changes you make will almost certainly degrade their quality. If you're determined to threaten the health of the opposing pitcher, go buy an illegal bat. Like illegal golf balls and ground effect lights for cars, they often have helpful labels like "Intended for experimental lab tests only!" or "Do not use to win your next round!" or "Show your boss you're the boss!"

If you insist on tampering with your aluminum bat, here you go:

Starting requirements: unrealistic amount of money, day job without pesky attendance requirements (ahhh, sinecure).

1) Buy an industrial aluminum forge facility.
2) Retain existing staff or hire new staff, as required.
3) Retool plant to support bat-related foo-foo stuff, like doing the markings and grips, or secure third-party production for those pieces.
4) Take existing bat to plant.
5) Melt bat down.
6) Reforge bat to illegal specifications like the ones you could have bought in the first place.
7) Send remaining fortune to Derek Zumsteg, c/o Houghton Mifflin Company.

the air during its swing. Objects move through chaotic air flows faster than normal ones, which is why golf balls are dimpled. Without them, a drive might go 150 yards instead of up to the 250 yards the modern superballs can go. Most bats are smooth and lacquered. On a bat, the effective use of this might make a swing faster without any sacrifice of weight. But the gain, if any, would be small and, depending on how it was accomplished, harm the transfer of energy in the bat-ball collision.

This situation almost begs for Nike to do what they've done with athletes' jerseys: they invest millions in wind tunnel testing, mate-

Opposite page: Home plate umpire Tim McClelland gingerly holds Sosa's corked bat with a world-weary expression. *AP*

rial research, off-season minor league hitters to test prototypes in game conditions, extremely smart scientists who bicker with one another, and a fabrication facility to make small test batches until they've perfected a wood bat, specially treated and jaw-droppingly expensive, to sell to baseball's elite and further their reputation as a quite frightening research operation.

More interesting is the possibility that advances in carbon fiber technology might make it possible to manufacture a bat that, on initial inspection, looks like and, better yet, sounds like a real bat when it makes contact, but combines improved hitting characteristics with almost user-definable weight.

The problem with that is the investment in carbon fiber crafting knowledge and experimentation is high. The good news is that aluminum bat manufacturers like Easton are already interested in fiber bats, because the ideal bat at the prep level would be an artificial, durable bat that doesn't break but has the characteristics of wood. Aluminum bats are too good at transferring energy to the ball and put fielders (and the pitcher in particular) in danger.

Carbon fiber could also conceivably be used to create bat inserts: you could hollow out a bat and insert a thin carbon fiber tube that could, as it does in bicycle frame tubes, provide directional strength and resiliency, keep the bat from deforming as much (or heck, allow it to deform more), all while saving significantly on weight.

From detecting corking to the cheating of the future, baseball could do much more preventive work. They could require bats to be inspected, even X-rayed or put through an MRI before being used in games. But who would administer the tests, and when? The umpires aren't going to do it before each at-bat, or even before each game. Major League Baseball is unlikely to hire technical crews to travel the country, inspecting team bats. And unless the check were made before a player goes to the plate, a team could always have the bats they wanted inspected kept in a different place than the bat they want used. Prevention then means an airport-like screening before anyone can take a bat onto the field or marking bats that have been inspected and approved, after which you'd seal them in some kind of tamper-resistant container until they are used. Neither is going to happen.

Batters who cork often know they're at risk of being discovered, and they also know that if they're discovered, baseball's going to X-ray all of their bats. So batters will keep one bat, marked differently from the others (say, a piece of tape on the handle) and a stock of legal bats. There are many reasons hitters might do this, but if you look into a team's dugout and see a player's got five bats and one has a taped "X," and that's the one he grabs when he goes up with men on and two out late in a game . . . well, pay attention.

Bat corking's an interesting case because, unlike other branches of cheating, doctoring the bat hasn't died out because of rule changes or draconian enforcement; it's simply fallen out of favor as players have adopted legal, lighter bats. But technology's catching up and should soon be able to help the cheating hitter without his being betrayed by corking's tendency to reveal itself. And that will be a fascinating escalation to watch.

Doctoring the Ball

> Don Sutton was asked if it was true that he used foreign substances on balls, and he replied, "Not true at all. Vaseline is manufactured right here in the United States."
>
> — Variations of this exchange have also been attributed to George Frazier (by AL president Bobby Brown, no less), Jim Kaat (to an umpire), and others

PITY TODAY'S PITCHER. The strike zone's the size of a mailbox. The seams on baseballs aren't as high as they used to be, so they're harder to grip and don't break as much when you throw a curve. The new ballparks are cozy, intimate affairs where last year's deep but easily caught fly ball is today's grand slam. Advances in weight training, nutrition, and the use of, uh, supplements make today's average second baseman a well-muscled guy who can drive a mistake pitch into the stands. Baseball's increased reach means that even with expansion, teams draw from a much greater talent pool, and while pitchers risk career-ending injuries every time they take the mound, those armies of hitters march relentlessly up from the minor leagues. Once a good portion of any major league lineup was free outs, and pitchers admitted they would give a pitch their full effort only against the best hitters or in situations that threatened the game's outcome, like with runners on. Today there are no breaks and few easy outs, so every pitch is thrown almost at full effort.

And yet Major League Baseball, those fat cats in New York, refuse to legalize the spitball! For years they've watched the offensive explosion — tolerating steroids, shrinking the strike zone — and they did nothing to retain the balance of the game, to restore to respectability one of its long-practiced techniques.

It's a shame.

Yet the spitball's still here. It's never gone away.

The Origin of the Spitball

There was a time a pitcher could lean over, in full view of the batter, umpire, and crowd, and spit right on a ball. Right on it! And if the pitcher didn't feel like spitting on the ball, he'd throw it around the horn, and the fielders would each unload a stream of tobacco juice on it — and juice means spit — and it would come back as slimy and disgusting as a newborn. And there was no need for scuffing. While today the lifespan of a ball might be as short as a few pitches, back then there were only a few balls to last the game. Those balls would be so torn up and battered, a pitcher couldn't be sure where they'd end up.

Those were the days.

The first spitter was thrown soon after the first pitch. There are reliable accounts of pitchers using spit on the ball when they were forced to throw underhand. Harnessing spit for a consistent advantage to get it to drop predictably didn't take off until much later.

Tommy Bond pitched from 1874 to 1884, and in addition to being one of the first curve ball pitchers, he also used glycerin on baseballs to get them to break. Bobby Mathews, though, may have been the first to throw a good spitter as far back as the late 1860s. While it wasn't widespread or a mainstay of any particular pitcher, pitchers used it occasionally as one of their many pitches, and almost all of them experimented with it, leading to interesting results. Al Orth, who started out pitching for the Philadelphia Nationals in 1895, was a right-hander who used "a sweeping underhand" motion (what today we'd call a submarine delivery), and he threw a spitball that would rise, which is rarely seen.

As a primary pitch, the spitball became popular in the 1900s, as future Hall of Famer Jack Chesbro of the New York Americans and Ed Walsh of the White Sox both enjoyed success with it. They had learned it from Elmer Stricklett, who is most commonly credited with inventing the pitch. Other pitchers, seeing the success of Chesbro and Walsh, imitated them, and soon spitballers were le-

What does a spitball do, anyway?

Spitballs have been used in two ways. First and most commonly, the pitcher uses a conventional fastball grip, with his fingertips on the wet spot. As the ball comes off the pitcher's hand, it slips off the fingers. The effect is almost the same as with a knuckleball, as the ball is thrown with little spin. And like a knuckleball, it's notorious for diving down toward the plate late in flight.

The second use of a spitball is entirely different. Using a lubricant that decreases air friction on one side, the pitch will generate the same kind of break a curve does, toward the side the lubricant is on, and can be thrown at full speed. You can see that this would be highly valued for a pitcher and amazingly frustrating for a hitter.

gion. Stricklett himself spent a few years playing for the Brooklyn Superbas but was out of the major leagues for good after the 1907 season.

Every pitch has a family tree, often with similarly vague beginnings, and you can trace its spread through pitchers and pitching coaches as they move through their careers, inspiring others when they don't teach them directly. This is especially true of unpredictable pitches like the spitter, which are best learned by direct instruction of someone with experience, compared to something like the split-fingered fastball or palmball, where the trick is in the way the ball is gripped.

Ed Cicotte, of Black Sox fame, threw the shineball. He'd learned it from Red Faber when they were both on the White Sox. Faber was one of the most notorious spitballers and kept up on other ways to get balls to do strange things. Cicotte is sometimes oddly credited as being the inventor of the spitball. Many veteran pitchers who've invested the time to tinker with trick pitches can pass on their knowledge, take a youngster aside and teach him how to use a dab of moisture to make the ball do strange things.

As Craig Counsell said, "You do see [pitch doctoring] more in older players. It could be that you've been around a long time and you've had a while to learn how to do it right, or you've had a teacher

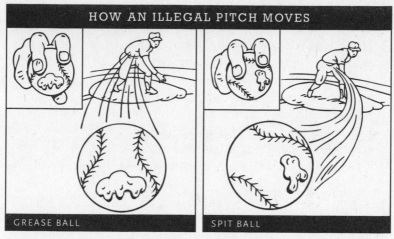

HOW AN ILLEGAL PITCH MOVES

GREASE BALL

SPIT BALL

A traditional Perry-like grease ball is thrown with a lubricant under the pitcher's fingers and comes out of the hand with little spin. Thrown correctly, it dives down as it approaches the plate. Spit can also be used on the ball itself (rather than on the contact patch between the pitcher's fingers and the ball). A little lubricant on the side will cause the ball to move toward that side. Lubricate the left side (from the batter's view) and the ball will tail to the left; lubricate the right side and it will move to the right.

CUT BALL

SCUFFED BALL

Cutting or scuffing a ball to create a rough spot has the opposite effect, causing the ball to move away from the direction of the rough spot. Scuff the left side (again, from the batter's view) and the ball will to go to the right; scuff the right side and it will move to the left.

— maybe another older pitcher from a few years earlier — teach you how to do it."

So the spitball emerged and soon, in the 1910s, all the tricks came out in a burst of innovation that baseball hasn't seen since:

- Shine ball (rub a smooth spot on the ball)
- Emery ball (use something to scrape the ball)
- Mud ball (slap some mud on a ball)
- Paraffin ball (use wax to create a smooth spot)
- Licorice ball (chew some licorice and use the particularly viscous spit)

All these tactics were designed to change a ball's aerodynamics by weighting one side unevenly or making the surface texture non-uniform. Since then, the list of innovations is limited, more or less, to the

- Grease ball (use a lubricant to create a slippery spot on the ball)
- Soap ball (use a detergent and a bit of moisture to create a slippery spot)

Take the shineball as an example of pioneering. Teams would spray an oily liquid on the infield to keep the dirt down in the heat and wind, preventing dustups that presaged the coming depression. Cicotte would put some of that oil on the ball, then rub it to a high shine (hence the name). That spot would have less aerodynamic resistance, and a good pitcher could get it to do the same kind of tricks a good spit- or greaseball would.

There were rules on the books to prevent these pitches, but they weren't enforced and were sometimes entirely contravened. American League president Ban Johnson ruled that because the shineball used substances that existed on the field, it was not a "foreign substance" and was okay. He used the same logic in ruling on spitballs, so it was open season, and in 1917 many pitchers adopted the spit- or shineball (or both), and baseball quickly acquired a reputation as a joke, an unsanitary and unsavory sport. Soon, protests that the pitch should be banned began to grow.

John McGraw, who as we know was no stranger to dirty tricks himself, was in favor of the ban.

"My position as regards the spitball is well known. I have always been opposed to it. It is disgusting, unscientific and dangerous. I was the last manager in the major leagues to sign a spitballer — Jeff Tesreau . . . Batting would be helped by a rule against the spitball, and the public wants batting. The chance of error making would be lessened, and the public wants cleanly fielded games. There would be less danger to batter and catcher with the freak deliveries out of the way, for not only are they hard to hit, but hard to catch."

It wasn't long before he got his wish.

The Roaring Twenties: The fall of the spitball

Freak Pitching Is Doomed in Majors
— *New York Times*, October 31, 1919

The 1920s brought the first serious crackdown on illegal pitches and deliveries. Pressure had been building for some time, led by figures like McGraw, who found the spitter in particular to be distasteful but didn't have much tolerance for other trick pitches either. After Prohibition passed in January 1919, all of those do-gooders didn't have anything else to do with their time and, emboldened, they started trying to clean up baseball. The nerve.

Baseball hadn't so much as tweaked the rules in years, but in February 1920 they implemented a whole slew of them, including the ban on spitballs and trick pitches:

> In the event of the ball being intentionally discolored by any player, either by rubbing it with the soil, or by applying rosin, paraffin, licorice, or any other foreign substance to it, or otherwise intentionally damaging or roughening the same with sandpaper or emery paper, or other substance, the umpire shall forthwith demand the return of that ball and substitute it for another legal ball, and the offending player shall be disbarred from further participation in the game.

That's just for the fielders. If you were a pitcher and you tried anything, you got ejected and suspended for ten days.

Each team could name two pitchers as spitballers, while others were not allowed to use the pitch. McGraw and others who wanted to see the pitch banned were gratified to see more run scoring immediately.

RUNS ALLOWED PER GAME, AMERICAN LEAGUE, 1910–30

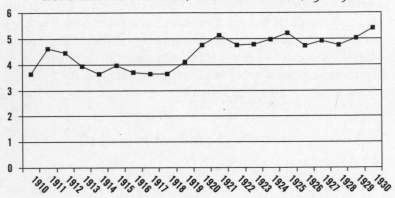

The shineball and other trick deliveries are frequently credited for the decline in league offense, but some of the dip in the 1915–18 seasons has to be attributed to the war. The huge jumps in 1920–21 are certainly due to the new ban on trick pitches and deliveries.

The National League, which at least didn't have Ban Johnson issuing strange definitions of a foreign substance, had a similar experience:

RUNS ALLOWED PER GAME, NATIONAL LEAGUE, 1910–30

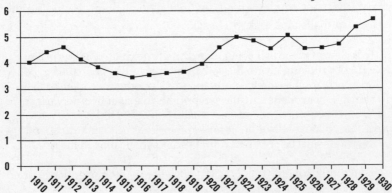

Another huge jump in scoring in the 1920 season went even further the following year. The spitball had been driven underground, where it remains today.

In 1921, the number of pitchers who could continue throwing the pitch was further reduced to eight NL and nine AL pitchers. Those so named were allowed to use the spitter for the rest of their career. Everyone else was spit outta luck.

Pittsburgh Pirates pitcher Hal Carlson is the most famous. Left off the list by his own team, Carlson suddenly had to rely on his other legal pitches to survive. Within a few years he was in the minors, where he worked on new pitches, like a screwball, and finally made himself into a major league pitcher again.

The grandfathered pitchers

American League

Name	1920 Team	Last year pitched
Doc Ayers	Detroit	1921
Ray Caldwell	Cleveland	1921
Stan Coveleski	Cleveland	1928
Red Faber	Chicago	1933
Dutch Leonard	Detroit	1925
Jack Quinn	New York	1933
Allan Russell	Boston	1925
Urban Shocker	St. Louis	1928
Allen Sothoron	St. Louis	1926

National League

Name	1920 Team	Last year pitched
Bill Doak	St. Louis	1929
Phil Douglas	New York	1922
Dana Fillingim	Boston	1925
Ray Fisher	Cincinnati	1920
Marv Goodwin	St Louis	1925
Burleigh Grimes	Brooklyn	1934
Clarence Mitchell	Brooklyn	1932
Dick Rudolph	Brooklyn	1927

Names in bold indicate Hall of Fame members.

Once it was illegal to throw a spitball, the pitch acquired a mystique, like the cool crime of burglary, and hitters started worrying about it. Pitchers weren't allowed to use it, but everyone knew that a year earlier they had, and they probably still were, only they'd be hiding it. It became as much about making the batters worry about it as being able to make the ball bend unnaturally.

This uncertainty led to a cycle of accusation and escalation that continues today. If Burleigh Grimes could get a ball to seemingly duck down as you swung at it and another pitcher got similar movement, well, Grimes threw the spitter . . .

Those few grandfathered spitballers didn't have to slink around and play hide-and-seek with the umpires. They could lick their hands openly and wipe them on the ball in full view of everyone if the mood struck. But they didn't; they valued the deception as much as the movement. Red Faber, who picked up the spitball to compensate for a dead arm, sometimes threw only a few spitballs in an entire game, preferring to keep the other side guessing. Grimes, known at the time as much for his combative personality and fondness for plunking opposing batters, enjoyed being known for his spitball without having to throw it very often.

Hall of Fame pitchers who doctored balls illegally

These pitchers frequently used illegal pitches after the pitch was banned and were not godfathered in.

Who	Career	HoF election	Threw	Denial	Admission
Don Drysdale	1956–1969	1984	Spitter	Y	Y
Whitey Ford	1950–1967	1974	All kinds of illegal pitches	Y	Y
Gaylord Perry	1962–1983	1991	Everything	Y	Y
"Bullet" Rogan*	1917–1938	1998	Spitter		
Don Sutton	1966–1988	1998	Cut ball	Y	Not in public

* Because of the racism prevalent at the time, Rogan pitched in the Negro Leagues, so this is kind of a cheat. No one followed him around writing biographies and interviewing him about whether, in addition to throwing ridiculously good legal pitches, he also mixed in the spitter. He did, though.

Every spitballer of note has been right-handed, just as nearly every pitcher into any kind of doctoring has been right-handed, far out of proportion to their numbers in the major leagues. Some might say this is because left-handers get more natural movement from their deliveries, but really, it's more likely just because historically there have been far fewer left-handers, and left-handers don't have to resort to those kind of tricks because being left-handed is, itself, an even better trick.

A history of spitballing after the ban

1930s

Nothing happened. A couple of the grandfathered pitchers finished out their careers, but by the second half of the decade, the spitball was pretty much dead.

1940s

The spitball rose from its grave with a vengeance, and soon there were as many pitchers throwing it as there had been in, say, 1925, when the grandfathered pitchers started to retire or leave the majors. The shortage of players during World War II resulted in a huge drop in the quality of play, and the new pitchers, who weren't as athletically talented, resorted to the old pitcher's friend.

Browns pitcher Nelson Potter was the first player suspended for throwing the spitball on July 20, 1944, when umpire Carl Hubbard reported him to the league. Potter protested that he'd only been blowing on his hand because it was cold, but the league suspended him for ten games. Potter denied he'd ever thrown a spitter in his career long afterward.

1950s

Lew Burdette was the greatest spitballer of the 1950s. He debuted in 1950 but didn't start pitching regularly until 1952 at the age of twenty-three. Everyone accused Burdette of throwing the spitball because of the dramatic downward break he could get on a pitch, but he always denied it. When he hung up his spikes in 1967, he had

Tampering through temperature

In the 1950s, the Chicago White Sox found a way to give their entire pitching staff an advantage without the trouble of cheating while they were on the mound. They froze the balls. The White Sox were pitching-rich and hitting-poor, and to try and negate visiting teams' offensive advantage, they found a way to deaden the ball. Freezing caused the rubber and cork center of the ball to remain dramatically less elastic and bounce far less, even if they were pulled out in time to bring their surface to room temperature. On the field, a hit ball didn't go as far, and home runs became deep fly outs, doubles became singles.

They stopped chilling the balls for a while but went back to it in the mid-60s. Pitchers complained that the balls were cold, wet, and slippery. In 1967, Joe Falls validated their suspicions when he wrote an article in the *Detroit Free Press*, alleging that the White Sox had for two years stored their baseballs in "a dark, dank area near their dressing room and let them get so mildewed that the boxes in which the balls came would decay and fall apart from the moisture." When the umpires investigated, the Sox set out fresh boxes of balls near the chamber of dankness and showed these off.

This seems, at best, a modest exaggeration. How would that work? Where would they get the replacement boxes? Would the umpires, who have to rub a game's balls down with mud before each game, really not notice if the balls were clammy, cold to the touch, and smelled of gym socks?

Recently, the Colorado Rockies revived the concept when they used a humidor for their balls in 2002. Since their first game, the Rockies have struggled with the unique challenge of playing in Denver. The thinner air makes it harder for pitchers to get their balls to move, and balls, once hit, travel farther. It's entertaining for a while, but the environment made building a successful team extremely difficult.

Back then, they used the humidor to keep the balls from drying out and making things worse, and it helped a little. But in 2006 they stored them longer,* and suddenly Coors Field turned into a pitcher-friendly park, almost entirely by deadening the ball — the same effect the White Sox enjoyed decades earlier. If legally making the balls a little wetter and a little heavier can turn the best environment for hitters into a neutral park, you can imagine how great an effect a pitcher can have working on one ball at a time.

---

* That's the story, anyway.

won 203 games, gone to two All-Star games (1957 and 1959), and in 1958 finished third in the Cy Young voting.

Burdette would get good hitters to come up to the plate and stare at him, waiting for the spitball, watching strike after strike go past them, right over the plate, and then they'd go sit down, angry they hadn't seen a spitter.

Burdette helped force a rule change that prohibited pitchers from going to their mouth while on the mound. Like some of the other great trick pitchers, eventually Burdette did admit he'd been putting something on the ball, but not what he was accused of: "I wet my fingers by bringing them to my mouth once in a while like a lot of other pitchers do. It's a nervous habit. But I go to my eyebrows a lot more, and that's when my fingers get real wet. I'm a pretty good perspirer, one of the best, and the sweat runs down my forehead and soaks my eyebrows."

Pedro Ramos was another 1950s spitballer, throwing a "Cuban palmball" as a complement to his fastball. Ramos was another wet-and-fake-wipe spitballer. He was also one of the first to court the reputation of a spitballer: while most other pitchers accused made angry denials, Ramos's denials still read as though he was winking. Ramos much later admitted that he was, as many suspected, throwing a spitter.

Not everyone was using spit. Clyde King, who later became a pitching coach and manager, recalled a game in 1951 (or, less likely, 1948) where he used bubble gum on a ball: "I was pitching for Brooklyn against the Giants at the Polo Grounds and Whitey Lockman was up with two out and two on in the ninth. The pitch I threw to strike him out had three pieces of bubble gum on it . . . not one but three. I don't know how they got there, but when [Dodgers catcher Roy] Campanella caught it, he fired it out into left field before anybody could look at it."

1960s

The 1960s was a great decade for the spitball, even with the repeated attempts to crack down on it. The rule changes drove much of the innovation that has defined spitballing ever since.

When the decade started, pitchers would get moisture on their

Gaylord Perry touches the brim of his cap, wets his fingers, and fakes the hand wipe. He would milk this for years. *National Baseball Hall of Fame/AP*

fingers by licking their fingers or actually spitting on them, or from perspiration, usually from their forehead, hair, or even forearms. They'd then fake the wipe (if they bothered to fake it at all) and put their moisture-laden fingers on the ball.

As the rules about going to the mouth became increasingly strict, pitchers moved away from sweat and spit to greasier substances that could be smeared on their uniform. Now, instead of licking their fingers, they'd tug on a section of their jersey and come away with a little bit of Vaseline on their fingers to serve the same purpose.

The 1960s showcased the greatest of all spitballers, Gaylord Perry. Perry started his career in 1962 with the Giants and was almost immediately accused of using the spitter. Which he was absolutely doing. A number of spitballers were using the pitch frequently at the time, possibly as many as a dozen, while perhaps twice that many dabbled in it. Perry outlasted them all.

"The hitters are given every advantage, so we need every trick we can get," Perry said in 1964, with two decades of spitballing still to go. But he gets his own section. Even with his debut, there might have been only four or five real masters of the spitball (including

Perry), with a dozen who used it frequently and another 30–40 who dabbled with it.

With Perry, the 1960s would result in rule changes.

Orlando Pena went to a spitball frequently in his outstanding 1964 season. He echoed Perry's sentiment: "A lot of guys in the big leagues throw spitballs. What the heck, pitchers gotta live, too."

Things really started to get heated in the middle of the decade. The year 1965 brought two incidents, both relating to Bob Shaw, who once said he was inspired to turn to the spitter by Lew Burdette. Shaw, like Perry, had an elaborate set of motions he would go through before each pitch: touch cap, touch lips, touch rosin bag, wipe or fake wiping hand on jersey.

On June 25, Gene Mauch, manager of the Phillies, coached at third so he could keep a close eye on the pitcher, and he ended up stopping play thirteen times during the game as umpires inspected balls. A manager or coach asking to have a ball inspected, even multiple times, happens rarely enough, but for a manager to put himself in a coach's box the better to stare at a pitcher and watch his pitches, and to stop play and ask for inspections thirteen times was unprecedented.

"It actually became funny and I couldn't stop laughing," Shaw said. Mauch was not amused.

If anything, it provided ammunition for every pitcher constantly hassled and inspected by the umpires on the mound. If Mauch, given that much latitude, was unable to catch Shaw even once — and remember, thirteen times he saw a pitch he thought was suspicious enough to ask for it to be inspected and the umps found nothing — why should the umpires listen to the other team's complaints at all, much less indulge their requests to scrutinize balls and search pitchers?

The next month, Milwaukee manager Bobby Bragan ordered his pitchers to throw spitters against the Giants because he felt the rules weren't being enforced against Bob Shaw. "I told the pitchers to throw the spitter and make no pretense of hiding it. The umpires didn't say anything."

Umpire Frank Secory, the crew chief, said, "If any pitcher threw a spitter, I didn't see it."

"It's a phase through which we have often have passed," National League president Warren Giles said that year. "I'm not naïve enough to think that the spitter is not being used or that it hasn't been since it was ruled illegal many, many years ago. But to prove it is something else. My umpires have their instructions — enforce the rule. But it isn't that simple."

Enforcement was wildly uneven throughout the 1960s. Many umpires, faced with the impossible task of making judgment calls on what pitches might be illegal, gave up as long as they weren't splattered when the ball hit the catcher's mitt.

Some umpires felt that because the league offices were reluctant to suspend pitchers suspected of cheating, the message was that spitballers were to be tolerated. Many umpires, in memoirs and interviews after retirement, talk about the difficulty of enforcing rules that were being changed season to season while instructions to the umpires themselves seemed to end with "but" and an implied "don't take that too seriously."

Those jaded umpires would search a pitcher once, find nothing, shrug, and let him throw whatever he wanted the rest of the night, no matter how much the opposing manager squealed.

The umpires were right about the lack of support: if Major League Baseball really wanted to pursue spitballers, how hard would it have been? Based on complaints or, even better, umpires' game reports, the leagues could have put observers in the stands, even used some good cameras. If it had forced a spitballer to lay off even only when he knew or suspected he was being watched, that would have been progress and a show of support for the umpires. But they didn't do anything of the kind.

Most umpires did their best to walk the wide, wide gray line the league painted for them; other umpires attempted to enforce the rules as strictly as they could. They would take a manager's complaint seriously and go out to the mound to inspect a pitcher, running their hands through his hair, down his forearms, along the sleeves of his uniform, looking for moisture or even unreasonable wetness, and they'd do it more than once if they felt it was justified.

Given time, those umps generally burned out and joined the jaded ones.

The second half of the decade brought Cubs pitcher Cal Koonce, who threw a great deceptive change and a sweatball. He was one of the few pitchers to admit to throwing a spitball while still active, saying in 1968 while with the Mets: "I threw half a dozen every game. A lot of pitchers did, but nobody would admit it because the spitball has been illegal since 1920. What was the point of all the hypocrisy? It was getting ridiculous, so I admitted it."

Koonce admitted that he'd used perspiration from his hand or wrist. Before he'd throw the ball, the catcher would signal him to ask if a pitch would be wet or dry if the situation or count seemed ripe for its use, and Koonce would signal his reply. This way, they made sure that the catcher was prepared for a pitch that would move more than usual and might need to be stopped after diving into the dirt.

Interestingly, while Koonce's illegal pitches were quite effective, the greatest spitballing firestorm that decade was over pitcher Jack Hamilton, who spent time on six teams between 1962 and 1969. Even throwing the pitch, Hamilton was no great shakes. In 1966, for instance, when he was regularly accused of cheating, he finished with a 6-13 record and a 3.93 ERA — higher than the league average — walked 88 batters, struck out 93, and allowed 13 home runs in his 148⅔ innings of mostly relief work.

When Hamilton pitched against the Washington Senators in June 1967 while with the California Angels, Gil Hodges, the manager of the Senators, stopped play five times to ask the umpires to inspect pitches he thought were suspicious. His batters did it another nine times. After the game, Hodges kept at it, protesting the loss to the league. "When a team wins a game on something the rules say is illegal, I protest," he said. He also called Hamilton a "disgrace to baseball" and said it was the most flagrant use of the spitball he'd ever seen. Joe Adcock, the manager of the Indians, said, "The only way he knows how to pitch is with a spitball."

It seemed as if every Hamilton appearance was accompanied by bitter accusations from opposing managers and hitters.

The umpires found nothing, however, and Hamilton kept on. When Dennis Ribant, a former teammate of Hamilton's, was accused of using a spitter against the Reds in a 4–2 win, he took a different approach: "I'm going to play this cute. I'm not going to admit it or deny it. This will give me a secret weapon."

The continuing accusations of spitballing and chicanery were wearing on the game. Babe Pinelli, a former National League umpire for twenty-two years, came out in favor of making the spitter legal: "That would end the charges of cheating. I'd like to see it tried out for a year or two, anyway, and get rid of the bickering."

Some had a sense of humor about the whole thing. The Tigers' Dave Wickersham was accused of throwing a spitball, but he insisted that while he has a good spitter, he wouldn't throw it as long as it was illegal. "In the first place," he said, "I think it's cheating. Besides, the last time I threw one, it got by the catcher."

Instead, there was another crackdown. Rule changes in the winter of 1967 essentially eliminated the spitter. An umpire was now instructed to call a suspect pitch a ball regardless of whether he was able to find any cut or substance on the ball, and repeated violations were punished by fines from the league. This was a giant leap forward in not requiring evidence, but it also put the burden on umpires to distinguish between when a ball had been loaded up and when the pitcher had managed to legally get a lot of spin on it. As a deterrent, though, the new power worked.

Cheating by pitchers wasn't eliminated, of course. It evolved, moving from saliva to greasy manmade substances, in particular Vaseline. Obviously, many pitchers still chose to adapt rather than go gently into retirement. Leo Durocher, then the manager of the Cubs, claimed there were two to three dozen pitchers who doctored pitches in the National League. We can safely assume "the Lip" was exaggerating a little, since that would have meant there were two or three cheaters on every team in the league, which would be an epidemic of spitters not seen since the pitch's ban. Even a few years earlier, Washington manager Gil Hodges estimated that there might be handful of pitchers throwing it. But they were out there, and they weren't anonymous.

San Francisco Giants manager Herman Franks complained in 1968 that "every one of the Dodger starting pitchers is throwing a Vaseline ball — Don Drysdale, Bill Singer and Don Sutton. The only difference between Drysdale and the other two is that Drysdale throws harder, so his Vaseline ball breaks more. He's thrown a spitter for years and knows how to handle stuff on the ball. Vaseline, spit — what's the difference? They've taken the spitter from the pitcher and given him the Vaseline ball. I've never seen so many guys with Vaseline in their hair — just plastered down. I've seen caps soaked with Vaseline."

Hall of Famer Drysdale is probably most notorious for beaning hitters, but toward the end of his career he did indeed throw more and more spitters and eventually admitted it. He picked his spots carefully for maximum effect. Don Sutton, another practitioner, described his approach:

"Don Drysdale was the master. He'd pick out the most vociferous guy on the team, do something funny with a ball he'd throw to him, and the guy would tell everyone on the bench. When the hitter believes the ball is going to do something crazy, you're halfway there."

Some umpires saw the new rules as encouragement. On August 18, 1968, reputed greaseballer Phil Regan faced the Cincinnati Reds and, as it turned out, a second opponent in umpire Chris Pelekoudas. Pelekoudas went so far as to call Reds batters back to the plate after they'd made an out if he thought the Regan's last pitch looked suspicious. Then Regan ran into Reds catcher Pat Corrales trying to score at home, and later in the game, Reds pitcher George Culver claimed he found a used tube of Vaseline and slippery elm tablets at home plate. Regan claimed they were a plant; Culver said there was no doubt they were Regan's. It does seem odd that the items would lie around for a while, out there in the open, waiting for the other team to discover them, and it's also strange that Regan would have both elm tablets, the traditional aid of spitballers, used for getting saliva going, and a tube of Vaseline, the weapon of the greaser. The league took no action.

Then, in 1969, baseball tried to crack down even further — there was an additional edict by the league — with ejection if the umpire was convinced a pitcher put a substance on the ball. Umpires rarely invoked this new enforcement tool, though as we'll see, it provided one particularly dramatic moment down the road.

1970s

At the start of the decade Chris Pelekoudas, already known for aggressively going after pitchers thought to be throwing doctored balls, led a crew of particularly active umps in pursuit of wrong-doers. They went after Gaylord Perry and Phil Regan, as well as others. In one game pitched by Regan, who had already tangled with Pelekoudas, the umpire's inspection was so thorough that Regan was allowed to skip his next physical, yet afterwards Pelekoudas still repeatedly stopped the game so that he could inspect balls.

Regan was miffed, saying, "I realize it's the umpire's job to come out and check me out, but when they have found nothing, that should be it. After that I don't believe they should be allowed to stop the game repeatedly to look at the ball. Then it becomes harassment and my concentration is being destroyed. Then I believe I have some rights in the matter too."

Regan, like other spitballers, understood that it could work to his advantage. "I like the batters to complain," he said, "because then they're disturbed enough so that they can't concentrate on what I'm throwing."

Perry was the subject of even worse dressing-downs, to the point that his team protested to the league and got the president to ask his umpires to stop inspecting pitchers at the request of the opposing manager. Things got better for suspected cheaters, and they didn't get any worse for hitters, since inspections had won them only excessive delays.

Pelekoudas did have a sense of humor, though. When Perry was traded to the Indians before the 1972 season, he showed up at a big going-away banquet for the pitcher and gave him a present of a one-pound jar of Vaseline. Perry, during spring training that year, got him back when he found Pelekoudas before a Giants-Indians exhibition game and greeted him, shaking his hand and sliming him outrageously with his own Vaseline-slick hand.

In the winter of 1973, baseball implemented new rules to try to crack down on Perry. Umpires could judge whether a pitch was illegal without finding any evidence on the ball or on the pitcher. The first violation was a called ball, a warning for the pitcher, and a PA system announcement. A second suspicious pitch meant an ejection and fine. This was an escalation from calling a suspicious pitch a ball without evidence and having repeated violations presented to the league. Now, an umpire, again using only his own observations, could eject the pitcher on the second strange thing he saw.

The next year, Perry's excellent book, *Me and the Spitter, An Autobiographical Confession,* appeared. In it, Perry describes in great detail how he threw both the spitball and the greaseball but declared that he was done with being an "outlaw pitcher." He was not.

Sometimes the battle between hitter and pitcher threatened to spill into the courts. Under the new rules, Drysdale protégé Don Sutton was thrown out in 1978 when umps found a third similarly scuffed ball in one game. Facing suspension, Sutton threatened to sue the league and was let off. He was also rumored to have gone back to the spitter that year as well and to have taught it to rookie Bob Welch (who went on to have a 17-year career and win a Cy Young Award in 1990 while with the A's). It's unusual for a pitcher to throw one illegal pitch, but if contemporary accounts can be believed, he was throwing two in 1978 and teaching the kids how to follow in his footsteps.

1980s

Seattle Mariner pitcher Rick Honeycutt was suspended for ten days near the end of the first season of the decade for scuffing the ball. The Royals had suspected that he was scuffing ever since their previous meeting a week earlier, when he threw eight innings allowing six hits, two walks, with two strikeouts. You'd think if he was cutting the ball he'd get better results, but still, the Royals had their eye on him. When the Royals' outfielder Willie Wilson tripled, he watched Honeycutt closely, and when he scored, he told the umpire to check the pitcher's glove hand. The ump found that Honeycutt had a tack sticking out from under some tape on his index finger — which had sandpaper on it.

He had also scraped his forehead when he'd wiped it, forgetting he had the tack on. The umpires noted this when they came out to inspect him. Honeycutt was ejected and suspended.

Tommy John was also accused of scuffing balls while with the

Yankees and Angels. The Royals collected the balls from one of his games, and manager Jim Frey joked, "I'm going to blame the groundskeeper right now. I think there's got to be a lot of gravel around home plate, because every time he throws a ball it ends up in our dugout, it ends up all scuffed up. I think the Yankee Stadium groundskeeper ought to take all the gravel and sandpaper out of the dirt around home plate." Other teams collected balls from Tommy John's starts and found them cut in exactly the same spot, but no one ever caught him at it.

In 1981, Billy Martin assembled a pitching staff of spitballers so brazen, it got noticed by executives with a long history of tolerating such pitchers. The A's pitching since the late 1970s had been widely rumored to lean heavily on illegal pitches that involved detergents, but Martin's A's were singled out in a memo to umpires on spitballs. The league also drew up a list of fourteen pitchers suspected of violating the rules. Four of them were A's (Mike Norris, Matt Keough, Rick Langford, and Steve McCatty).

The '80s were most notable for the milestone achievement of May 6, 1982, when Gaylord Perry won his 300th game and, equally remarkable, his first and only career ejection for doctoring the ball on August 23, 1982.

In 1983 in Kansas City, Perry reached back for an old trick he'd used earlier in his career and turned it into a new pitch — the puff ball. Perry would load up his hand with rosin from the bag. When he threw, the ball would come out of his hands in a cloud of rosin dust. For hitters who depend on picking up the speed and rotation of the ball as it comes out of the pitcher's hand, the explosion of dust was distracting and made it almost impossible to see the ball in those crucial first moments.

"One good resin bag can make an entire game for me," Perry said.

Perry retired after the 1983 season. Unlike the situation after the retirement of the great pitching cheaters of the past, there was no one to take his place.

Pitchers did learn from Perry, though. On May 26, 1985, Mike Scott of the Astros was accused by Cubs manager Jim Frey of scuffing the ball. Frey submitted to the league a small piece of sandpaper he claimed that his first baseman, Leon Durham, had found on the mound. Frey said that Scott had ditched the sandpaper when home plate umpire John Kibler (at Frey's request) went to the mound to search him.

Scott reasonably pointed out that the umpire checked balls during the game and didn't throw any out or raise any concerns about unusual scuffing or movement. Whether he was scuffing or not, Scott went on to play it like Perry: "This could help me. All this does is put thoughts in people's minds. Hitters will be looking for all sorts of things now. Maybe I'll go out there with a portable workbench and power tools next time."

In 1987, an umpiring crew went out to look over Minnesota Twins pitcher Joe Niekro. Ordered to empty his pockets, he tossed an emery board and a bit of sandpaper away from the umpires as he complied. They noticed and threw him out.

"I always carry two things out there with me," Niekro said. "An emery board and a small piece of sandpaper. I've done that ever since I started throwing the knuckleball. Being a knuckleball pitcher, I sometimes have to file my nails between innings."

It's an entirely valid reason, though you'd think he'd leave the equipment on the bench. And it's not, by itself, an ejectionable offense to have those objects on your person. The rule is that you're allowed to carry whatever you want within reason as long as you behave.

"They can carry a chainsaw as long as they don't use it on the ball," said umpire Steve Palermo. The umpires, inspecting Niekro because they believed he was doctoring the balls, thought the emery board he tossed aside was the instrument of that tampering. They sent several sample balls into the league office, and Niekro was suspended for ten days.

In 1987, pitcher Kevin Gross was caught with sandpaper and ejected. The incident inspired an enduring bit of hand-wringing from National League president (and future commissioner of baseball) Bart Giamatti. In denying Gross's appeal of his suspension, Giamatti wrote a long piece that appears in his collected essays, *A*

Nail care no, dental care yes

On July 16, 1969, Chicago Cubs manager Leo Durocher was convinced that Dodgers pitcher Bill Singer was using something on his balls. When Singer was running the bases in his jacket (as you commonly see pitchers do), a tube of toothpaste popped out. Durocher ran out of the dugout, seized it, and yelled, "Aha, I've got the son of the bitch. He's loading the ball with toothpaste."

"I like to brush my teeth when I come to the park," Singer said. "It's pretty hard to brush your teeth without a toothbrush and toothpaste, unless you do it with your fingers and water."

No action was taken against Singer.

Great and Glorious Game, which is A Boring and Horrible Book. Still, he provides a nice summary of why some people get so worked up about cheating:

> Unlike acts of impulse or violence, intended at the moment to vent frustration or abuse another, acts of cheating are intended to alter the very conditions of play to favor one person. They are secretive, covert acts that strike at and seek to undermine the basic foundation of any contest declaring the winner — that all participants play under identical rules and conditions. Acts of cheating destroy that necessary foundation and thus strike at the essence of a contest. They destroy faith in the game's integrity and fairness; if participants and spectators alike cannot assume integrity and fairness, and proceed from there, the contest cannot in its essence exist.

The obvious question is why, if Giamatti's concern was truly about "secretive, covert" acts that undermine the sport, was he suspending Kevin Gross for ten games for sandpaper while twiddling his thumbs and ignoring the exploding use of steroids and other drugs?

"Cheating, on the other hand, has no organic basis in the game and no origins in the act of playing."

What halcyon vision of baseball was Giamatti brought up on that this was a shocker? Some of the greatest cheaters in the game were operating in his youth — why, the Giants were stealing signs on their way to a miracle pennant when he was thirteen. Giamatti, like

Landis long before him, wanted to sell the sport as clean and gentle-manly, and ignored its rich and fascinating history if it contradicted that sales pitch.

That was the '80s for you.

In 1988, reliever Jay Howell got caught with pine tar on his glove in a playoff game — the National League Championship Series against the Mets. He was ejected and suspended for three games.

1990s

The best incident of a largely boring decade happened on May 1, 1999. Tampa Bay Devil Rays manager Larry Rothschild convinced the umpires to inspect Detroit Tigers pitcher Brian Moehler, and home plate umpire Larry Barnette found a small piece of sandpaper glued to the thumb of Moehler's left (glove) hand.

Moehler claimed that it was dirt, not sandpaper, but didn't appeal his ejection and subsequent ten-game suspension.

Controversy around pitchers' cheating, though much reduced from its peak, still went on. "When we played the Braves — it must have been the late '90s — I was with Florida, and Pat Corrales was the first base coach with the Braves," Diamondbacks shortstop Craig Counsell said. "He would yell at [Marlins pitcher] Dennis Cook when he'd come into the game. Cook rubbed the baseball real hard, and Corrales thought he was raising the seams with his finger-nails. He wasn't actually doing anything illegal, I don't think — he may have been taking his fingernails to the ball a little, though. It seemed to happen every time we played them and Cook was pitch-ing, Corrales would really yell at him, really loud."

Marlins manager Jim Leyland was livid at Corrales, but not about what you'd think.

"If you're going to stand five or six feet outside of the coach's box trying to steal signals every night . . . get in the damn box. He's right on the [ball-scuffing] rule, but do what you're supposed to do your-self. Don't throw stones and live in glass houses."

2000s

Pitching in this bright new millennium has been a snoozer so far. Some pitchers have been mentioned as throwing a spitball once in a while, but after games, the losing team never jumps up and down in front of reporters, screaming that the other pitcher threw a hundred spitters that game.

Back in the heyday of pitchers loading up baseballs, writers would regularly produce speculative articles on pitchers like Perry, Regan, and even suspected ones like Sutton and Tommy John, asking, "Do they or don't they?" Managers and opposing hitters would rant and rave in postgame interviews, pointing fingers and throwing chairs.

We know that pitchers still go for it every once in a while, but today the most we hear is "some hitters think this guy's slider slides a little too much, if you know what I'm saying" during a game broadcast. No one carries a reputation for using a doctored pitch as a regular part of his game. Does that mean there just aren't pitchers who rely on it so heavily, or does it mean that everyone's scared of being sued?

We've seen only a few relatively minor controversies, as in May 2003, when Zach Day was ejected for using glue on a blister between the second and third innings. Day then walked the first batter and attempted to get the glue off. The Expos trainer came out of the dugout, and home plate umpire Bill Miller saw what was happening and ejected Day immediately, arguing that under rule 8.02(b), a pitcher can't "have on his person, or in his possession, any foreign substance."

The rules were (and are) unclear on this point, except in saying that the umpire has sole discretion in these decisions. Is it really illegal for a pitcher to use any kind of glue or bandage on a blister or other cut? Especially in a case like that one, where the substance can't be applied to the ball and doesn't give the pitcher any advantage (if anything, having a blister glued down is likely to degrade a pitcher's ability, rather than enhance it).

In 2004, St. Louis Cardinals reliever Julian Tavarez was ejected for having pine tar on his hat and suspended for eight days. The next year, Angels reliever Brendan Donnelly was ejected for having pine tar in his glove. In a fun twist, his manager Mike Scioscia dusted off and used the old 1920s Ban Johnson argument, saying that pine tar wasn't against the rules.

"The rulebook says that you can't have any foreign substance on a

---

How to spot a spitter

Look for warning signs:

- an unusual break compared to other pitches from the same player
- far less spin on the ball than a normal curve or slider, but it still moves
- ball is thrown at the same speed as a normal fastball but moves way in or out
- batter glares and/or yells unusually foul curse words at the pitcher after striking out

Watch the pitcher closely if you're not sure and look for a tug at an odd spot on his uniform or the old spit-to-ball routine: hand to mouth, fake wipe, fingers to ball.

---

glove," Scioscia said. "Pine tar is an accepted practice among pitchers."

Donnelly said, "I don't have anything to apologize for. Pine tar is used the same way resin is used. People think you're loading up the ball, but it keeps your fingers dry. I'm not trying to cheat or doctor the ball. Just to get a grip. Nothing more, nothing less."

"Pine tar is not doctoring the ball. Pine tar does not alter the flight of the ball," Scioscia asserted. This is made funnier since, as a former catcher who at one point caught Don Sutton, Scioscia knows that anything on the ball can alter its flight.

There is support for Donnelly's view, though. Todd Jones, a longtime reliever, wrote after the Donnelly ejection that he'd used pine tar every time he had to pitch at Coors Field because "it's very dry in Denver, and that makes the baseball slippery. I needed the tar to hold on to the ball. I didn't want the ball to slip and hit a hitter. At least, that was my thinking. I never considered it cheating; I was breaking even."

Craig Counsell agreed: "They'll come up with anything if they think they can get a better grip on the baseball. You'll see the bill of their hat is black, the rest of the hat's red, and you're saying to yourself, 'That's not sweat.' If something is done just to get a better grip on the baseball, that's no big deal to me. But if they're loading the ball up with saliva or whatever, and their pitches don't do what normal pitches do, then you start to wonder."

Donnelly wasn't ejected for throwing a ball with pine tar on it, though, just for having it on his person.

The problem with this line of thinking is that even getting a better grip means that a player's getting an edge through the use of a substance that's against the rules. Further, if pine tar substantially improves a pitcher's grip, that does more than prevent slips and improve control. It can also, by maintaining better finger contact longer, improve the break a pitcher gets on a curve ball, for instance.

In Game 2 of the 2006 World Series, Detroit Tigers starter Kenny Rogers had a brown substance on the palm of his pitching hand during the first inning. When the inning ended, the smudge sparked a series of conversations, including a soft complaint to the umpires from Cardinals manager Tony LaRussa.

When Rogers returned to pitch the second inning, his hand was clean.

"It was dirt and rosin put together," Rogers said after the game. "That's what happens when you rub it up . . . I just went and wiped it off. I didn't think it was an issue. After the first inning, it was fine. I felt I was pretty comfortable after that."

Looking past the sheer implausibility of Rogers's explanation and ignoring that the smear looked like pine tar, broadcasters found footage from other games earlier in the season of pine tar — dirt, sorry — in exactly the same place on his hand. It's even more ludicrous to think that Rogers would not notice he had dirt (that looked like pine tar) on his pitching hand in the same spot repeatedly during the season.

If it's true that he was using pine tar, though, why didn't the umpires do anything? Surely they could see that Rogers had something on his hand. And why didn't LaRussa ask for an inspection that might have resulted in Rogers's ejection?

The reason is that, as we've seen, the use of pine tar by pitchers is a baseball tradition. As long as a pitcher's using it to get a better grip on the ball in poor conditions, especially where the rosin bag isn't going to help much — like the Detroit weather for Game 2 — the umpires will let it go unless the other side complains, as LaRussa did, or if it's overly obvious, as it was that night.

As for LaRussa's motivations and why he didn't request an inspection, he was in a difficult position. In such bad conditions, his own pitchers were probably also using something technically illegal to get a decent grip, and he didn't want to have everyone inspected. But with his hitters complaining that the ball was moving strangely, he had to stand up for them or risk having them snap after a strikeout and say something unfortunate to the umpire that would result in an ejection.

So LaRussa didn't want the rule strictly enforced as much as he wanted Rogers to stop being so flagrant about it, and if that meant Rogers was less effective, that would be a nice bonus. Rogers then pitched another seven innings of shutout ball, so whether he was using the strange mystery substance for grip or to get unnatural movement on his pitches, Rogers either didn't need it that much or he found a suitable alternative.

The future or lack thereof

At the major league level, there isn't much of a future for the spitball or any similar cheating. Even the most modest of baseball broadcasts uses three cameras (center field, first base camera pit, third base camera pit), and many get over a half dozen, not including hand-held units. With every camera feed stored and accessible, it's easy for someone at MLB headquarters to review a complaint by quickly scanning all of a pitcher's actions in a game and then hand out fines or suspensions as appropriate.

Gaylord Perry labored under this toward the end of his career, and it was a pain in the neck for him. But if you've watched old games, you know that they were limited by not just the lower number of cameras but also the quality of the picture they could take and how close they could zoom in.

This is a much stronger deterrent. The leagues are much more aggressive now in using video to review protests and investigate incidents on the field. Where a pitcher once had to worry only about

How to become a master spitballer

If you decide to get into loading the ball, experiment. Perry tried everything, no matter how nutty. Whether you're using sweat, spit, or applying a food-grade synthetic grease with PTFE,* you also need to work on your control so that you can throw it consistently for strikes. A trick pitch you can't control might freak a batter out, which can be useful, but it's not an effective part of your repertoire until you can throw it on a full count with confidence.

You need to be able to put the substance on the ball before you throw it, though. Work on misdirection — if you can get people to watch you touch your hat, for instance, while you're cutting up the ball like it was a teenager in a slasher movie, all the better.

Enlist as many accomplices as you can. The catcher doesn't have to be the one who applies a spot of grease for you. Any infielder who touches the ball can do it. The first baseman, because he's involved in almost every play, is an ideal candidate to slip something on the ball before returning it.

---

* "Fill surface irregularities, forming a smooth, waterproof, lubricated surface" and only $2.57 for each easily concealable half-ounce tube when you buy a standard pack of twelve from McMaster-Carr.

pulling it off in front of the umpires and other team, now he knows that if he blows a move and no one sees it, there's still a good chance it'll show up on the night's highlight reel, and he'll be facing possible disciplinary action. At that point, it's harder to justify using the spitter even in the most important situations.

What's more, there's not as much need for the spitter now. A pitcher who can throw a good split-fingered fastball or a forkball doesn't need to risk ejection and suspension for the marginal edge, and his time is better spent on working on other breaking pitches than trying to master a pitch he might get away with throwing only a few times a game unless they're in Kansas City for a day game and the visiting team is from the West Coast, so no one's televising it at all.

And yet baseball runs in circles. Technology doesn't eliminate the possibility of someone throwing a ball with something on it. Every year, many talented pitchers out of high school are taken late in baseball's annual draft, or go undrafted entirely. They then have a choice: accept a team's offer of a ham sandwich to sign as a thirtieth-round pick (or, if they're undrafted, trotting themselves out for teams at open tryouts), or accept an athletic scholarship to a junior or technical college. If they go the latter route, they have a chance to take some classes, hang out, and succeed on the field against a higher level of competition, maybe attracting more attention from teams. There are many talented, smart pitchers who spend a year or two bored out of their minds at places like Southeastern Virginia Technical College of Carrollton, surrounded by some of the most interesting chemicals modern industry can produce.

Why, look at the McMaster-Carr catalogue (which is an outstandingly well done piece of work and makes for excellent reading). They've got *seventeen pages* of the wackiest industrial lubricants you can imagine, many of them clear, odorless, water-based, with ratings and codes . . . Oh, it's glorious. Modern technology provides the wannabe cheater with an unprecedented arsenal of weapons.

At some point, someone's going to have an idea. And if he can figure out how to get away with it while cameras watch and record his moves on the mound, others will follow.

Gaylord Perry: Greatest cheater ever

THE MOST NOTORIOUS admitted and successful cheater in baseball history was Gaylord Perry. For his entire career, Perry was the center of attention. When he came to town, the local papers ran stories on whether he threw the spitter or not. He was not always the best pitcher in baseball, though he was the first pitcher to win a Cy Young Award as the league's best pitcher in both the National and American leagues, but he was by far the most notorious and famous pitcher in baseball. Everyone knew that spitballer, that cheater, that crafty veteran.

Gaylord Perry was born to poor tenant farmers on September 15, 1938, in North Carolina. He first saw indoor plumbing at his high school. He and his brother, Jim Perry, were both encouraged by their father and became successful major league pitchers. Both won a Cy Young Award. But only one of them cheated, and only one is in the Hall of Fame.

Perry threw the spitter growing up, shown first at the age of ten by pitcher Slim Gardner, who played on a local team with his dad. But Perry really figured out how to throw it from pitching coach Frank Shellenback and his teammate Bob Shaw while in the Giants minor league system.

But he only became Gaylord Perry, Spitballer, on May 31, 1964, when the San Francisco Giants played two games against the New York Mets. In the first, the Giants won, 5–3, behind Juan Marichal, who threw a complete game. The second went into extra innings, and in the thirteenth, manager Al Dark called in the last man on his pitching staff, a once–highly regarded prospect who hadn't done much against major league hitting and, at twenty-four, might have

KNOWN AND SUSPECTED PERRY STASH LOCATIONS

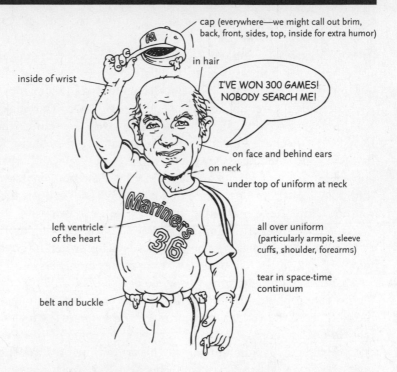

cap (everywhere—we might call out brim, back, front, sides, top, inside for extra humor)

in hair

inside of wrist

I'VE WON 300 GAMES! NOBODY SEARCH ME!

on face and behind ears

on neck

under top of uniform at neck

left ventricle of the heart

all over uniform (particularly armpit, sleeve cuffs, shoulder, forearms)

tear in space-time continuum

belt and buckle

At some point during his long career, Perry probably hid grease everywhere his free hand could reach.

shown that he couldn't win at the highest levels. Or at least he couldn't win the way he'd been trying.

In the fifteenth inning, facing trouble, his catcher Tommy Haller told Perry, "It's time to try it out," and Gaylord Perry, master spitballer, made his first appearance in a game. Before he'd only used it with large, safe leads, to experiment; now a mistake could cost his team a marathon game.

He threw ten shutout innings of relief with the spitter that night, striking out nine batters. He was accused of using the pitch, but Perry denied then and for years to come that he did anything illegal. His increasingly frustrated opposition screamed and opposing managers demanded that umpires inspect him to the point that he was regularly stripped down on the mound, but from that first game, where he tried it under duress, until his retirement, Perry was never caught in the act.

Not for lack of trying, either. Perry endured a level of scrutiny usually reserved for presidential candidates.

Umpires asked him to take off his hat so they could look it over, then they might carefully inspect his nearly bald head. They looked his glove over and wiped his arms off with a towel. Sometimes they forced Perry to change his uniform top, or pants, if they suspected he was hiding something they couldn't find. And Perry would make sure he came out of the clubhouse again with something on it, even if he'd been pitching clean up to that point, because he knew there was no chance they'd make him change his uniform twice.

Yet Perry never got caught. There was no doctored ball, no uniform, no stash. His one ejection was on suspicion, when he got astounding movement following a warning earlier in the game.

When Perry came to town, press photographers would try to get incriminating photos of him on the mound or in the dugout, and the pictures would run on the front page of the sports section with incredulous captions. Television networks put cameras on Perry and claimed they caught him going to his armpits before throwing a pitch they judged as a greaseball. The *New York Times* once published a pitch chart of a Perry start, where some anonymous benefactor marked Perry's pitches and location, using — scandal of scandals — a mark to indicate the spitball. The *Times* took the sheet to ABC, went through the tape of the game, and proudly announced that before each spitball, Perry touched the inside of his left sleeve with his pitching hand. The league took no action.

But for all the attention, all the cameras, and the constant scrutiny of his every move, no one ever caught him at it in the twenty seasons between that extra-inning game in 1964 and his final appearance in 1983.

Hard work was Perry's secret more than anything else. He honed his mound routine through practice, from his early trick of wetting his fingers and then faking a wipeoff to the late career production he'd put on, fidgeting, stretching, twitching, touching, adjusting,

Blood is thicker than Vaseline

Perry writes in his autobiography of a game in 1971 where a reporter grilled his five-year-old daughter, Allison, in the stands.
"Where does your daddy keep the grease?" he asked her.
"In the garage, by the car," she said.
"Does your daddy throw a greaseball?"
"It's a hard slider," Allison replied.

pulling at different parts of his uniform, until he had the delivery of substance to ball undetectable. He was always willing to try different substances, so he was able to move from throwing spitballs to using a dab of Vaseline to K-Y Jelly, always staying one step ahead of the law.

He would experiment, store the result away, and go back to it later. He played around with putting a lot of resin on his hand and ball so that it would come off his hands in a thin white cloud of resin powder — the puffball — against the Oakland A's in 1974, then tried it out again in spring training in 1979; then in 1980, with his legal pitches on the wane, he started to throw the puffball more frequently until baseball changed the rules to outlaw his creative use of the rosin bag.

He also cultivated his reputation, going so far as to write an autobiography that described how he'd used spit and grease and everything else on the mound. But he swore that he'd given up being an outlaw pitcher — which was about as true as all his previous denials. It played havoc with hitters.

"Sometimes I'd shake hands with opposing ballplayers before a game," Perry said. "But I'd grease my hand with Vaseline. The player would say: 'Are you starting the spitball stuff already?'"

Perry could adapt too. He knew which umps he could push things with and which ones required restraint. He seized every opportunity. "If your ball does something funny, it doesn't mean it's a spitball or a greaseball. It might just be a cut-up ball. Like that pitch I threw to John Ellis that he hollered about, that was just a cut-up ball, a ball with a little nick in it. You can make a cut-up ball look like a spitball or a greaseball. You get a cut-up ball out there in a real game, you're not going to turn it over to the umpire. You're going to use it."

But Perry wasn't all smoke-and-mirrors and psychological games. He was a good pitcher without the spitter.

In his last game of the season in 1973, Perry threw a 1–0 five-hit shutout for the Indians against the Red Sox, striking out seven. For the entire game, he did none of his fidgeting or other crazy motions that drove hitters nuts. "Did it on purpose," he said. "I had a feeling they were going to change the spitball rule — either legalize it or make it tougher. I wanted to prove to the front office I could pitch just as well without all the monkey business. Didn't do too bad, did I?"

In 1989, Perry appeared on his first Hall of Fame ballot. There was surprisingly little controversy over his election. Thomas Boswell, one of the most prominent baseball writers, made an aside in a Hall of Fame column ("another of our recent and somewhat dubious applicants for permanent glory"), and there was sniping from lesser writers and letters to editors, but in general his accomplishments were acknowledged and his methods regaled with fondness. On a ballot with Johnny Bench and Carl Yastrzemski, two amazingly good players (who both got over 90 percent of the vote), Perry was third, at 68 percent, and his support increased until he was elected in 1991.

It's not a slight on Perry that he wasn't elected instantly. He was good for a long career but rarely displayed the kind of dominance Hall of Fame voters really like to see — he won the Cy Young Award twice, once in each league, but he was only in the top ten vote-getters another three times — and he only appeared in one postseason, which meant there were no memorable playoff theatrics in his legend.

If there were voters who wouldn't put him on their ballot because he used the spitter, we know that there weren't more than 25 percent of them, because 75 percent of the voters saw fit to enshrine him.

Part III
Thrown Off
the Varsity Team

If everyone threw the spitter, the game would be wetter, but it would still be our national pastime. Past rule changes around the composition and construction of bats haven't threatened the integrity of the game. Banning the spitball and the corked bat while being lax in enforcing the bans hasn't caused ticket sales to flag nor fans to question the fairness of the games they see. But other forms of cheating could each, in its own way, threaten the very essence of the game.

These are the unforgivable crimes of baseball. Here we'll look at game-fixing and gambling on games and, the most recent sportwide crisis, the use of drugs by some players that forces a horrible choice on all the rest. They threaten the sport's integrity and the public's confidence in fair competition, and they can't be tolerated.

Gambling and game-fixing: The good old days

You might think the Black Sox was the first team to throw a game. Would you care to bet on that?*

Baseball's early history isn't tainted with gambling. The sport was born and grew up beside gambling, and their close relationship almost snuffed the game entirely. Given the level of influence that gambling had, it's amazing baseball survived to become a national sport. Game-fixing scandals were common. Teams paying other teams to beat a rival, or rough them up, happened all the time.

When organized baseball began, it was a social game between people with spare time and money to indulge their hobby, and they placed friendly wagers. Baseball drew spectators, who also bet on the games, attracting people who took bets to make a living. Then, shockingly, the amateur players took money to win — and lose — games. In 1865, when the players were still paid secretly, a gambler bribed members of the New York Mutuals to roll over for the Brooklyn Eckfords. An investigation found them out, and the league suspended them, only to let them back in over the next few years.

The players learned a lesson: if they were so obvious in their poor play that their team immediately knew what was up, they might be forced to play elsewhere for a while. Needless to say, it was not an effective deterrent.

Schemes to make money through collusion with gamblers became more common. In 1869, the Troy Haymakers threw games to get better odds for betting on themselves when they played the Red Stockings. The result was nearly a riot.

---

* If yes, quick! Send your bet — any amount will do — to Derek Zumsteg, c/o the publisher at the address at the front of this book.

The Haymakers' owner, along with his players, bet $60,000 (in 1869!) on a much-anticipated game against the Red Sox. But he feared they might not pull off a straight win, so he instructed his team to cut the game short if they weren't sure they could win but had a lead or tied the game. At the top of the sixth inning, tied at 17, some of the team, including the pitcher, put their equipment away. The decision to stomp off the field was expensive. With five innings played and the score tied, they had a decent chance of winning outright. But the angry Cincinnati crowd spilled onto the field, the umpire declared a forfeit in favor of the Red Stockings, and they lost their money.

As was normal at the time, no action was taken. Discipline was light and erratically enforced. Clubs cut some players who took payoffs and the leagues banned some, but others escaped any punishment. Even when they were banned, players might still be signed by other clubs and return to the league.

When the professional leagues were established, bets of all kinds were rampant. Players would bet one another during a game, there'd be bets on whether they'd have a hit that night, they'd bet on whether their team would finish first or third or whether they'd win three of five or five of seven. Generally the bets were small: a hat, a cigar, a few dollars. But the players and managers also bet cash on themselves in an effort to supplement their income, and the owners bet on their own teams to make more money. A league's president might bet on games or pennants. Whole teams bought into pools on their pennant chances.

This was all in the open. Newspapers printed the bets as encouraging news. For the fans, it was both a sign of your team's confidence and an assurance that they probably weren't on the take. It also meant that the players were regularly in contact with gambling and those unsavory elements who fixed games, but as long as they were betting on themselves, it was no big deal . . . right?

Eventually, that close connection with gambling brought down the first openly, truly professional league, the National Association, which started in 1871. The interest in games by bettors and rumors of fixes real and imagined hurt the league's reputation. Soon even the most innocent misplay was the object of suspicion and whis-

Betting for the fan

With the country fixated on its counterproductive and tiring crusade against gambling (who will protect the children from sports betting?), many fans are itching for a way to liven up baseball with a little friendly betting action. I'm here to scratchy, scratchy that itch.

Scratchy, scratchy, picky picky

Every bettor picks a player standing against the dugout rail, watching the game. The bettor then makes money on the actions of this player.

The player scratches or otherwise reaches down to adjust his crotch or athletic supporter, the owning bettor wins $1 from all other bettors.

Picking the nose is worth $2 (maximum, one payout per minute), but if it's followed by booger-eating it's worth $10 (when accepting the money, the winner must shrug and say, "He was hungry").

If the player leaves the rail, the owning bettor picks a replacement. If no replacements are available, that bettor is excused from payouts. Otherwise no switches are allowed. If only one player is on the rail, all action is off. Alternates: advanced bettors can pick more than one player. Picks of players can be persistent. If only one player is at the rail and is owned, he can still pay off.

pering. Henry Chadwick, a Hall of Fame *writer* (the only one) in New York, opined regularly about the gambling and corruption that dogged the league and the damage that even a few players could do: "No positive proof can be brought forward in support of any direct charges of collusion among players for fraudulent purposes, but not one man out of ten who witnessed the majority of games of October last can be persuaded that the contests were fairly or honorably contested. In this respect, just one player of the nine can be guilty of the mischief, one club can do mischief enough to taint the reputation of a dozen."

Chadwick predicted that the wide misconduct, left unchecked, would result in the league's demise. It took only three more seasons.

Things got worse. There was frenzied betting on underdogs before they would squeak out a win. Managers would have terrible tantrums and accuse their players of not giving an honest effort. Umpires were offered hefty bribes to make calls in one team's favor.

Past a diving Derek Jeter

Suitable for two bettors. Each bettor picks one of the unfortunate ballgirls who sit in foul territory next to the right and left field to demonstrate an important life lesson.

Boys: know someone or be well born and the world will come to you, rewarding you with a lifetime of secret handshakes, open doors, and all the cool jobs like being a ballboy.

Girls: work hard enough and you'll get the awful jobs boys don't want, like sitting along the foul lines and looking bad trying to get up and sprint after fouls.

If a foul ball is hit to their side *and they leave their seat to try to make a play:*

The ballgirl does not stop the ball — either because it skips past her or bounces off her: owner pays $2.

The ballgirl manages to stop the ball: owner wins $5.

The ballgirl dives for the ball but does not stop it: owner pays $10.

As season ticket–holders know, this is an area where experience and attention pay off. After a few games, the perceptive fan will notice that Katy is a reliable fielder but Catie is easily excitable, jumping up and diving for every ball no matter what her chances. And as no fielding statistics are printed (or available), it's easy to take advantage of the rube you're treating to the game.

If the ballgirls switch sides at midgame, payouts follow the girl and are not fixed on the side they originally took.

Even pennants were fixed, with the second-place team losing on purpose for pay. On July 24, 1873, Jim Ferguson of the Brooklyn Atlantics umpired a game between the New York Mutuals and the Lord Baltimores. Ferguson's temper was already short, as he was convinced that some of his own players were fixing games. Disgusted by the terrible and suspicious play he saw (the Lord Baltimores won, 4–1), Ferguson charged the stands, confronted the gamblers, and swore revenge on them. Then he got into a fight with the players and broke one of their arms with a bat.

No action was taken, either for that game or against the Atlantics team that was betraying him on the field. In subsequent seasons,

"Did we give up when the Germans bombed Pearl Harbor?"

Before the game, bettors should agree on the odds that an inspirational video will be played to rev up the home crowd before the ninth inning. Bluto's speech from *Animal House* pays double.

too, individual teams and the association stood by and did nothing. They launched no investigations of specific games; no matter how obvious a fix was, they didn't look into allegations that particular players were readily available for sale.

Teams like the New York Mutuals were so frequently involved in throwing games that its backers were almost certainly involved. An umpire bribery scandal involving several players was investigated by the league and resulted in the expulsion of only one player, John Radcliffe, who'd directly approached the umpire with the offer. Radcliffe was then reinstated. Rules in the National Association against players, managers, and umpires betting on games were not enforced.

The league ended in 1875. Before one game, Dick Higham, the captain of the Chicago White Stockings, found out that their opponents, the Philadelphia Athletics, had been paid off to lose. Higham demanded that the gamblers pay him a cut as well. Denied, he convinced his own team to conspire to lose to the team that had been paid off to lose. The farce went twelve innings and was dominated by awful defensive play on both sides. Philadelphia won, 5–2. Higham was suspended (only to be reinstated).

Later in the season, caught associating with gamblers, betting, and throwing a game, Higham at last received his walking papers. Though talented, he was widely considered one of the most corrupt players in baseball, involved with almost every serious fixing scandal the National Association endured. The horribly corrupt Mutuals signed him immediately. It was a perfect match: they were so bad that they were useless on either side of a fix: no one would bet on them to win, so they couldn't lose on purpose, and they couldn't win on purpose even if the other team had been bought. Dick Higham was a good enough player so that he could help his team win games and flexible enough morally that he could be paid not to.

> **We're so patriotic**
>
> Two bettors: will the seventh-inning stretch be the amusing and funny
> "Take Me Out to the Ball Game" or the ponderous stupidity of "God
> Bless America"? This can be a straight bet or negotiated odds. It's not
> valid in Yankee Stadium or Toronto, though you're welcome to try and
> get an out-of-towner to bet with you.
>
> Insider tip: this is another one where being a season ticket–holder
> pays off, because you'll know what your team's habit is. Baseball's
> been retreating from playing "God Bless America" every day, but
> you're generally well off betting yes on Sundays, the first game of
> homestands, and any day honoring or associated with the armed
> forces. Because what troops on leave from getting shot at really want
> isn't competent elected leadership to get them home, it's a tinny PA
> announcement and hearing "God Bless America."

After the season, teams left the National Association to form the
National League, which was intended to be better organized, more
businesslike, and set higher standards than the National Association (which folded). However, the new league's dedication to better
morals met with skepticism when it allowed the most notorious
crooked players to participate, and its constitution prohibited only
betting against your own team.

One of those players, Mike McGeary, was the first National League
player accused of game-fixing. The league suspended him and investigated the matter but could find no evidence, so McGeary was
reinstated. But when George Bechtel solicited another player to try
and get his manager to throw a game for $500, it ended his career. It
was a start.

The next year, the National League showed that it was entirely serious about pursuing corruption. In 1877 players on the Louisville
Grays threw exhibition games for money; they confessed and were
banned from the game permanently. (They may have thrown regular-
season games as well, but evidence never came to light.) They were
found out when a league investigation turned up a series of weird
telegrams to unremarkable utility man Al Nichols, some from a

Ooooh, say are you bored?

Suitable for two bettors. Over/under on the singing (or playing) of the national anthem is 1:30s, so one wins if it's longer, one wins if it's shorter. Set the amount high enough to make the betting interesting. Advanced bettors may wish to negotiate the over/under time based on this insider's tip: always bet the over on long-haired saxophonists and anyone described as a "local recording artist." Opera stars are good bets on the over, but sometimes they'll belt it out fast, the way it was meant to be sung, and you'll be paying out.

man who ran gambling pools in Brooklyn. They leaned on Nichols, and soon the scheme was cracked.

The league suspended and later banned four players, including a legitimate star in George Hall. Shortstop Bill Craver, who had previously been connected with many problems in the National Association, was thrown out, not for conspiring but for refusing to allow his telegrams to be inspected.

This was the first time the new league and possibly any professional league took such an action: conspiring with other players to throw games would result in the end of a player's career. Even refusing to cooperate with an investigation, as Craver did, would end a career.

Al Spalding, who published the *Spalding Guides* that frequently denounced excessive arguing, dirty and tricky play, and player drinking and gambling, wrote of being with William Hulbert when Grays pitcher Jim Devlin asked to be let back in the game, as he and his family were in terrible straits after his expulsion. Hulbert gave him $50 and said, "Devlin, that's what I think of you personally; but damn you, you have sold a game; you are dishonest and this National League will not stand for it. We are going to expel you."

Because it was the first public gambling scandal with clear evidence that players were involved, some thought it would damage the league. But the league's investigation and the severe action taken helped to establish that the NL was going to be much more zealous in its pursuit of wrongdoing that threatened the game.

The league showed a mean streak. When the fledgling International Association, which started that same year, decided to allow those players in, even signing them to contracts, the NL pressured the rival league until it reversed course and kept them out. Al Nichols went on to play for independent and semipro teams under fake names; he was discovered and thrown off his last team on suspicion of taking money to play poorly as "Al Williams" of the Long Island City Senators.

Craver's ejection, if possibly unjust, made a great difference to the league. Some of the harshest critics of the admittance of problem players from the old association sang the praises of the NL. The game experienced a resurgence, as fans returned to the game they'd soured on after years watching unseemly conduct.

Still, gambling was not banished from the game by that one act. Attempts to bribe players were thwarted. Some efforts at enforcement were overzealous, and players who were almost certainly innocent suffered. Lipman Pike, for example, had become disgusted by the corruption of the Washington Mutuals and quit the team, but he was briefly expelled from the National League after the 1881 season for no good reason. He was eventually reinstated.

Dick Higham (yes, the same Dick Higham) was hired as an umpire for the NL (no, really) in 1881 and immediately raised suspicions in his game calls. But it took a year for evidence to come to light. In 1882 Mike McGeary (yes, that Mike McGeary) accused Higham of unfair judging, and the investigation turned up a letter that revealed that Higham, in collusion with a gambler named Todd Jones, was placing bets on the likely winners of games he was umpiring. Higham was tossed and banned permanently. He remains the only umpire found to be working to affect game outcomes in baseball's history.

The next great scandal occurred outside the National League. Established in 1882, the upstart American Association tried to fill the void left by this new, high-falutin' NL. It played on Sundays (where legal) and served alcohol at games — and lots of it, as many of the teams were owned by brewing interests. There were rumors of fixing from the group's inception, and they came to a head in 1886,

Hate that song

Bettors can each pick one song they think will be played during the game. "YMCA," "Cotton-Eyed Joe," "Thank God I'm a Country Boy" — whatever craptastic melody you think you're going to be subjected to. The first one played wins. The remaining bettors can stay in, renewing bets for the second-played song.

Bet on the song you hate the most. That way, when you hear those awful first notes, your resignation will be tempered by the cash influx that will buy you your next alcoholic beverage, which might ease your pain.

when a Cincinnati paper accused five players of involvement with throwing games, with direct testimony against pitcher Tony Mullane of the Louisville Eclipse. Mullane mounted a counterattack. He noted that the *Cincinnati Enquirer* was owned by a man forced out of the club's ownership, so he naturally had an ax to grind and he'd been grinding it ever since, publishing attacks on the team and even funding the brief existence of the Cincinnati Outlaw Reds, of the Union Association.

Mullane and the other players were cleared.

Later that season, baseball had its first World Series controversy. The two teams, the Chicago White Stockings (who, and I don't want to spoil anything, will appear again later in this chapter) and the St. Louis Browns agreed that the winning team would take home all of the gate receipts of the best-of-seven series.

The White Sox then realized that the most lucrative thing to do was to make sure the Series went to seven games, even if it meant they flirted with defeat: the more games played, the more gate money for the winner. Rumors began quickly after the Sox went down, 12–0, in the second game, and after the fourth, when the White Sox lost another game to tie the Series, the team hung around the hotel, joking and drinking, not seeming concerned about the day's loss or the difficulty they'd had so far. Then they lost Game Five, 10–3, behind a weak start on the mound by the team's shortstop, who didn't get out of the first inning. Down 3–2, the White Sox dropped the sixth game to the Browns to lose the Series. If the Sox had indeed been trying to prolong the Series, it ended up granting the gains of their scheme to their opponents.

In 1888, the owner of those same Browns accused the umpires of favoring the New York Giants when they got to 5-1 (it was a best-of-eleven); when faced with the ensuing uproar, he promptly claimed he'd been misquoted. No evidence proved that his accusations were anything but bluster. Which was how things went until the turn of the century: infrequent accusations investigated, dismissed, and quickly forgotten.

Though the White Sox may have tried to prolong a World Series for financial gain in 1886, it was years before anyone attempted to fix the outcome. In 1903, Ban Johnson prohibited betting from American League ballparks, and the same year gamblers were exposed when they tried to buy off two Boston Pilgrim players. In 1904, former White Sox pitcher Jack Taylor, now with the St. Louis Cardinals, was taunted in Chicago by fans over his poor play the year before in the city series. Taylor responded, "Why should I have won? I got $100 from Hart for winning and I got $500 for losing." Taylor was fined, but a National Commission consisting of the commissioner and both league presidents found that saying you'd thrown games wasn't sufficient evidence to take action.

Taylor, playing for the St. Louis Cardinals, got in trouble the very next season when he was accused of laying down in *that* city's series between the Cardinals and the Browns. The effect on baseball went beyond the allegations, though. After the National League's tough line against gambling initially, the treatment of Taylor was a significant step backward and emboldened gamblers.

In 1908, there was an attempt to buy the umpire in a World Series. The Giants team physician, Joseph Creamer, a close friend of manager John McGraw's, approached Hall of Fame umpire Bill Klem under the stands with $2,500. Klem reported that Creamer said, "It's yours if you'll give all the close decisions to the Giants and see that they win for sure. You know who is behind me and needn't be afraid of anything. You will have a good job for the rest of your life."

Creamer denied he talked to Klem or that he'd ever tried to bribe anyone. Creamer was banished from the game, and Klem's reputation for integrity remained untainted. The incident was made public to show how incorruptible the sport was, but the failure to investigate the incident to see if McGraw was involved hurt the sport. It was unlikely that anyone involved with the Giants would attempt such a thing without McGraw's knowledge, particularly someone as close to the manager as Creamer. But fear of McGraw's legal retaliation stayed the league's hand.

Later, players on the second-place Philadelphia team would allege that they had been approached to lose games so that the Giants could win the championship and go on to the World Series. The money offered was immense — said to be tens of thousands of dollars. This makes the World Series incident even more suspicious: if gambling interests had worked during the season to ensure the Giants would win the pennant, then what were the chances that a control freak like McGraw was unaware of this plan — and if he knew, he did nothing to inform the league or otherwise deter the gamblers.

McGraw tasted the fruits of his involvement (or, at least, tolerance) of the fix when eight years later he became convinced his own team had been bought out from under him. He stormed off the field in 1916, accusing his players of having given up — specifically, that they ignored signs, instruction, and prepared strategies. It was almost a direct accusation that they had been paid off. Why else, the thinking went, would a team coached by McGraw play so badly and not follow his orders in the heat of a pennant race?

Nothing happened. The influence of gambling grew, and soon baseball would see its greatest event toppled.

The worst thing ever to happen to baseball:
The Black Sox scandal

I don't know why I did it.
— Eddie Cicotte, Chicago White Sox pitcher

WITH GAMBLING PREVALENT and game-fixing tolerated, things got still worse during the First World War. When the horse tracks closed, the bettors, bookies, runners, and all their hangers-on moved to their local baseball fields, where they took and made bets and generally scuzzed up the place. They spread rumors of injuries or fixes to move the odds in one direction or another, and they'd brag that they could arrange a game's result. As disruptive and ominous as their presence was, the owners did little.

The intimacy between gamblers, bookies, and other unsavory characters with fans, players, and teams made possible the greatest cheating scandal in baseball history: the fix of a championship. The underdog Cincinnati Reds beat the Chicago White Sox in the 1919 World Series, five games to three in a best-of-nine contest, because players on the White Sox accepted money to lose.

The events of that Series are now confused with popular, soothing myths, films that portray figures of the scandal with needless sympathy, and the deluded and dishonest defenders of the fixers — all playing their part in obscuring that essential truth. As briefly as possible, this will set the record straight.

The setup

It would have happened eventually on some team, but Charles Comiskey, the notoriously tight-fisted owner of the White Sox, fostered an atmosphere particularly conducive to discontent. In such a place, unhappy players are more susceptible to dark thoughts of sabotage or throwing games, and they're able to find others who nurture similar designs. Then Comiskey brought in a crooked player, with predictable results.

It's important to reiterate: Comiskey was cheap. Horribly, horribly cheap. He cut expenses everywhere, from the per-day meal allowance of $3 (other teams gave $4) to charging players a daily fee for laundry service. His players refused to pay and went out, game after game, in increasingly grimy duds, which was how they earned the nickname Black Sox. Of course the derisive nickname would stick, to take on an entirely different meaning.

In 1917 Comiskey promised his team a bonus if they beat the New York Giants in the World Series. They expected thousands of dollars, which was reasonable for a team with a different owner, but when they won it all, Comiskey bought them only a case of champagne.

He exploited his players with their salaries as well. At the time, players were little more than cattle, branded with the insignia of the team that held their contract. Every year, the team would offer them a contract, and the players could either accept it or threaten to retire to start the coal dealership they had always dreamed of. There was no free agency, no matter how long or how good a player's career. While all the owners used their leverage to keep salaries down, no one kept them low like Comiskey, and no one was as needlessly confrontational, offering players their contracts with a curt "take it or leave it."

In 1918, there was a draft and a "work or fight" order. Adult men were expected to either enlist in the armed forces or find a job in an industry supporting the war effort, such as a munitions manufacturer or a shipyard. While baseball had permission to finish that year's season, many players left their teams to join the military or, like Chicago's Joe Jackson and Lefty Williams, take suitable jobs. Many players got their pick of positions and found places to work where they could play baseball on the weekend for the local team.

The losses hurt the White Sox particularly, as the 1918 team finished badly, and all across baseball, attendance dropped. While Comiskey was not alone in criticizing the players who chose civilian employment over enlistment, he was particularly bitter in his grandstanding, saying things like "There is no room on my club for players who wish to evade the army by entering the employ of shipbuilders" and singling Joe Jackson out for being the first on the team to take up employment. When the war ended, though, Comiskey welcomed them back without a word of apology.

As hard as the war years were for players, the armistice did not improve things. The baseball owners worried whether attendance would pick up, so they shortened the season and reduced player salaries for the upcoming year. These cuts were particular unwelcome to White Sox players and were a crucial early incident setting up the later fix.

Joe Jackson escaped a pay cut for that 1919 season only because cutting his $6,000 contract might have caused him to retire in disgust or take a bat to whoever delivered the news. He was one of the best hitters in baseball, at the top or among the league leaders in hits, doubles, triples, and home runs every year. His career batting average still stands as the third best of all time. The year 1919 was Joe Jackson's twelfth in the major leagues, and even discounting the 1918 war year, he had seven seasons as an outstanding, full-time player.

But Jackson received half as much as the players on other teams who were even close to his talents. At the time, salaries went up only if a player had a good season, and they could be cut drastically after only one off year. Generally, the only way to improve your pay was through year after year of success, earning a modest raise with each new contract. Jackson, despite his long record of success, made very little money because he'd been signed to a terrible long-term deal before he was sold to the White Sox, who held him to it.

Compare Jackson and his $6,000 to Babe Ruth of the Red Sox, who made $10,000 that year. While Ruth, a pitcher, was such a good hitter that he often played the field when not scheduled to start — and once he became a full-time hitter proved one of the best in baseball's history — 1919 was the first season he played over 100 games in the field. Yet he was paid far more than Jackson, who had proven himself as an elite hitter for many years.

Or consider Edd Roush, the center fielder for the Reds team Jackson would face in the World Series, who wasn't nearly as good a hitter and had three fewer years experience. Roush also made $10,000 in 1919.

When the season started, the owners' fear of low attendance proved unfounded. Enthusiastic crowds once again filled parks to see their favorites. When Comiskey didn't volunteer to restore his team's pay, the players asked manager Kid Gleason to lobby on their behalf. Comiskey would not even discuss it. When Gleason reported back, the furious players nearly refused to take the field. Chick Gandil, the first baseman, watched his teammates' reactions closely. Gandil had a dark idea, and with his team angry and mutinous, he would find the coconspirators he needed.

Gandil had likely nursed his design for throwing a World Series for years. Earlier, playing for the Washington Senators, he had met Joseph "Sport" Sullivan, and Sullivan cultivated their relationship like a farmer tending his crops. He introduced Gandil to members of society and showed him around, and Gandil returned the favor by passing Sullivan information, going so far as to call long-distance if there was a pitching change or a key player fell ill. The information brought Sullivan money and a reputation as a savvy baseball bettor. But Gandil had to wait for a chance at larger larceny: as he played for the Senators from 1912 to 1915, the team declined from contender to also-ran.

The White Sox, though, were perfect. They won the World Series in his second season there, and the 1919 team would contend. In July, when Comiskey refused their request for raises, they led the Yankees by four and a half games. An angry, underpaid squad, fairly certain to reach the World Series — Gandil could not have imagined a better opportunity. Knowing he needed pitchers first, he started with Eddie Cicotte, the team's ace (29-7 in the regular season, with a 1.82 ERA). Cicotte eventually agreed but wanted $10,000 before the Series started.

Then Gandil recruited others from the rural, largely uneducated,

The Fixers

Chick Gandil was a great defensive first baseman, a teenage runaway who had once boxed for money. He enjoyed the status and access to social circles that his friendship with Sport Sullivan gained him.

Eddie Cicotte threw the then-legal shineball and was one of the best pitchers of his time. But he was also thirty-five and nervous about his financial future.

Lefty Williams, a Southerner, was twenty-six and finally coming into his own as a pitcher. He had shown promise but not excelled until 1919, when his control improved and he went 23-11.

Oscar Felsch was a smiling, relaxed Milwaukee kid, the team's center fielder known for his great range. Like the others, he had little education and didn't much care.

Joe Jackson, the left fielder, was born in South Carolina and was illiterate (he signed even his contracts with an X).

Charles "Swede" Risberg, the shortstop, had great reflexes. Like Gandil, he came from California, which had barely over a million people in the whole state, and he too hated the educated, refined Eddie Collins.

Buck Weaver was so fast at third base that he was the only fielder Ty Cobb wouldn't bunt at. He was well known for his constant smile and optimism.

Fred McMullin was a scrub, and when he demanded a piece of the pie, it's surprising that they didn't haul him out to the countryside, brain him with a shovel, and bury him. He was so superfluous to the team that they sent him ahead to do scouting on the Reds, which we can safely assume he did as badly as possible in order to handicap the players who weren't in on the conspiracy.

rough-edged players that formed one faction of the contentious White Sox clubhouse. He played on their discontent, relishing the chance to stick it to Comiskey and Eddie Collins, the refined, educated team captain who led the other faction of the clubhouse and was also Comiskey's pet (and the only well-paid member of the team: at $14,500, over twice again Jackson's salary). With Cicotte in, Gandil didn't have to try hard to convince the others it could be done.

Defensively, here's the team:

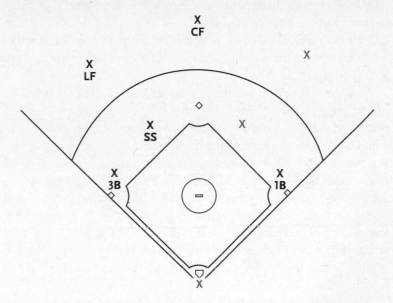

The conspirators controlled three of the four most important defensive positions (shortstop, center field, and third base, leaving only the catcher), the whole of the left side of the diamond, and the person at first base, involved in every infield play.

Offensively they had the team's star hitter and two of the other top five hitters. They also included the team's first two starters, the best pitchers on the team. A quality Series fix could have been carried off with half these players.

Gandil met with Sullivan in the middle of September, three weeks before the first game of the World Series. He said he could put together a fix. For Sullivan, all of the introductions, drinks, and cigars he'd invested was finally yielding something so lucrative it was almost priceless, and Gandil wanted only $80,000 for it.

The eight players met in a hotel room. They worried about ensuring their payment, and Buck Weaver suggested they ask for it in advance, with an eye toward double-crossing the gamblers if things got too hot. As Gandil later put it, "We agreed this was a hell of a brainy plan." The fix was in.

But brainy Buck Weaver dropped out. He didn't show up for meetings or even discuss things again with the players. He didn't demand money, and he played his best in every game. But he also didn't turn them in. Weaver would tell Commissioner Landis that while he needed the money, he'd been unable to either go through with it or inform on his friends.

As Weaver dropped out, though, the chance to get paid twice for one fix presented itself. Former pitcher Bill "Sleepy" Burns heard rumors and wanted part of the profits. He approached Cicotte, and with Gandil, the players told Burns they could work something out, but they needed $100,000 before the Series started (a full $20,000 more than Gandil had asked from his friend Sport Sullivan). Burns agreed. He had some money of his own and a clean reputation but no connections with gambling interests. Burns thrashed around unfamiliar circles looking for backers while his C-grade partner-in-crime Billy Maharg asked everyone he saw if they'd back their fix. Whispers that the Series' outcome was already determined spread rapidly.

Burns even told Hal Fullerton, the reporter who would later doggedly pursue the story: "Get wise and get yourself some money." Fullerton, having heard rumors and even having Chicago gamblers tell him "flat-footedly that the series was fixed for Cincinnati to win," went to both Comiskey and Ban Johnson, going as far as "calling them a bunch of whitewashing bastards who were letting a bunch of crooks get away with it because they were afraid of losing money." Neither Comiskey, Johnson, or any of their people took any action.

Then things got complicated. It may have gone something like this.

Act One

Scene 1: The Jamaica Race Track stands, New York

SLEEPY BURNS: Hello, Arnold Rothstein. I hope you're enjoying the races here at your box at the Jamaica Race Track. This is my friend Billy Maharg.

MAHARG: Hello. We would like to talk to you about a business proposition.

ROTHSTEIN: I am busy watching these honest horse races, but wait in the restaurant and I may come by.

Scene 2: The Jamaica Race Track restaurant, New York
BURNS: Well, Billy, here we are in the track restaurant.
MAHARG: But Mr. Rothstein is nowhere to be found.
ABE ATTELL: Hello, I am Abe Attell, former prizefighter and able and loyal lieutenant to Mr. Rothstein. What would you like to discuss?
BURNS: We wish to have his support in throwing the World Series.
ATTELL: This is interesting. Tell me more, and I will present it to Mr. Rothstein.

Scene 3: Somewhere.
ATTELL: . . . and that is their plan.
ROTHSTEIN: I do not think it will work.
ATTELL: Okay.

Scene 4: Somewhere else.
ATTELL: Mr. Burns, Rothstein declines your generous offer.
BURNS: Drat.

Scene 5: The Astor Hotel, Times Square
BURNS: Mr. Rothstein, we have cornered you here at your hotel.
MAHARG: We intend to fix the World Series.
ROTHSTEIN: My able and loyal lieutenant Mr. Attell informed me as much, and I am not interested.
BURNS: Oh well, we will stop our plotting then.

ACT TWO

Scene 1: A fictional location that represents what was probably a telephone conversation.
ATTELL: Mr. Burns, I am happy to report that Mr. Rothstein has reconsidered and is willing to fund the fix.
BURNS: Wow, that is great news. Mr. Rothstein really said that?

ATTELL: Oh yes. But you're not to mention his name. You must only deal with me.

BURNS: Using intermediaries certainly does seem like something that a smart, prominent gambler like Mr. Rothstein would do.

ATTELL: Yes.

BURNS: Just to reassure me, though . . . You're not just trying make us think Mr. Rothstein agreed to fund the fix because you see an opportunity to make some money by lying to us, having us set up the fix, and then burning us later, without Mr. Rothstein's permission or knowledge?

ATTELL: Perish the thought!

BURNS: I certainly will. Thanks for getting back to me. I will now proceed to fix the World Series, believing in good faith that Mr. Rothstein is funding it.

ATTELL: Yes. Mr. Rothstein.

Scene 2: Somewhere in New York.

SPORT SULLIVAN: Hi, Mr. Rothstein.

ROTHSTEIN: Hello, Mr. Sullivan, a well-known gambler I respect.

SULLIVAN: I have hatched a plot with Gandil of the White Sox to fix the World Series.

ROTHSTEIN: This is a fix I can get behind. Sign me up.

SULLIVAN: Wait, had you heard previous proposals to fix this Series?

ROTHSTEIN: I had but was not interested, as they did not come from people of your reputation and standing. This is good, though, as the more rumors circulate, the harder it will be for them to pin anything on us!

SULLIVAN: Ha ha ha ha ha ha!

ROTHSTEIN: Ha ha ha ha ha ha!

SULLIVAN: Heh. Good one, sir.

ROTHSTEIN: I will arrange for $40,000 to pay the players beforehand, and I'll save another $40,000 to give them when the loss is complete.

SULLIVAN: Great! I certainly won't go gamble this money away myself.

THE END.

When the dust settled, there were at least two fixes in:

Fix	Backed by	Player contact	Amount	Payment plan
Gandil-Sullivan	Rothstein	Gandil	$80,000	$40k now, $40k afterward
Burns-Cicotte	Attell	Cicotte	$100,000	Up front

Things went bad in a hurry. Rothstein placed massive wagers on the Series, which drove the odds down. Sullivan feared rumors would move the odds even further, so he took $30,000 of the first $40,000 Rothstein had given him and used it to place bets. Meanwhile, Attell put his own money against the White Sox while he leaked news of the fix all over, and Burns told a Chicago sportswriter who was worried the rumors were true that he'd be smart to get his money in line with his suspicions. The chaos pleased only Rothstein. For all the whispering and suspicion, baseball took no action, even to investigate.

Sullivan gave his remaining $10,000 to Gandil, who in turn gave it to Cicotte to satisfy his long and unwavering demand for up-front money. The other players got nothing. Angry at being shorted so early, Gandil and other players met in Cincinnati the day before the Series with Attell, looking for their $100,000 in advance. Attell changed the deal. He'd give them $20,000 after each loss for a total of $100,000, he said. The players decided to throw the first two games, try to lose Game Three, and then get Cicotte a win in Game Four.

Pre-Series payout:

Fix	Backed by	Amount	Paid out
Sullivan	Rothstein	$80,000	$10,000
Burns	Attell	$100,000	$0

GAME 1, OCTOBER 1, 1919

Before the game, Joe Jackson told his manager he did not want to play that night. Gleason, who had heard the rumors but could not bring himself to believe them, put him in left field.

Rothstein arranged for Cicotte to plunk the first Reds batter in the game to show that the fix was in. Cicotte nailed Maurice Rath in the back with the second pitch in the bottom of the first inning. Cicotte's pitching was awful, and the Reds were helped by a key defensive misplay by outfielders Joe Jackson and Happy Felsch early in the game that allowed two runs to score. The White Sox lost, 9–1.

After the game Attell, flush with money, refused to give any to Burns and Maharg so that they could pay off the players.

Gleason exploded when he ran into Risberg and Cicotte in the team's hotel lobby. In front of a crowd, he accused them of intentionally playing badly. Later that night, Comiskey asked Gleason if he thought the team was throwing the Series; Gleason replied that he thought something was wrong but was not certain.

Comiskey agonized, but he feared the reaction of his rival, Ban Johnson, president of the American League, and instead went late at night to the National League president. The two of them woke Johnson and told him their suspicions. Johnson, as Comiskey had feared, was as satisfied over the owner's plight as he was concerned for baseball. The three retired for the night. They would take no action.

GAME 2, OCTOBER 2

That morning, Gandil and Lefty Williams, the day's starting pitcher, met with the figures of the Burns-Attell fix. Again they demanded the promised $20,000 for the first loss. Attell refused but encouraged Williams to throw the game in a less obvious way than Cicotte had the day before. Sport Sullivan and his crew were nowhere to be found. The original and better-supported fix was letting the amateurs Burns and Maharg pay out and, if things went badly, take the blame.

The conspirators, trying to lose, succeeded. Williams showed surprisingly bad control. In a normal start he might walk a man or two (in the whole 1919 season, he walked 58 in 40 starts), but here he walked 6. Worse, he gave up critical hits when all season he'd wiggled out of trouble. The White Sox lost, 4–2.

After the game, White Sox catcher Schalk complained to Gleason that when he'd called for a curve, Williams had refused to throw it. Tempers flared, and Gleason tried to fight Gandil in the clubhouse but was held back; Schalk fought Williams on the way out of the park but was pulled off.

Burns went to Attell again, now seeking $40,000 for two losses. In a hotel room filled with money, Attell gave up $10,000. To make more money, he wanted the odds to swing back toward the White Sox, so he asked Burns to get the players to win the third game. Burns paid Gandil the $10,000, but it only fueled Gandil's anger. The players had thrown two games, their poor play earned them harsh criticism, yet they were not being paid.

Fix	Backed by	Amount	Paid out
Sullivan	Rothstein	$80,000	$10,000
Burns	Attell	$100,000	$10,000

GAME 3, OCTOBER 3

The Series moved to Chicago. Huge throngs of fans turned out; boisterous Cincinnati fans made the trip and were well mocked by the locals. The city was excited despite the two losses.

Before the game, Attell refused to cough up any more of the money he owed. Instead, he got Burns to ask Gandil what the players would do. Though they hadn't decided, Gandil told Burns they were going to lose. Burns went to bet money on the Reds again. Attell, wary, put bets on Chicago.

The players hadn't discussed how to lose the game — they hadn't met to decide what they'd do at all. They seethed over the broken and bent promises of money and nursed their injured reputations. Gandil wanted a win to demonstrate that they could still take the Series, hopefully scaring their backers into paying up. There would be no lying down.

Starting pitcher Dickie Kerr threw a complete-game shutout, allowing only three hits and one walk and striking out four. Gandil singled Jackson home in the second inning for a lead that held up as the White Sox won, 3–0, in an hour and a half. The Series stood at 2-1 Reds.

It was the team Chicago fans knew and wanted to see. The hero of the game was Gandil, who'd choked in previous games. The pitching was strong, having looked horrible in the first two games. There was hope.

Burns and Maharg went broke betting on Gandil's pregame assurance. Attell made money betting against it. He wanted the White Sox to lose the next game and promised $20,000. Burns approached the players with Attell's offer. They laughed. Attell was behind $30,000 after two losses, so a promise to pay another $20,000 for a third meant nothing. Broke and equally frustrated, Burns offered to "drop the whole business," but he wanted a thousand back of the original $10,000. The players laughed at that too. Burns threatened to go public and left. With Burns quitting and Sullivan still nowhere to be found, the fixes were off.

GAME 4, OCTOBER 4

That morning, Sullivan called Gandil. Gandil said they were mad, didn't trust anyone — in particular, Sullivan's disappearing self — and they wouldn't lose any more games. Sullivan knew that a Sox win would ruin him. More important, though, Rothstein might have him killed to ease the pain of his own losses. Sullivan produced $20,000 immediately (it's hard to be a well-to-do gambler and live the good life while dead). He promised Gandil he'd come up with another $20,000 before the next game.

With money coming in again, the players agreed to lie down. Cicotte pitched well but made two huge defensive errors in the fifth inning, allowing the Reds to score two, which was all they'd need, winning 2–0.

After the game, Gandil broke out Sullivan's money and gave $5,000 to Risberg, Felsch, Williams, and Jackson. McMullin got nothing. The Burns fix was dead, but the Sullivan fix was alive again.

Fix	Backed by	Amount	Paid out
Sullivan	Rothstein	$80,000	$30,000
Burns	Attell	$100,000	$10,000

GAME 5, OCTOBER 6

After rain delayed the game for a day, the White Sox set out to lose again. Williams wanted to look good and pitched well to start. In the sixth inning, a set of poor defensive plays by the team members who'd just been paid off allowed four runs to score. The White Sox, meanwhile, were held to three hits and lost again, 5–0. The Reds needed only one more win for the championship.

GAME 6, OCTOBER 7

The Series returned to Cincinnati. With the mighty White Sox offense nearly silent, their vaunted defense porous, and their outstanding pitchers unreliable, victory was assured.

But Sullivan didn't make the second payment of $20,000 or travel to Cincinnati as he'd promised. The players decided that without the money, they would play it straight. Kerr was not nearly as good as he'd been in Game 3, but he managed to go all ten innings, allowing only four runs. The offense looked like the regular-season version, chasing the starter out after five innings. The White Sox won, 5–4, in extra innings.

The Reds still led the Series, 4–2.

GAME 7, OCTOBER 8

The White Sox were revived, the gloomy atmosphere around them gone. Few Reds fans attended, either fearing defeat or the crowds of previous games, and they quietly watched the Reds lose.

Eddie Cicotte, the first person to join Gandil's conspiracy, having already pitched two losses, wanted the ball. He didn't pitch much better than in the games he'd been trying to lose — seven hits with three walks in nine innings — but he didn't groove pitches in critical situations, and he played defense well. The White Sox won, 4–1.

The victory persuaded even reporters who'd believed in the fix. Gleason, so depressed before, was ebullient. A one-game deficit to the Reds was no obstacle to a team playing this well.

However, Rothstein would lose just shy of $300,000 if the White Sox won the last two games to take the Series. He called Sullivan to his apartment to talk about his strong desire for the Series to end immediately — with the Reds winning. Sullivan needed to make absolutely certain that the next game was a loss; he knew the players might not take his money, and even if they did, they might not cooperate. So he paid local talent in Chicago to make it clear to Lefty Williams that he should lose and lose fast.

GAME 8, OCTOBER 9

The Series moved back to Chicago for the final games. The White Sox had played two games in a row to the best of their ability and won both. If that team showed up, they couldn't lose.

But the goons got through to Williams, and he threw hittable fastballs, one after another. The first batter flew out; then the Reds got four hits, two of them doubles. Williams's intent was so obvious that Gleason pulled him after only 15 pitches, with three runs scored and a runner on second who would score. The Reds, spotted four runs in the first, continued to hit off the White Sox relievers and won, 10–5, taking the World Series.

After the game, a furious Gleason said the Reds shouldn't have beaten them and that something was wrong, even mentioning the crazy betting odds.

The aftermath

Gleason told Comiskey later that night that seven players were in on the fix (whether he left out Weaver because he had played well or McMullin because he wasn't worth noting and didn't play much is unclear).

Baseball writers hinted at the dark rumors even as they attributed the defeat to poor play, or overconfidence, or the phase of the moon.

Sullivan delivered $40,000 to Gandil, Risberg, and McMullin. Risberg took $10,000. McMullin took $5,000 (which is a pretty good take considering he only pinch-hit twice). That left $25,000 for Gandil, who kept it.

Fix	Backed by	Amount Promised	Amount Paid
Sullivan	Rothstein	$80,000	$70,000
Burns	Attell	$100,000	$10,000

Or, to look at this another way:

The screw-o-meter

Conspirator	Money made
Gandil	$35,000
Risberg	$15,000
Cicotte	$10,000
Filch	$5,000
Jackson	$5,000
McMullin	$5,000
Williams	$5,000
Weaver	$0

Many of the players later testified to the amounts they received directly. They may also have bet against themselves through accomplices to make more.

Meanwhile, on the opposite side:

The money-making backers

Fixer	Backed by	Amount spent	Profit
Sullivan	Rothstein	$0	At least $30,000
Rothstein		$80,000	At least $220,000
Burns	Attell	Tons	$0
Attell		$10,000	Tons

It's hard to tell how much Burns lost on Gandil's betrayal. It's impossible to know how well Attell made out, but he may have made the most profit of anyone involved — even Rothstein, who had the resources to place huge bets on games and the entire Series, paid (as far as he knew) $80,000 to the fixers.

Those with the most capital successfully exploited the workers and those with less capital.* The players, by trusting untrustworthy people from the backers to Chick Gandil, risked everything and made little. It could have been much different: had the players refused Attell when he wanted to move to a per-loss payment schedule

---

* So has it been through history.

(which turned out to be a never-pay schedule), Sullivan's early disappearance might have led the conspirators to turn around and win earlier, possibly changing the outcome of the Series. Though it's just as likely that would only have pushed Rothstein to make his move to force the conclusion earlier.

It's certainly not sad, though, that the fixers found themselves betrayed. That most of them were barely rewarded for their wrongdoing is, if anything, an appropriate consequence of their actions, both in inception and in their poor execution.

After the World Series was lost, as he'd been warned, Comiskey chose to protect himself and his team, even though it meant shielding players who had betrayed him. He announced that there was no evidence of a fix and offered a $20,000 cash reward for information. The reward brought results. Joe Gedeon, a player for the St. Louis Browns and a friend of Swede Risberg's, knew of the fix and had placed bets for Risberg. Another St. Louis man knew of Attell's involvement. Even Joe Jackson had his wife write Comiskey a letter saying that the Series was fixed and offering to tell what he knew. Comiskey paid no one and would not talk to Jackson.

Comiskey hired a private investigator, John Hunter,* to look into the seven men involved in the fix (Weaver was left out), then did nothing with the information.

In December, the World Series wasn't discussed at the league meetings.

Still, while papers were afraid to run stories that addressed the fix or even hinted at it too directly, some reporters continued to pursue the truth. First among them was Hal Fullerton, still after the story.

Meanwhile, Comiskey tried to bring back all the players he knew had betrayed him, offering many of them substantial raises. Gandil, one step ahead of the scandal, retired to California. Jackson threatened to retire, and when Comiskey sent one of his men to negotiate, he asked why the owner had not responded to his letter. Comiskey's man told Jackson that the fix was nothing to worry about and offered him a new contract for almost twice the money he'd been making. Weaver got a raise to $7,500.

---

* Which is a great name for a private detective.

They may have wished they had refused to return, though. The fallout from the World Series dogged the players and the team. Gamblers pressured them into throwing important games, offering a little money and a little more time without exposure. In a bar, Attell apologized at length to Gleason as two reporters summoned by the manager listened. Their papers would not print the story. After a particularly horribly played series late in the season in Boston that cost the team the division lead, Eddie Collins went to Comiskey and told him the games had been bought. Comiskey did nothing.

The scandal breaks

Eventually, a meaningless and unrelated game in their home city exposed the 1919 White Sox fix. The Chicago Cubs were facing the Philadelphia Phillies, and Bill Veeck, the Cubs owner, received phone and telegraph warnings that the game was fixed and his team would lose. Meanwhile, the White Sox, having apparently settled quite comfortably into their game-fixing ways, were rolling over for the Red Sox. Veeck pulled the scheduled starter for the Cubs, figuring he would have to be a key part of any potential plan, but the Cubs lost anyway. Veeck released the telegrams to the press and asked for their help. A grand jury was convened to look into that game, along with allegations of a World Series fix the year before and corruption in baseball generally. American League president Ban Johnson offered the judge much of the evidence he had accumulated to use against Comiskey.

Comiskey angrily denied that a fix existed or that he knew of any conspiracy — though he clearly did. The grand jury stalled until New York Giants pitcher Rube Benton testified for a second time. He revealed that he had seen a telegram from Burns stating that the White Sox were going to lose the Series. Benton also claimed that Hal Chase knew of the fix and had won money by betting on Cincinnati. Other revelations quickly emerged.

In late September, the Philadelphia *North American* ran an interview with Billy Maharg (of the Burns fix) that gave a full account of what had happened when, from start to finish, including how Attell had double-crossed Maharg, Burns, and the players.

Hal Chase was a good-looking, talented baseball player who was involved in many game-fixing scandals during and after his career. *National Baseball Hall of Fame*

The first conspirator to sing was Eddie Cicotte. "I must have been crazy," he said. "Risberg, Gandil, and McMullin were at me for a week before the Series began. They wanted me to go crooked. I don't know. I needed the money. I had the wife and the kids. The wife and the kids don't know about this. I don't know what they'll think." He described how the scheme had developed and how he'd thrown games, and he admitted that his defensive blunders were intentional.

Then the others broke down. Jackson verified that he had been promised $20,000 but received only $5,000 because of Attell's cross. At the time, he was still unaware that Gandil had pocketed the final payment rather than cut him in.

Lefty Williams testified, then Oscar Felsch spilled his story in an interview. Rothstein began to work against the grand jury, arranging for Sullivan to go to Mexico and Attell to go to Canada to avoid testifying. Then Rothstein appeared before the jury and said he had

In this 1921 photo, Judge Kenesaw Mountain Landis (back left) questions Swede Risberg (back center) and Chick Gandil (back right). It appears the camera is more interesting than the inquiry. *AP*

been approached to join the fix and declined (true), that Attell had used Rothstein's name on his own (true, though deceptive), and that he had not bet on the Series at all (not at all true).

The mounting evidence forced Comiskey to suspend the eight players. The team faltered and finished second behind the Indians.

The players were indicted and the hijinks began. Everything that might have implicated Rothstein disappeared. The confessions of Eddie Cicotte, Lefty Williams, and Joe Jackson, along with other important court documents, found their way to the offices of the attorneys representing Comiskey and Attell. The confession and other papers only reappeared in court when Jackson sued Comiskey for lost pay. Comiskey, when asked in court how the lost grand jury records had suddenly turned up in his lawyer's briefcase after all that time, said, "I don't know."

Some records of the trial have still not resurfaced. The prosecution was forced to again file indictments, and the players were charged with conspiracy in five different ways — defrauding the public, defrauding White Sox catcher Ray Schalk, committing a confidence game, injuring the business of the American League, and injuring poor Mr. Charles Comiskey.

The best lawyers the shadowy figures could hire defended the players, assisted by disappearing evidence and bribed witnesses changing their stories. Further, the jury had specific instructions on the charges: "The State must prove that it was the intent of the ballplayers and gamblers charged with conspiracy through the throwing of the World Series, to defraud the public and others, and not merely to throw ballgames."

The players could have conspired to throw the games for money, but as long as their intent was limited to self-enrichment, it was not grounds for conviction. Thanks to this convenient loophole, the players were acquitted.

The verdict

The White Sox players struck a deal to lose the World Series. There is nothing anyone could do that could do more damage to the game's integrity.

Stealing signs, watering the mound — these things all spice up the game and are done in the service of winning a contest. A fan can cheer a contest between a spitballer and a guy with a corked bat, but if the outcome has already been determined, it's all pointless. They might as well take their entertainment dollar and check out what's playing at the community theater.

The players who took the money for their actions in determining the outcome of the World Series did this. Arguments about how particular players, like Joe Jackson, performed over the course of the World Series or whether a particular defensive misplay was intentional or not — all of them are irrelevant. The players took money, and in the games they wanted to lose, they played badly and lost. Amid the details, that essential truth should be remembered..

Joe Jackson, out of all the conspirators, has many defenders. They argue that he was a good-natured hick who played his best throughout the Series and so could not possibly have been involved in any conspiracy. Instead, Jackson was the victim of a great injus-

Collusion

The Black Sox are despised for throwing a World Series for money. What if the whole league were rigged and teams got together to agree who would win and who would remain in the cellar? Wouldn't that be far worse?

In the mid-1980s, two owners convinced the others that simply by not bidding on free agents, they could reduce the cost of labor and everyone would make more money. Teams agreed not to offer contracts to any free agents except their own, on terms to the team's liking. Bad teams didn't sign players to help them improve. Good teams didn't sign players to help them compete for division titles. No team had to worry about losing a star. The previous year's final standings would become, with minimal disturbance, the next year's final standings.

The 1986 Rangers had a talented club with average pitching. Two good pitchers (Ron Guidry and Doyle Alexander) were available, but the club passed on both, and both returned to their previous teams. With below-average pitching, the Rangers finished five games off the division lead. Had they not colluded, they may well have won the AL West title and made the playoffs.

The owners sacrificed competition season after season in order to make more money, and only the players getting screwed cared.* They sued and won $280 million, but the seasons remained lost, and the massive coordinated subversion of their agreement poisoned the relationship between players and owners, leading to bitter labor fights and work stoppages for the next fifteen years. Rather than pay for their actions, the owners raised the money through expansion fees, and baseball grew to thirty teams.

The two leaders of this astounding attempt to prevent the basic premise of the sport were the owner of the Chicago White Sox, Jerry Reisdorf, and the owner of the Milwaukee Brewers, now the commissioner of baseball, Bud Selig.

---

* There's no proof that collusion had anything to do with the explosive nationwide growth of professional wrestling after the first WrestleMania in 1985, but it sure seems related.

tice — essentially, he's Buck Weaver. But this is willfully ignorant, a conscious choice to believe a romantic myth over fact. Even in the most generous interpretation of the events, Jackson knew about the conspiracy, was a key participant in its inception, took money in return for his promise to participate and play poorly, and did play poorly in at least some of the games that they wanted to throw, contributing to those losses.

Any honest argument for his induction into the Hall of Fame needs to start with an acknowledgment of his actions and then move to whether any player who engages in the one act of cheating that could end the sport entirely should be admitted on the basis of his playing talent.

No, they shouldn't. Would you tip a grocery store clerk who expertly bagged your week's purchases, pushed the cart out to your car, then took you hostage and used you as a human shield in a cross-country series of liquor store heists, leaving you to die of dehydration in the Utah desert? Even if he did a great job bagging? Of course not.

Baseball reserves its greatest penalties for conduct that threatens the integrity of the game. Whether or not baseball looked away from other thrown games and let known corrupt players like Hal Chase go about the business of playing and fixing without fear, it was those eight players, to different degrees, who destroyed baseball's most important contest and created a scandal that almost entirely eroded the public's confidence. They knew what they were doing was wrong. If they were all surprised to be the first players caught and thrown out of the game, too bad for them.

The Black Sox scandal is another example of how cheating forced baseball's evolution. The sport's increasing flirtation with destruction, moving from participants betting on contests to payoffs to other teams to players throwing games, resulted in a scandal. It forced the sport to reconsider its attitude toward gambling in the same way that the previous decades forced a decision between a well-played game or a contest between thugs. The sport today is healthier and stronger for the protections that have stood since 1919 as a result of the team's transgression.

For whatever reason, you want to throw a World Series

When assembling your conspiracy, be discreet. A clubhouse attendant or scrappy bench player who overhears the planning will demand a huge cut of the take to not squeal, and you never know if those kids will discover a hidden talent for blackmail.

Once you have a conspiracy, you need to use it to make money. You could solicit sponsors from crime or gambling figures. However, while they will have money, you'll always be at cross-purposes. They'll want to divide the payments to ensure that they get results, while you'll want it all up front. You'll want to use cutouts and secure, anonymous means of communicating, while they'll insist on meeting in person, to make it as intimate an affair as possible. After you accept a payment, they have evidence against you. They may be willing to give you money up front and make their payments after each loss to ensure that you do throw the games, because they can reclaim it by threatening to expose you.

Of course, you could find some clean, honest crime figures who won't try to blackmail you or screw you out of any of the money. They're on aisle 6, next to the unicorns, fairies, sprites, and leprechauns.

You're better off placing bets on the Series yourself. This offers you all the money without the risk of having others involved.

Be prepared to get caught. Once rumors start to circulate, cell phone records will leak, e-mails get into the wild, and evidence will pour out. The question will be: Can you get off?

Find someone to make an emotional, cloying movie about your terrible plight as soon as possible. It can offer a sympathetic, even false, interpretation of events (you had a dying mother and wanted to save her orphanage). You may have to help finance it yourself (the movie, not the orphanage), but after fixing the series, you should have no trouble with that. The movie and books need to come out as soon as possible in order to taint jury pools, give members of Congress an excuse to give flowery speeches defending you, their most generous supporter, and so forth. With the groundwork laid, researchers and historians will appear to prove your innocence. Publications will be flooded with scholarly essays that include stats that prove your performance was within expected statistical variance and that dissect the evidence with a forensic examiner's eye for minutiae and a mother's sympathy for your case.

Soon you'll be able to go out in public, even sign baseball memorabilia at card shows. You might, after a discrete period of years, start a lobbying campaign to get yourself into the Hall of Fame (though your career achievements may make this difficult).

Pete Rose: The only undeterred gambler

SINCE THE BLACK SOX SCANDAL, there's been little gambling excitement. The severity of the punishment, combined with the wider distancing of the game from the interests that corrupted it, has kept things clean. There were minor incidents, and from time to time rumors have circulated that this coach or that player got a stern word from the commissioner about his too-close association with this mobster or that convicted felon, or his excessive nonbaseball gambling, but there's not much worth talking about until we get to Pete Rose.

Pete Rose bet on baseball games. He bet on the games of the teams he was managing and playing for. Both acts were strictly and totally forbidden in the wake of the 1919 scandal and ever since.

Baseball even puts up little plaques in clubhouses with that rule on it. Rose missed the writing on the wall* and, while in one of those clubhouses, he regularly placed bets on baseball games and on his own team.

Baseball started to investigate one of its most prominent figures when two men, Rose's friend Paul Janszen and Rose's sometime-bookie Ron Peters, facing other prosecutions, offered testimony and evidence that Rose had bet on baseball. On May 9, 1990, John Dowd, the investigator hired by MLB to look into the allegations, presented his findings (now known as the Dowd Report) to Bart Giamatti, then the commissioner of baseball; they presented overwhelming evidence that Rose had bet on his own team, often from his clubhouse. Rose sued the league to try and stop baseball from punishing

---

* My editor made me put that pun in. She says she couldn't resist.

Rule 21, Misconduct

(d) BETTING ON BALL GAMES. Any player, umpire, or club official or employee, who shall bet any sum whatsoever upon any baseball game in connection with which the bettor has no duty to perform shall be declared ineligible for one year.

Any player, umpire, or club or league official or employee, who shall bet any sum whatsoever upon any baseball game in connection with which the bettor has a duty to perform shall be declared permanently ineligible.

him, they wrangled for months, and eventually Rose signed what amounted to a plea bargain. He agreed to be placed on the "permanently ineligible" list for violating Rule 21, and MLB agreed that there would be no formal ruling on whether Rose had bet on baseball.

The penalty had a hidden barb. The Baseball Hall of Fame, a private institution that is not controlled by MLB, passed a rule that any "permanently ineligible" people could not be considered for induction. Pete Rose could not appear on a ballot.

However, Pete Rose holds the major league record for career hits: 4,256. He was a 17-time All-Star, the 1963 Rookie of the Year. He won the National League's Most Valuable Player Award in 1973 and finished in the top ten of voting another nine times. He was the MVP of the 1975 World Series. He led the NL in batting average three times and was in the top ten another ten times. He played ridiculously hard, winning the admiration of fans and fellow players, running out every ball he put into play — he even ran to first when he walked. Rose played defense not spectacularly but with equal effort, sacrificing his body by running flat out for even the most meaningless pop fly.

So that means he's innocent, right? With that career, on the sliding scale for professional athlete justice, he should be able to get away with killing as many as three people as long as it's in the same incident and only one of them is a celebrity of any kind.

Like Shoeless Joe Jackson and other members of the 1919 White

> **How we know Rose bet on baseball: an extremely quick summary**
>
> Testimony about Rose's betting on baseball from his cutouts.
> Testimony about Rose's betting on baseball from his bookies.
> Bank records of payments to his cutouts and bookies, including times when baseball was the only game going.
> Phone records of him calling his cutouts and bookies, including times when baseball was the only game going.
> Rose's handwritten betting records.
> Matches between the phone records, betting records, bank records, and testimony.
> Rose's testimony during the investigation offered no good explanation for any of the allegations.
> Rose's admission that he bet on baseball.

Sox, Rose had ardent defenders who, refusing to really look at the evidence, defended him angrily. The evidence against him proved nothing, they said, though it proved much. They said the investigation was biased, a witch-hunt to get him. But they ignored the tremendous damage baseball's active investigation did to the game's reputation.

Then Rose admitted it. Sort of. He told Bud Selig, the commissioner of baseball, that he had bet on the sport but swore he had never done it from the clubhouse, which he had. He repeated the half-admission in his autobiography, *My Prison Without Bars,* which contradicted denials in his previous biographies.

Here's how Rose did this:

1. Rose would talk to someone and tell them who to bet on for the night's games.
2. The cutout would then call a bookie, place the bets, and confirm them with Rose.
3. Rose would then lose money because he wasn't very good at betting.
4. Repeat.

What a conversation with Pete Rose would be like if he hit your car while you were standing next to it and you caught the whole thing on video:

"You hit my car."

"No, I didn't."

"Yes, you did, I was right here. You slammed right into it."

"I don't know what you're talking about."

"I have video footage of your car ramming mine."

"I wasn't driving."

"You're clearly visible in the tape."

"Maybe that tape's from some other car I hit, I don't know."

"You can see today's newspaper on the dash of my car."

"Maybe it was some guy who looks like me."

"When you got out of the car, your wallet flopped open to your driver's license."

"I don't know why you're persecuting me like this. I don't deserve this kind of treatment."

"You hit my car!"

As required, Rose would then cut a check to an intermediary or the bookie directly for an amount just shy of the IRS reporting limit; sometimes he wrote several checks under that limit.

The mechanics changed periodically. The cutouts and bookies would change because Rose wasn't good about paying up. Sometimes he called the bookies directly. Sometimes the locations changed: during the season, he might call from the clubhouse, then get called back there. Through it all, he bet heavily on whatever sports were being played, including baseball, including the team he managed.

So Pete Rose bet on baseball. Why does this matter?

Baseball made the penalty so high for several reasons. The first and most obvious is that when a player is betting money on the outcome of his own game, especially illegally, he's associating with exactly the kind of people who early in the century almost brought the game down. Giving them blackmail material, much less owing them huge sums of money, offers them a tremendous amount of leverage they can use to force the player to do bad things, start-

> **What a conversation with Pete Rose would be like a year after he hit your car while you were standing next to it and you caught the whole thing on video:**
>
> "It's possible I hit someone else's car. I don't really remember. I've hit different cars but not yours. Maybe it was my car but not me. I have different people drive my cars around, and sometimes they hit things."
>
> "It was you! I saw you! I videotaped you!"
>
> "You've got videotape — who knows what it shows, right? I think I was in a different state that week."
>
> "You hit my car outside the card show you were scheduled to appear at!"
>
> "I go to a lot of card shows. I can't be expected to remember which one I was at that day, can I?"
>
> "You hit my car!"

ing with leaking injury information and escalating into throwing games.

A second reason is more subtle. If a manager has money on the outcome of a game he controls, he might make decisions that could hurt his team in the long run in order to collect on his bet. For instance, say a star player is nursing an injured hamstring. A cautious manager might rest him, to make sure that he doesn't aggravate the injury and make it worse. But if the manager has a substantial bet, he's going to play that guy and face the consequences later. And it's the same thing with pitchers: someone with money on that game is a risk to ride a good starter hard or to use all the best relievers as long as required, even if it means they won't be available for a while. If the star player goes down for a week and the best relievers can't pick up a ball for three days, well, those are games the bettor doesn't have to wager on.

And if he has an incentive of $2,000 every day they bet to win, the manager has a reason to arrange losses to fall on the days he doesn't have wagers: push out a pitcher he doesn't like to start, rest the stars and the best relievers, and watch the fireworks.

Third, the very fact that the player or manager bets on the games offers information to the gambling community. Let's say you've got

Pete Rose betting on games, and he bets against a certain pitcher every time. While he may not have given the reason — he doesn't like the guy, the pitcher's nursing an injury, he thinks the guy is bad luck, whatever it might be — he was in a position to have inside information. As a major league manager he had access to advance scouts, other managers, and media sources. That Rose's inside knowledge told him that pitcher was worth betting against was valuable knowledge to a bookie, even without knowing the exact information that caused Rose to decide against the pitcher.

Now, Rose did not get in trouble that we know of. The Dowd Report contains a conversation that mentions a serious threat against one of Rose's runners and the runner's mom, but the bookies didn't ever come up with a good strategy to deal with Rose or use their connection toward a nefarious end. If anything, they seemed a little stymied by Rose's importance, knowing that Rose's use of cutouts meant that it would be difficult to blackmail him.

There's also nothing in the evidence we have available that Rose ever bet against his team or that he didn't bet on his team to win regularly — there is only one game in the time covered by the Dowd Report where he did not bet on them when they played. But baseball's documents cover only a short period of time, and we know Rose bet on baseball long before then. We just don't know what happened, and given his previous false denials, it seems better to leave it an open question than accept his blanket denial.

And that the bookies never figured out how to get to Rose to recover their money or to turn him into their puppet doesn't mean he should get to prance off into the sunset because he was lucky enough to avoid sufficiently ruthless and cunning gangsters. Given the scope and frequency of his gambling, it's surprising that no one ever took the next step.

Rose may have almost been forgiven. He and his allies (particularly Mike Schmidt) lobbied Commissioner Selig in 2002 for forgiveness, and that was when he personally confessed to the commissioner. As Rose relates it in his book, Selig asked, "I want to know one thing. Did you bet on baseball?" And Rose replied, "Sir, my daddy taught me two things in life — how to play baseball and how to take responsibility for my actions. I learned the first one pretty well. The other, I've had some trouble with. Yes, sir, I did bet on baseball."

"How often?"

"Four or five times a week. But I never bet against my own team, and I never made any bets from the clubhouse."

Early in 2003 they were hinting at an agreement to put Rose on a kind of tiered rehabilitation that would eventually remove him from the permanently ineligible list. It was widely rumored within baseball that Rose was on a one-year "keep your nose clean" secret probation, with instructions to stay away from casinos and gambling and not get into trouble. Then the deal would be announced and Rose would be able to return to baseball and, depending on your interpretation of the eligibility rules, possibly be voted into the Hall of Fame.

Rose then moved up the release date of his autobiography to come out during the 2004 Hall of Fame induction week, traditionally a time when baseball celebrates its history and the players who've made it great (like Gaylord Perry!).

The book paired the story of his admission with baffling statements like: "I'm sure that I'm supposed to act all sorry or sad or guilty now that I've accepted that I've done something wrong. But you see, I'm just not built that way . . . So let's leave it like this: I'm sorry it happened, and I'm sorry for all the people, fans and family that it hurt. Let's move on." And it included unbelievable statements, such as he started betting on baseball only in 1987 and never bet from a clubhouse.

The media firestorm around the admission started with Rose's inability to apologize or even understand why betting on his own team could be considered bad. It somehow got worse when, trying to control the damage, he made another television appearance to say, entirely unconvincingly, what people wanted him to say: he knew it was wrong and he apologized. He spoke with all the conviction of a bored schoolkid writing out his hundredth "I will not run in the hallway" sentence, looking over to see if it was time to go.

Many who'd always believed he was guilty weren't satisfied with his half-assed admission and lack of repentance.

Those who'd believed he was innocent were either stunned or horrified at his betrayal.

What a conversation with Pete Rose would be like several years after he hit your car while you were standing next to it and you caught the whole thing on video:

"Okay, okay, I admit I hit your car, but I didn't do all that damage. Someone must have hit it before me to total it, because there's no way —"

"You can determine your car's speed from the tape. You were clearly going over thirty!"

"Nope, I'll admit I hit your car, but there's no way I did any damage to it."

"You can see on the video that my car is intact before you hit it and then afterward it's destroyed!"

"Look here, I admitted that I hit your car. Isn't that enough for you? Can't we stop this witch-hunt and get on with our lives?"

"No."

"Why is this such a big deal? I didn't murder anyone."

"You hit my car!"

"I know what you want, you want me to apologize. Well, I can't do that. I'm sorry, it's just the way I am."

"I want you to pay for the car you destroyed!"

Many who'd long thought Rose's punishment was far too harsh were horrified at his timing and conduct and threw up their hands.

Any consideration of reinstatement died. The commissioner would have nothing to do with him, saying there "was no next step" in Rose's campaign for reinstatement.

He's made no further progress in the years since.

What does it mean?

Gambling on your own team to win isn't the worst thing a player can do. It's clear that it's not as serious as conspiring to throw a game.

But in the wake of the Black Sox scandal, baseball decided to set rules that would prevent a repeat. And it decided that gambling on games you participated in was serious enough to warrant the most severe punishment it could mete out.

That there has been only one high-profile lapse is a powerful testament to how effective that clear standard has been.

Steroids: Blame enough to go around

> We didn't get beat, we got out-milligrammed. And when you
> found out what they were taking, you started taking them.
>
> — Tom House, former pitcher and pitching coach,
> on drug use in the 1960s and 1970s

THIS SHOULD SEEM FAMILIAR. Baseball had a growing problem. Players, coaches, managers — the teams — all were involved. It had been winked at for decades but then turned dangerous and threatening. Some fans screamed that it was ruining the game, but it took a huge, impossible-to-ignore scandal for any action to be taken.

Widespread gambling turned into a World Series fix; rampant drug use turned into widespread steroid scandals.

It's hard to write about baseball's long history with drugs, and particularly with steroids, for several reasons. The issue is emotionally charged, there's so much blame to be handed out, and by the time this book reaches you, the story will have changed substantially.

Fans

"I'm so disgusted at the players. These hitters are all on steroids, everyone knows it. It's tainting the game."

"And yet here you are at the ballpark, wearing a hundred dollars in team gear."

"I'm not disgusted enough to stop going. You bums suck, you sucky bums!"

"Uh-huh. What do you think about this guy on your team, who gained twenty pounds of muscle in a hundred days through what he claims was an intensive off-season weight training program?"

"He's pretty good this year. Oh! Oh! Home run! Gooooo team!"

Reporters

"So, player with whom I must build a relationship as part of my job, you seem to have grown in size dramatically since last season in only, what, three months. It almost seems as if you have eaten the player I knew only last September and used his protein content to form muscles."

"Yes. I engaged in an intensive off-season weight training plan."

"Hey, I thought of a good headline — 'Previously Puny Player Pumps, Practices, Proclaims Power to Pound Pitches.' I notice that you seem to have an unusual amount of disgusting back acne there."

"That's from the bench press."

"Of course. Now, since I depend on you for quotes to put in my stories and don't want to anger you by asking about steroids —"

"Arrrghhhh! Me smash reporter!"

"Whoa there, big guy."

"Sorry. I don't know what came over me. Can we keep this between you and me, since we have a mutually dependent relationship?"

"Oh, no problem."

"You're not going to talk to your editor or anything and tell them you suspect the home team's got a bunch of steroid users, are you?"

"Heavens, no! Besides which, our sports section depends on access. You might lock the clubhouse, throw us out of the press box."

"Whew, that's a relief. Hey, can you excuse me for a second while I pick up this syringe and head for a toilet? I've got a vitamin injection I'm overdue for."

"Certainly. Have a good game tonight!"

As if the conflict of interest wasn't enough, reporters who did try to broach the issue were treated badly. When Mark McGwire had a bottle of then-legal androstenedione (generously termed a "steroid precursor"; while it was not technically a steroid, the body turned it into one, so it had the same practical effect) sitting in his locker, a reporter for the Associated Press noted it. Both MLB and the players' union responded with the same excuse ("Hey, it's legal"), and Cardinals manager Tony LaRussa tried to have the AP banned from the clubhouse.

Teams

"So how's my $200 million investment going to do this season?"

"Good, good, the team's shaping up well. The pitching's looking much better, we've got a kid up from the triple-A team, looks like he'll be competing to be the number three, number four, starter."

"I didn't know we had any good starters down there."

"Yeah, well, he picked up about three miles on his fastball last year, went from maybe 88 to consistently over 90."

"Really."

"Yes."

"That works out well for us."

"It does. And there's a couple other guys coming up to fill in the bullpen, bunch of flame-throwers."

"Wow. What are we putting in the water down there? What. Why are you giving me that look? Are we . . . We're not actually . . ."

"That reminds me. While you're here, I need you to authorize an additional office expense."

"Sure, lemme just — four hundred thousand dollars for a year's supply of coffee? This better be some kind of super coffee."

"Oh, it is. Anyway, you know we needed some more power guys in the lineup?"

"Uh-huh."

"You should see your second baseman."

"I have a new second baseman?"

"Yeah. You won't recognize him. Put on twenty pounds of muscle, all in the upper body. I saw him take some swings in the batting cage — he actually drove some of the balls through the netting and into the parking lot."

"Great news, great. Keep up the good work."

"And your Escalade needs a new windshield."

If the reporters only ignored the story, the teams were complicit. Teams supplied amphetamines, and some team personnel even helped players acquire steroids or find sources. Teams knew of players using personal trainers who were reputed to be involved with steroids and did nothing. The owners, whether they nudged the game toward becoming more offense-centered or stood by and counted the money pouring in, helped make power so lucrative that an arms race of drug use ensued. And as more and more players began to use steroids, nearly every team was happy to acquire suspected steroid users or look the other way when their own players started to inject themselves in the clubhouse.

What's worse is that early action by the owners or other team personnel could have averted this whole crisis. Before baseball had mandatory testing for everyone, it had an agreement, reached in 1984, that allowed the commissioner to take action against players who were arrested or otherwise detected using illegal drugs. The agreement centered on recreational drugs because cocaine was the issue of the day, but it was there.

The mid-1980s Athletics teams presented the first serious incursion of steroids into baseball, and they feigned ignorance. And if Jose Canseco, as he alleges, was heading into the clubhouse bathroom with Mark McGwire to shoot each other up, it must have taken some effort to ignore what was going on.

What if someone on the team, especially someone with authority and direct knowledge, like Tony LaRussa, had done something? They could have turned the whole lot into the police for the possession of controlled substances or even simply gone to the league and laid out all their evidence and suspicion, arguing that it met the detection standard of the drug policy as it existed then.

Turning in your own players takes some courage. It would have set off a huge fight, with Canseco calling in the union and everyone getting lawyered up. But then one of two things happens: They get a test done and Canseco flunks it and baseball confronts its steroid problem fifteen years early, in 1987 (or whenever LaRussa suffers this hypothetical attack of morals). It might not have prevented the use of drugs designed to escape the tests (for instance, the NFL, which had a much more comprehensive steroid testing program, saw several players test positive for THG when a test was created for that). But it certainly would have slowed the spread of drugs. Or Canseco and company might have escaped the test and punishment, but baseball would have fought the first battle over a player everyone then would know was using steroids. Instead of focusing so much on cocaine, baseball would have started far earlier to pursue its long argument about how to deal with performance-enhancing drugs. In the meantime, players would have been much more wary about using steroids in their clubhouses, which at least would slow (even a little) the spread of abuse from players like Canseco to others.

Either way, it would have given baseball a chance. The failure of teams to raise concern about their own players for fear they would be the only ones harmed ensured that everyone ended up paying a high price. Fans who look at the records of recent years as tainted should also look at the people who could have prevented it.

Players

"Hi, I'm here to talk to you about anabolic steroids and why you shouldn't use them."

"I've heard if I take them, I'll recover faster after a start, they'll reduce the shoulder inflammation that comes from pitching, and they might even make my fastballs quicker."

"Yup."

"Why, that could make me more effective and prevent injuries. It could be a great help to my career."

"It could."

"Wait. Will this affect my chances of getting a job? Will teams shun me if they suspect I'm doing it?"

"Not at all. If you pick the right team, they won't just look the other way, they'll help."

"There's no rule against it?"

"Nope."

"No policy or anything."

"None."

"No testing?"

"No testing."

"Is it illegal?"

"It would probably be illegal if anyone knew about it."

"Why wouldn't I take this wonder drug?"

"Depending on what drugs you choose and how crazy you go with them, you could elevate your blood pressure, get some pretty bad acne, and damage your liver."

"And?"

"Possibly prostate cancer? Premature baldness? Sexual dysfunction? Higher cholesterol levels? We don't really know. The long-term effects aren't clear."

"Uh-huh. Well, it's been nice talking to you, but I'm going to go find some of the new steroids now. Thanks for the tip."

"That didn't go as well as I'd hoped."

Players who feared they wouldn't come back from injuries took steroids. Players who feared they'd never make the majors on their own merits took steroids. Players who saw an opportunity to be better without breaking the rules took steroids. They all made quite reasonable decisions, given what baseball set up before them.

As a group, though, those individual decisions created the problem for all the players and all of baseball.

We should acknowledge that for too long the locker room culture and the players' loyalty to the union meant that they didn't speak publicly about their concerns and certainly didn't turn their fellow players in. That players would complain that they were forced to consider taking steroids to compete but never tried to trip the alarm boggles my mind. At some point, you fink the bad guys out or you're partly responsible for their actions.

The League

"Commissioner, surveys show that fans rate steroids as the number-one problem in baseball today."

"Have you seen the latest attendance figures? They're great!"

"If you've read this week's columns, there are reporters following stars around with urine cups, asking them to prove they're clean by offering a sample to be tested."

"And we're close to reaching a new broadcast deal! Have you seen

the numbers on this thing? I'm going to build a giant vault in the basement of the building so I can swim around in the money like Scrooge McDuck."

"And I've had some informal talks with the players union representatives. I can't be sure, of course, but they're hinting that they're interested in talking about testing if we bring it to the table."

"There's going to be a diving board, a depth gauge so you can look to see how much we've got, little hashmarks at every obsquatumatillion, little pool toys —"

"Sir, we've ignored this problem for too long. Sir? You're ignoring me now. Great."

"Oh! We'll get a rubber duckie for the money vault, only a Scrooge McDuck rubber duckie! You want to swim in the money vault, don't you kid?"

"Yessir."

There's another way the rise of these drugs could have been stemmed far earlier. Baseball implemented a drug policy in 1984 without mandatory or random testing that both players and owners agreed to. It included treatment, limited testing, and wide powers for the commissioner to use at his discretion, which he did use when players were named in drug trafficking trials, for instance.

When Peter Ueberroth took over as baseball's commissioner, cocaine use by players was a big issue, and he decided to go after it by imposing mandatory drug tests for all players just before the 1986 season, a move promptly nixed in court as a violation of the labor agreement. Then he sent letters to each player, asking him to submit to confidential, consequence-free, voluntary drug tests during the season. When Donald Fehr, the head of the players union, met Ueberroth after the two embarrassments, the commissioner asked if the union would agree to testing, "even if it was just for the sake of public relations."

Major League Baseball would make no significant progress on

Opposite page: For years, nearly every public appearance by Commissioner Bud Selig has turned into an impromptu press conference on baseball's steroid policies. *AP*

the issue for the next fifteen years. Instead of trying to build a consensus with players or address the rising use of steroids, Ueberroth
alienated what support he had from the player rank-and-file for a
drug testing program. So he declared victory.

"We're going to have a season that's virtually drug-free," Ueberroth said in April 1986. "We'll be the first sport that can say that."

Jose Canseco, in his first full season in the majors, would hit 33
home runs that season, fourth highest in the American League, and
win the Rookie of the Year award.

Are steroids bad? Really?

It's important to give a nuanced answer here, but anything besides
"yes" means that my publisher and I will be sued into the ground by
the parents of the next kid to OD mainlining horse testosterone before the big game, so yes. Yes, they are.

You probably know someone on steroids. It's most likely an
asthma sufferer, and he's taking small doses. It helps reduce inflammation, reduces the amount of asthma medication he needs, and
has other beneficial effects. There are corticosteroids, sure, not anabolic steroids, but they're all hormones that regulate different body
functions like blood production, immune system response, and
muscle growth. They all have legitimate, beneficial medical uses as
well as harmful effects, particularly when abused.

Yeah, yeah, obviously, you say. But this is an important point. Steroids themselves aren't evil. They don't load themselves up into syringes in excessive doses and inject themselves into someone's innocent butt.

The horrible side effects, like the scarring and disgusting ab-
scesses from the injections, the acne, the liver damage — the whole
mess is due to abuse. The goal can be understood, as in the case of a
borderline player scared he will never get his job back if he's slow to
come off an injury, or it can be ridiculous, like the professional
wrestler looking for a little more definition in the pythonal muscle
group.

Steroids aren't bad. Steroid abuse is bad.

Was it cheating?

Yes, if the steroids were illegal, it was barely cheating. Until 2003, all baseball had was a weak policy focused on recreational drugs. As outlined in memos to teams: "The possession, sale, or use of any illegal drug or controlled substance by Major League players and personnel is strictly prohibited." Players were not tested, though, unless they admitted using illegal drugs or were "detected" using them, and then they were subject to testing for the remainder of their career. And testing only covered "cocaine, marijuana, amphetamines, opiates and phencyclidine (PCP)."

So if a player was arrested for dealing cocaine, he could be regularly tested. And while the memos threatened the players with lifetime bans, as long as there was no testing and no agreed-upon schedule for punishment, baseball's policy was pretty much useless in dealing with illegal steroids.

What's all the fuss about, then?

Steroids and other drugs are not the greatest threat baseball has ever faced (see "Gambling and game-fixing"), and much of the outrage about the game's problems is manufactured. Alleging widespread steroid use or bemoaning the larger issue is an easy column for sportswriters, and it's an easy way to get a lot of press if you're in Congress and don't want to hold hearings on more substantial issues (like crippling corruption in Congress).

The argument about the integrity of records is overwrought. A record is only a story of what happened. A hitter on steroids hit those home runs, just as a spitballer struck out those hitters and a bat corker got those extra hits. The statistics aren't tainted; they just require us to remember their context, as has always been true. Every era's statistics are skewed. Barry Bonds took drugs for a few years. Babe Ruth is a spot below him on the all-time home run leader board, and Ruth never had to face a pitcher who wasn't white as a lily. Who had the bigger advantage? All the triple leaders played in gigantic parks, where line drives could drop and roll forever and the fielders had poor equipment. Pitchers before 1920 could use trick pitches to their heart's content. And so on, through the last game that was played.

The real problem is that if even a few players are using performance-enhancing drugs, all players are forced to make a decision between accepting the risks and trying to keep up with the users or refusing to follow them and potentially putting their careers at risk.

Where's the line? Why is it so large and gray?

The fuzzy line between cheating and allowable training seems to be: "Does taking this drug allow you to do things you couldn't naturally do?"

Taking a crazy set of drugs so you can become the greatest hitter ever late in your career — yeah, that's over the line.

But this presents a real problem, one that all sports are starting to face. Today's athletes have training methods available, like a detailed motion analysis of their performances, that previous generations didn't. Runners once trained at a high altitude to increase their ability to take in oxygen, then realized they could "live high, train low" for maximum benefit. Now it's possible to use a tent or other method to simulate high altitudes at night, giving athletes the benefits of altitude without requiring them to commute up and down a mountain.

Creatine is a substance (a nitrogenous organic acid) that's particularly helpful in building twitch muscles. Twitch muscles are used in physical activities that require more impulse power, like swinging a bat, which is why hitters went crazy for the stuff when it became commercially available. It's been cited as the force behind Brady Anderson's out-of-nowhere 50–home run season in 1996, though of course there are more ominous whispers.

Normally, you get about half of it from the liver and about half from meat or fish unless you're a vegetarian, and then you're in trouble. During training, a two-hundred-pound athlete might take up to 10 grams of creatine a day. That's a big scoop of creatine from a commercial supplement or five pounds of fish or beef. Is the supplement cheating? You could eat that much meat normally, though it wouldn't be pleasant.

Or for a baseball-specific example, take ligament replacement surgery. Not that long ago, if a pitcher tore his elbow ligament, it meant he might never pitch again. Then, in 1974, Tommy John underwent the first ligament replacement surgery and recovered to pitch from 1976 through 1989. He never would have been able to win those games without an operation unavailable to all the generations of pitchers before him. Today, the surgery is almost routine: even high school pitchers, horribly overused by their abusive coaches, break down and have it done.

If pitchers were allowed to do only what they can do naturally, their careers would end. But the game is better for having those talented pitchers return to the mound. Who would want to deny them that?

Pitchers often report they throw faster after the surgery, with the new, fresh tendon taking over for the old, frayed one that had so many pitches on the odometer. Pitchers faced with a difficult rest and rehabilitation schedule or surgery are increasingly eager to choose the surgical option.

Now we're getting into uncomfortable territory. What do you do about players who choose surgery in part because they believe it will help their performance?

This is a very hazy area, and any distinction is by necessity going to be arbitrary and in some instances unfair.

What about the children?

One of the reasons given for banning steroids is that young kids competing in high school look at their heroes and emulate their use, and steroids have undeniably terrible effects on adolescents.

It's true that if kids believe that they have to use steroids to compete as professional baseball players, they might roll up their sleeves (drop their pants, actually) and say, "May as well get started."

But is the converse true? The NFL's had a steroids policy for decades, for instance, but amateur football players still inject themselves with whatever they can buy out of some scuzzy guy's Camaro in the parking lot of the neighborhood gym. Will high school boys hoping to compete in their sport of choice, with access to these drugs and with the same incentives to take them, decide against taking them because they're banned in the major leagues? It was a dangerous behavior for them before, and it's a dangerous behavior for them now.

Or will the temptation of being a prep star walking down the halls, adoring girls (or guys) hanging from each massive biceps, prove too great?

There's no evidence that prep athletes decide to use or pass on steroids based on the policies of a sport. You could as well make the reverse argument, that by banning steroids, a sport acknowledges that they make players who take them too good and so encourages younger athletes looking for an edge to turn to them.

The worst part about this may be that steroids — or anything that messes with the body — are bad drugs to abuse for anyone, but for kids who are growing, with their blood 90 percent hormones and 10 percent angst and with all their glands working overtime to produce some chemical to counteract what the gland one over is trying to do, steroids are insanely bad. It's like some fraction of the benefits and a hundred times the catastrophic consequences.

Which is to say, it's understandable that the issue is so emotionally charged, but it's not why baseball should have a rigorous testing policy with real penalties.

An extremely short history of drug use by major league players

For a long time, players drank a lot, and the most noxious chemical in their bodies was nitrates from all the hot dogs.* Nothing really happened until the late 1940s, when pilots returning from World

---

* Of course, they were quaffing Dr. Phineas Q. McFaddington's All-Purpose Elixir for Athletic Strengthening along with whatever else they could get their hands on, but as long as it didn't work, it didn't spread or affect anything.

War II had tasted the wonder of amphetamines. Baseball's rigorous schedule made it an ideal "pick-me-up" drug, and it quickly spread through the game. While the increase seems trivial, the addition in 1961 of eight games to the schedule — expanding the season from 154 games to 162 and making a long grind that much harder — helped the use of amphetamines grow.

In the 1980s, baseball was rife with cocaine abuse, and it was embarrassed by a high-profile trial that ensnared many major-leaguers. Cocaine use then subsided, as it did across American society.

The late 1980s saw the first serious use of steroids. Baseball had long been prejudiced against any kind of weight-lifting, teams even banning serious training, but that began to erode from the '70s into the late 1980s, when a huge Oakland Athletics team weight-trained constantly, scared other teams that even glanced at them, and won titles. Some of those guys, like Jose Canseco, used steroids.

Players and trainers began to adopt the workout methods and long hours of the bodybuilders, increasingly turning the lovably fat, beer-league softball sluggers into the kind of cut, defined athletes more associated with football and basketball. With the new training culture came other innovations, like supplements. Soon came the explosion of creatine use in the late 1990s, in addition to the less publicized spread of many illegal steroids that were already in wide use in bodybuilding.

A giant steroid scandal began when a new anabolic steroid, THG, was discovered when a sample was sent anonymously to the United States Anti-Doping Agency. Previously undetectable, the steroid is quite similar to two known and banned anabolic steroids, but it was also entirely legal, not recognized by legislation covering known steroids. THG was traced to the Bay Area Laboratory Cooperative (BALCO), which had ties to many top baseball hitters, particularly Jason Giambi and Barry Bonds. Legislation caught up to the drug soon after it was uncovered.

In 2003, baseball began testing for steroid use but without penalties. When over 5 percent of tests were refused or came back with positive results, penalties were instituted. MLB and the players later agreed to revisions, including much harsher penalties. In 2006, they began to test for amphetamines.

A discussion of Jason Giambi with Fulbright scholar Jeff Shaw

"Jeff, you're a prestigious Fulbright scholar. What's the deal with Jason Giambi? Early in his career, he starts taking steroids. Then, in 2004, he has a series of really strange injuries, including a pituitary tumor and a bout with intestinal parasites. He seems utterly helpless at the plate. Then, suddenly, he starts to hit again."

"From a strictly clinical, scholarly perspective, Jason Giambi is an interesting case. A case of what we might call 'intestinal parasites.' In the halls of academe, we might term this affliction 'the Oakland–New York marathon,' because we can only imagine the type of runs he had."

"I see. I found it odd that Kevin Brown also had an intestinal parasite issue at the same time."

"Kevin Brown is an intestinal parasite issue. The real issue with Giambi remains unexplored. Remember how, after he signed with the Yankees, Steinbrenner had him shave, shower, buy a new suit, and start generally comporting himself like a metrosexual? Could there be a causal link here? Why blame the cocktail of HGH, Winstrol, and whatever else he was on? Did anybody test the gnarly new colognes he used?"

"Didn't he endorse a deodorant? What if the underarm germs were keeping the parasites at bay? And what about the intestinal parasites — were they cured or did Giambi get them to swear allegiance to him and convert them to his cause? A colony of allied parasites, keeping the system clean, rallying tired muscles . . . it'd be quite an advantage."

"Plus, who would know the internal workings of the man's body better? It would be like Dennis Quaid in InnerSpace, but with parasites."

"Yeah, how did that pituitary tumor get resolved?"

"Clearly, it was excised by the parasites. Supply the little buggers with the occasional Jack in the Box hamburger, and they become your own private security system or Green Lantern power ring."

"You think that's enough? I'd think you'd have to promise them more than that."

"Maybe some hot female parasites? The same thing that was apparently promised to Kris Benson."

"Are parasites sexual?"

"Several I dated were. Hoo-boy, I could tell you stories. But that's not the point. The point is, from a scholarly perspective, Jason Giambi has clearly stayed one step ahead of the testers with help from an army of leechlike organisms."

Who uses?

For steroids, the stereotype was always that it was the hitters, the power hitters especially. But the suspensions have hit pitchers just as hard. One of the greatest benefits of steroids for all players is that they help in recovery. A hitter can work out and be ready to hit the weights again the next day. Players heal from injuries faster. That's particularly good news for older hitters, fighting nicks and long-nagging strains that might otherwise keep them out of the lineup for a week each time they flared up.

Pitchers see additional benefits. By suppressing inflammation, steroids help them not only get through their appearances but bounce back to pitch again. For starters, it may not mean they can pitch deeper into any particular game, but it means they'll be much fresher for their next start. For relievers, it might mean the differ- ence between being able to appear in two games out of three or be- ing back in the minors. For both types of pitcher, who constantly face the specter of career-ending injuries, the benefits of steroids in preventing shoulder tears might make it worthwhile all on its own.

Also surprising, most players who were suspended weren't the names most often bandied around. Of the hitters caught, only Rafael Palmeiro ever made an All-Star team. From the leaked grand jury testimony, we know that a few top hitters were using, but still, it does appear that performance enhancers are used most at the bot-tom of the roster, for players who might not otherwise put together a career.

It does make sense, economically: the difference between a mi-nor league contract and being even a fringe major league player is a ton of money and a much nicer life in general. But average to better? Not quite as life-changing, and users aren't as common.

For hitters in general, the benefits have been well discussed. Players can quickly put on a lot of muscle in the off-season using steroids and aggressive workout programs, and then, by continuing whatever cocktail of drugs they're on, maintain that muscle de-spite having much less time to work out during baseball's grinding season.

Identifying the user

An absolutely scientific guide to identifying users of performance-enhancing drugs like steroids and HGH:

Does he have a large head? (+10)
Is the player bald or rapidly losing his hair? (+10)
Is the player developing feminine features, like breasts? (+10)
Does he look puffy? (+10)
Does the player have braces or other orthodontic work despite being old? (+10)
Does he suffer from muscle strains and tendon tears? (+10)
Does he recover from injuries with frightening speed? (+10)
Is the player much heavier than he was when younger? (+10)
Is the player much leaner than he was when younger? (+10)
Does he play for a team besides your favorite? (+10)
(pitchers) Did he pick up an extra 2–3 miles on the fastball one year? (+10)
(hitters) Did he start hitting an extra 15 home runs one year? (+10)
Did he angrily deny using steroids in front of Congress/grand jury/etc.? (+10)
Did he angrily deny knowingly using steroids in front of Congress/a grand jury/etc.? (+10)
Does he bench-press a car during the between-innings promotion for a local dealership? (+20)
Does he have a good relationship with the media and fans? (−10)

Scoring:

0–50 points: Not on steroids. How dare you even suggest such a thing.
51 or more points: There's no doubt the player is on steroids.

How many players were using?

The more sensational estimates were extremely high: Canseco said that 85 percent of players were using steroids. Ken Caminiti thought at least half were, though he later backed off that figure. But take those two as the worst-case scenario: there would have to be be-

Using our exclusive test on these players testifying at a congressional hearing, we find that they're (from left) . . . guilty, guilty, guilty, innocent — in that order. *AP*

tween about 375 and 640 players (out of the 750 on active rosters) who were using steroids at any point in the season. There's just no way it was that high.

In the first year of minor league testing, 2001, 11 percent of minor-leaguers failed. That testing covered all players in the minor leagues except those on a major-league roster, like players on injury rehabs and some prospects.

In 2003, the first year of major league steroid testing but without penalties for failing, players were tested once during the season and again a week later. To establish how many players were on steroids, anonymous testing is quite helpful. Because there was no punishment, players had no incentive to stop using. They could happily pee a sample that was 50 percent Winstrol and walk away whistling happily. There was no need to go off their favorite drug, try out masking agents, or anything like that. Use away.

The exact percentage is unknown, but between 5 and 7 percent failed, enough to trigger further testing backed up with (weak) penalties. By contrast, in 1986, when the NFL began testing, it nailed 30 percent of the players.

Five to 7 percent means that maybe 80 players failed or refused to take a steroid test in 2003. That's a lot fewer than 750 or even 375. Not that 80 is good, but it's not the kind of massive epidemic that threatened the very foundations of the game in the way throwing the World Series did.

And still, even if there were no epidemic, the perception by fans that steroids are a serious and widespread problem is itself a serious threat to the game, as no sport can exist without fans (except the WNBA). If sixty to eighty players created a crisis of confidence, it was enough to demand action.

Did steroid use help players?

Yes, but maybe not as much as seems to be generally believed. There are two major arguments here, and they focus more on hitters because their statistics are much easier to work with, since the benefits to pitchers are mostly in recovery and preventing injury.

First, there's the appeal to example. All the huge home run hitters have been implicated in steroid scandals. Some have been caught, some have admitted their use to the BALCO grand jury, others haven't cracked yet but the evidence is damning.

If it didn't work, then why would anyone do it? If it didn't work, why were the guys setting home run records?

While these drugs may or may not help individual players, it's pretty clear that they do help some players — a lot. However, take Jason Giambi. If the grand jury testimony that's been published is accurate, Giambi used steroids for much of his career, including his MVP season; he went off them and had a horrible season, then regained his power and started to hit again. Unless you believe that he found another lab that could give him undetectable steroids (or that Giambi discovered another way to get back on performance-enhancers without being caught), he's as good a power hitter clean as is he was using steroids.

Looking at the larger group of players who were caught, though, the effect isn't great. A study by Nate Silver of *Baseball Prospectus* showed that hitters who tested positive for performance-enhancing drugs lost about 10 points of batting average and a little bit of power after their suspension. However, the suspended players were mostly marginal major-leaguers and didn't include any star but Rafael Palmeiro.

Pitchers saw their walk rate go up, their strikeout rate drop (minimally), and they allowed more home runs.

The differences aren't much. It certainly doesn't turn an average player into a great one, or anything like it. But when you think about it, 10 points of batting average, or .13 points of ERA, can be the difference between a marginal major-leaguer and a career, however modest. This helps to explain why so many of the players caught are fighting for the last spot on a roster, not the spotlight on ESPN.

Let's look at this in a different way, though. Barry Bonds is the most prominent player linked to steroids still playing, the holder of the single-season home run record, one of the most talented hitters in baseball history, and one of the most tainted players due to his central role in the BALCO scandal.

According to the book *Game of Shadows*, Bonds reportedly complains that when he went off his cycle, he felt much worse: he wasn't getting as much power on the ball, and so forth, to the point that he wanted to stop cycling and take the drugs constantly; he was willing to dose himself if he had to. The book alleges that Bonds was on a three-week-on, one-week-off cycle, and while it makes all kinds of allusions to the dosing calendars and whatever else, right now the only people who have them are the government, the *San Francisco Chronicle* writers, it seems, and possibly Bonds or his trainer, unless they were seized.

However, we can still take a look, using Bonds's 2002 season. Steroid users take their drug of choice only for several weeks and then stop because constant doses over a long period of time cause the body to shut down the natural production of testosterone, with potentially disastrous effects for the user. What we might expect to see is that when the player is feeling the effects of the drugs, whether they kick in on the first day of the cycle or there's a delay, is an improvement in performance, with a relative decrease in performance at other times.

Set April 2, the first day of the season, as the first day of the cycle. Count the performance over the next three weeks as "on," the performance the week after as "off," and repeat through the end of the season, totaling his performances for "on" and "off." What we'd expect to see, if a player isn't using or doesn't perform better while on steroids, is that the "on" weeks would look, more or less, like the "off" weeks. If they were on, we'd expect to see not only an increase in performance during the "on" weeks but that the dates we suspect the cycles start on would be fairly tightly grouped.

Barry Bonds's 2002 statistics by hypothetical starting date of four-week cycle

Starts cycle on	Batting average while "on"	Batting average while "off"	Slugging percentage, "on"	Slugging percentage, "off"	Percentage of hits that were home runs, "on"	Percentage of hits that were home runs, "off"
4/1/02	.392	.293	.878	.533	34	19
4/2/02	.388	.313	.859	.616	32	26
4/3/02	.368	.375	.814	.750	32	28
4/4/02	.369	.374	.798	.802	30	32
4/5/02	.370	.367	.807	.776	31	31
4/6/02	.384	.327	.811	.762	28	39
4/7/02	.386	.320	.817	.742	29	39
4/8/02	.369	.371	.775	.876	28	39
4/9/02	.375	.354	.818	.740	31	29
4/10/02	.377	.347	.810	.765	30	32
4/11/02	.377	.351	.808	.775	31	31
4/12/02	.371	.366	.780	.848	30	34
4/13/02	.366	.378	.784	.838	31	31
4/14/02	.360	.392	.753	.908	28	36
4/15/02	.360	.393	.748	.923	27	39
4/16/02	.364	.385	.741	.940	26	42
4/17/02	.361	.394	.759	.908	28	37
4/18/02	.361	.396	.765	.901	28	38
4/19/02	.355	.419	.761	.925	29	36
4/20/02	.346	.443	.742	.979	30	33
4/21/02	.343	.457	.754	.947	33	26
4/22/02	.356	.412	.791	.825	34	23
4/23/02	.353	.429	.776	.879	34	23
4/24/02	.373	.360	.812	.760	33	25
4/25/02	.373	.360	.825	.720	34	22

Barry Bonds's 2002 statistics by hypothetical starting date of four-week cycle (cont.)

Starts cycle on	Batting average while "on"	Batting average while "off"	Slugging percentage, "on"	Slugging percentage, "off"	Percentage of hits that were home runs, "on"	Percentage of hits that were home runs, "off"
4/26/02	.383	.330	.848	.650	34	21
4/27/02	.382	.330	.858	.606	34	19
4/28/02	.389	.304	.868	.565	33	21

Top ten most probable cycle start dates and how big the difference was, Barry Bonds 2002

Date	Batting average while "on"	Batting average while "off"	Slugging percentage "on"	Slugging percentage "off"	Percentage of hits that were home runs, "on"	Percentage of hits that were home runs, "off"
4/29/2002	.392	.293	.878	.533	34	19
4/28/2002	.389	.304	.868	.565	33	21
4/27/2002	.382	.330	.858	.606	34	19
4/2/2002	.388	.313	.859	.616	32	26
4/26/2002	.383	.330	.848	.650	34	21
4/25/2002	.373	.360	.825	.720	34	22
4/9/2002	.375	.354	.818	.740	31	29
4/7/2002	.386	.320	.817	.742	29	39
4/3/2002	.368	.375	.814	.750	32	28
4/24/2002	.373	.360	.812	.760	33	25

And that's what we see. The first two columns are batting averages. So if we assume that April 1 was the first day of his "on" cycle, Bonds hit .392 while "on" and .293 while "off." The next two columns are slugging percentage, a good rough measure of raw power. It's measured as total bases divided by at-bats. A player who hit a single every four at-bats would have a .250 slugging percentage, while a player who hit a home run every at-bat would have a 4.000 slugging percentage. The major league average is about .430. Slugging percentage is a good measure of how much power a hitter has. Here, Bonds hit for a .878 slugging percentage "on" and .533 "off." The next two columns are simpler: of the hits he got, how many were home runs? During the "on" period, an amazing 34 percent of his hits were home runs; during the "off" period, 19 percent were.

These numbers support the contention in *Game of Shadows* that Bonds was on a regular three-week cycle when he felt great and then a week off when he would find his power gone.

If we apply the cycle to a season in which a player is experiencing surges in performance while "on" and decreases while "off," we would see the dates that fit best very close to each other.

Here, we see that. The best fit is 4/1, and the next best fit is the day before (4/28, because the cycle loops), followed by 4/27, 4/2, 4/26, and 4/25.

If we tried to apply this three-week/one-week grouping to a season in which a player was not experiencing actual cycles of good and relatively poor performances, we'd still see some dates where the "on" was much stronger than the "off" and the best-fit dates would be more or less randomly scattered.

To test this schedule, I went to Keith Woolner at *Baseball Prospectus* and had him run it for other Bonds seasons using their detailed game logs. In 1997 and 1998, before Bonds supposedly decided to take up steroids, we find that there are no strong patterns; the difference from even the best candidate dates shows about half the difference in power as found in 2002.

In another supposed steroid year, 2001, the best-fit dates clump together again: 4/5, 4/4, 4/6, 4/8, 4/13 (#6 is 4/9).

Then, a moment of frank awe. Looking at the numbers, it appears that, first, we can reasonably assume that Bonds was right: there was a dramatic difference between the Bonds who felt the power and the Bonds who complained that his hits weren't traveling. Bonds wasn't much more of a contact hitter, only a little better at getting hits, but he was a far, far more dangerous power hitter when the steroids were coursing through his veins. One hitter was what you might reasonably expect of Bonds as an amazingly talented but aging thirty-seven-year-old hitter, and the other is the greatest hitter baseball has ever seen.

Kids, don't try that at home.

It appears, in general, that using the steroids and performance-enhancing drugs we know about don't help a player swing a bat and hit a ball more effectively, which is a traditional "why steroids don't help" argument. Where they do seem to help, and help dramatically, is to help a player hit for massive power. Historic power, the likes of which the game had never seen before. Steroids indeed were a powerful, wish-granting genie, at least for the biggest, best player of the modern era, and baseball will struggle forever after with how to stuff that djinn back in its lamp.

Untangling the long-term effects of drug use in baseball players may never be possible. We can't know what Jason Giambi would have hit if he'd never taken steroids, or how many home runs Babe Ruth might have hit if he had had access to HGH. We don't know if, overall, the power benefits are worth the cost the body pays — and that might not be something anyone not facing the decision can determine.

We can say that, unlike bat-corking, it's clear there is a benefit.

How many players are using now?

Forty-two.
By team, alphabetically:
[REDACTED BY LAWYERS]

What happens next?

Two problems are facing baseball right now, and neither can be solved immediately.

Many players who used steroids have moved to HGH. While it doesn't help building the massive muscle bulk that anabolic steroids do, it has many of the beneficial effects that players, especially older ones, generally look to steroids for. It's not that hard to get, though it can be quite expensive. Most important, while HGH is banned, there's no proven test for it. If a test can be found, the players will almost certainly have to sign up for blood draws, which would have to go through the collective bargaining process. While players on the whole were willing to agree to urine tests to help their sport, regular blood draws could be another matter entirely.

The future of performance-enhancing drugs is that the world will become more stratified. BALCO didn't sell to anyone: it actively worked with the elite athletes in different sports. BALCO was both blessed and cursed by Victor Conte. He was charismatic, able to make friends with anyone and turn them into clients, but he could not stop talking: about current clients to outsiders and about his operation to people who could betray him or who were investigating him, and that lack of discretion played a large part in the downfall of his operation.

If other chemistry labs like BALCO are out in the wild, not discovered by current testing methods and government investigations (and we would be silly to presume there are not), they will be even more paranoid and expensive. They will be selling the next secret designer steroid at prices someone making the major league minimum couldn't afford.

Then what is the marginal guy trying to scrape by on his minor league salary and willing to make the gamble going to do? Baseball would hope he gives up looking for chemical solutions, but if he's dedicated, he'll likely try to use mainstream (and thus cheap) steroids and try to use other drugs to mask their presence in his system or cheat the system in another way. These players are the ones who are still going to get caught when it turns out that Pepto-Bismol tablets combined with two daily packs of Pop Rocks does not allow them to test negative for the Deca they were taking all year.

We can't know yet how effective baseball's new drug policy will be in fighting new threats, but there's reason to be hopeful. Baseball waited for twenty years to take action, but in the last few years it's made tremendous strides. Both the testing program, with multiple random checks that can fall outside the season, and the punishment schedule were unthinkable not long ago, and today we're looking ahead to improving the system. Hopefully both players and owners can continue to be civil and rational about this issue and work together to pursue their goal of making baseball a safe sport to offer a living.

I hope it works. If there's one chapter I would hate to revise for future editions with new scandals, it'd be gambling and game-fixing, but if there were two, this would be the second.

Is it wrong?

The test offered at the start of this book is whether, when widely adopted, the act would hurt baseball. Steroid use certainly does. It is not nearly as wrong as game-fixing, for instance, because someone using steroids is trying to play better, not tamper with the essential nature of the contest.

We can argue about how bad the problem is, how much of the horror is manufactured and how much has merit, whether the effect of steroid use is marginal or outrageous. But no one would say that an athlete who spends his career honing his skills to reach the highest levels of competition should then be told that he can either take a devil's cocktail of drugs to keep moving up or remain clean and fail. It is absolutely not what sports should be about.

What makes steroids particularly galling, though, is that it's gross and boring. Syringes, secret labs, chemists trying to outwit other chemists in the artful mediums of urine and blood samples . . . it all has nothing to do with baseball. It has none of the outlaw charm that spitballing does, for instance. Gaylord Perry applying a dab of Vaseline while a packed stadium, umpires, and the other team all stare at him is interesting. Injecting yourself in the butt in a toilet stall requires some similar contortions but none of the courage, chutzpah, or skill, and that's as good a reason to drive performance-enhancing drugs from baseball as any other.

Part IV
Cheating Our Way into the Sunset

BASEBALL WITHOUT CHEATING would be a terrible sport, as popular as beer league kickball but not as much fun. Without cheating by teams to hire and pay the best players, teams would still consist of amateurs. Without the professional leagues, the best players wouldn't play against one another because there would be no league that made being professional lucrative, so they would be scattered, playing baseball as a hobby in their off-hours.

Batters might still be calling for high or low pitches. There would be none of the competition between pitcher and batter if pitchers had not continuously undermined the rules to help their team win. Once on base, there would be little to do, as without the Orioles and the other early teams working the rules like a punching bag, we'd have no hit-and-run, no sacrifice bunting, nothing interesting. Crowds would watch mutely and applaud quietly at the conclusion of a victory. Without crowds or interest, it's unlikely gambling would ever have been a problem, and without a financial incentive to succeed (or even the attention that success at a popular sport would have brought), there wouldn't have been a reason for athletes to use performance-enhancing drugs. Even assuming there were amateur tournaments where the best local teams could play each other, the umpiring would be horrible, with only one or two barely trained, easily intimidated umpires pulled from random passersby.

Without the influence of cheating, baseball might not have survived. Maybe some wilder variant of stickball would have arisen, or cricket, or maybe we'd have seen the rise of American football much earlier. But if not dead, baseball would most likely be a fringe hobby.

Baseball purists are half-blind. They applaud a runner's hard slide into second, taking out the shortstop to break up a double play, but are saddened at allegations that a pitcher scuffs a ball. Both are cheating, both are long-held traditions. Baseball has never been a clean sport.

What makes cheating in baseball special? Other sports have cheating, from the steroids and illegal plays of football to the out-of-specification restrictor plates NASCAR teams would love to get onto their cars. There are many reasons: it is such a difficult sport that the incentive to find tiny, illegal advantages is great, the pitcher has possession of the ball before each pitch, baseball's pace results in hundreds of short moments in which each side can think of how they can advance their chances of winning, but the most important is baseball's pedigree. No avenue of cheating has ever been shut off entirely but rather controlled, defined, adapted, made legal, and accepted. It's assimilated and welcomed into the fold.

Cheating makes baseball a more colorful, interesting sport, where outlaws can flourish if they're smart and skilled enough. They become not just successful players but heroes of a kind, inducted into the Hall of Fame and greeted warmly everywhere they go for their ability to flaunt the law and win.

Cheating makes the sport stronger. The most important crises in baseball's history have been forced by the worst kind of underhanded conduct. The rampant rough play of the early years forced baseball to decide to become a cleaner game that focused less on the ability to fight and more on athletic skills. The long association with gambling cost the game a World Series but resulted in a clear goal against betting and a set of clear rules that have almost entirely prevented any further scandal. And while baseball winked at the use of drugs for decades, the explosion of steroids from the 1980s finally forced the game to establish a policy with testing and penalties, and now, as with all other rules, it's begun what will be a long quest to draw a fine line between the acceptable and the illegal in an increasingly complex world.

Baseball doesn't have a cheating problem. Baseball is and always will be inseparable from cheating, and because of that it's found success, grown, and become the national pastime. Knowing more about the cheating that has shaped and built the sport makes us appreciate the game, in all its glory and subtle nuances, ever more.

Now go look for it. You'll be happily surprised.

Acknowledgments

First and foremost, this book wouldn't exist if not for the tolerance and support of my wife, Jill, who put up with so much I'm better off not reminding her, even here. Jill feels baseball would be better if it ended after seven innings, yet spent a week with me in snowy Cooperstown doing research at the Hall of Fame.

Thanks to all the librarians and everyone who's walked through a stack for InterLibrary Loan (or whatever your institution calls it) for helping me and countless others with their research. Hi, Mom!

Many thanks to my friends:

Jonah Keri conducted several interviews that appear in quotes and inform the chapters, and he lent his golden retriever–like boundless energy at times when I really needed it.

Jeff Shaw, for letting me bounce chapters, jokes, approaches, and anecdotes off him throughout this project. This book would not be nearly as funny without Jeff as a test audience.

Joel Reiter, who generously spent a lot of his valuable time explaining things like "angular momentum" to me and proofread some critical chapters. The science of the book is far stronger for his effort in trying to steer me toward the light.

Steve Goldman gave some timely assists with research, answered questions selflessly, and, through his Casey Stengel biography, inspired me to do the best work possible for its own sake.

My coauthors at U.S.S. Mariner (ussmariner.com): Dave Cameron, Jason Barker, and Jeff Shaw (again), and our dear readers. It's been awesome, and I owe you much for your support these last few years.

And to all my friends who haven't seen me since I started working on this: I'm alive. Thanks for your patience. Call me, we'll go have a beer, and you can tell me what you've been up to these last few years.

Thanks are due to my agent, Sydelle Kramer, who was willing to help me figure out which book idea I could do well with, whip up a good proposal, and find it a home.

Thanks to Susan Canavan, my editor at Houghton Mifflin, for pushing me to make sure everyone's clearly identified throughout the book and for supporting the crazy digressions, the jokes, and for having the patience to let me spend the time to make this a book we both wanted to publish.

I'd like to thank my cat, Maddie, for making sure that during this long production I didn't lose sight of the important things, like playing with bits of string and ensuring that she receive satisfactory brushing. If my house is ever burglarized by a giant piece of string, that string's in for the thrashing of a lifetime.

I'd like to acknowledge the unintentional contributions of the Anchor Steam Brewery in San Francisco, California, the Deschutes Brewery in Bend, Oregon, the Sierra Nevada Brewing Company in Chico, California, and my local favorite, the Redhook Brewery in Woodinville, Washington. Many, many beers were harmed over the years it took to write this book.

Notes

I, along with every modern baseball writer and fan, owe a great debt to resources that make our job much easier. First among these is Retrosheet (retrosheet.org). Retrosheet is trying to provide complete play-by-play accounts of every game ever played. I checked Retrosheet throughout, both for facts and to find interesting angles. It is invaluable.

Similarly, Baseball Reference (baseballreference.com) contains all the baseball stats for all the teams since baseball turned professional.

Total Baseball was an invaluable reference in tracing rule changes through baseball's history.

The other resource I turned to over and over was the *Sporting News*. It was for almost a century a national source of baseball news and analysis.

On the malleability of truth

Many of the things I expected to include in this book have been left out. There were no historical records for some of my favorite stories and widely circulated anecdotes.

I'll mention some of these here in the notes, but in general I chose what I considered the best-supported version. This will, I'm sure, prove to be imperfect, and I hope my best effort in striving for contemporary accounts and primary sources makes the fewest of the inevitable errors in a project like this.

Toward a philosophy of cheating

Obviously, this ends up looking a lot like Immanuel Kant's Categorical Imperative, laid out in *Groundwork of the Metaphysic of Morals* (1785), *Critique of Practical Reason* (1788), and *Metaphysics of Morals* (1798).

Delay of game

"sent to a grocery store for some candles, and after lighting them placed them in front of the bench occupied by his player. . . ." is from the *New York Times*, 8/8/1941.

The *Brooklyn Eagle* being appalled is from 9/8/1889, which I found in *Early Innings* by Dean Sullivan.

The Washington-Boston game is reported as the seventh inning by some sources, which it wasn't.

It will probably take a playoff game being affected by the relevant rules to force MLB to fix the rainout rules, but a high-enough-profile disaster during a pennant race might suffice (say, a Boston–New York series to decide the AL East title that prevents one team from getting there). The postseason games are played in locations vulnerable to extremely bad weather, and the stakes are so high in those games that a chance at a cheap win (or a cheap restart of a game) is absolutely worth fines and public scorn.

Or we could see the World Series moved, like the Super Bowl, to neutral ground in a fair-weather city. Who knows? In Bud Selig's time as commissioner, we've seen other seemingly sacred traditions broken.

The Hidden Ball Trick

There are additional, undiscovered Matt Williams hidden ball trick attempts. We'd know about a successful one, but if it was blown by the pitcher or the umpire's lack of attention, it may have escaped being written up. They're out there — Matt Williams even told Bill Deane they were, then didn't get back to him.

The "what are friends for" comes from the *Los Angeles Times*, 7/1/86.

On Slagle: there are slightly different versions of what happened on the play.

Groundskeeping

The Bossard quotes come from a variety of articles I found at the Hall of Fame. The most helpful one was "They Doctor the Diamond" by Hal Lebovitz, *Baseball Digest*, July 1955, 31–40.

I don't know if I'm just a total geek about this stuff, but I would love to read a great book on Bossard and groundskeeping that gets into things like his grass mix choices.

The Metrodome revelations, including study, were found in "Did the Dome's Air Flow Turn Pop Flies into Home Runs?" by Randy Furst, *Minneapolis Star Tribune*, 7/27/2003.

Stealing Signs

The "Manila Bay" exchange comes from an unsourced newspaper clipping from the Hall of Fame files.

There's a belief for some reason that baseball passed a rule in 1961 banning the use of mechanical devices to steal signs. It's been circulated in different contexts and in fact is quoted in Prager's WSJ article. But if it went in in 1961, it came out between then and now, because it doesn't stand as a currently enacted rule. MLB, unfortunately, did not respond to my requests for information about rules around this and, if so, what they are. I asked Prager, and he said that in an interview with Bud Selig, the commissioner confirmed there is no rule on the books against stealing signs in any manner.

I have an entirely unsupported theory that baseball may have issued a memo at some point that laid out what it would consider illegal conduct, and that standard has sat out there ever since, an off-the-rulebook rule. If there were no rule or standard, why would teams file complaints with the league when they think themselves victims?

Similarly, there's no rule that says a manager can't use a radio transmitter or other electronic means to convey signs to his coaches if he was so inclined.

McGraw

This was by far the hardest chapter to investigate. So many of the myths are false, repeated and exaggerated over generations of writers. This is a frustration in any historical project, I suspect, but particularly here, because many of the stories about McGraw have been repeated, embellished, and printed, at which point they're cited as sources — even though using a hard-to-believe anecdote published in 1960 to back up your view of baseball in the 1890s is at best lazy.

I am greatly in debt to Howard Rosenberg's "Cap Anson" books for this chapter, and particularly the third book in that series. Rosenberg's methodical reliance on contemporary sources shatters many of the contemporary myths about how bad things were while demonstrating vividly how interesting and colorful baseball was then. It encouraged me to spend the time to go back myself and read the old *Spalding Guides*, the old issues of the *Sporting News*, dig through the *New York Times* archives, and hit the microfiche. The more I did that, the more modern books I discarded entirely.

In 2100, I'm sure books will be written that allege John McGraw used the just-invented telephone to steal signs from his opponents, was a key financier of the Republic of Hawaii, testified against Oscar Wilde during spring training, sparked the First World War by spiking Archduke Ferdinand, and killed the last passenger pigeon in a close play at third.

It's hard to prove whether much of what he's accused of happened or not. If I want to prove that McGraw punched someone, game stories written at the time offer proof, and biographies describe the fight. Proving that someone didn't do something, such as proving I don't have an undetectable magic dragon, can be impossible. The larger problem — trying to determine what really happened a hundred years ago — is made more difficult by the state of sports coverage at the time.

Contemporary accounts are often unreliable and exaggerated. Few writers traveled with their team, and hometown writers were extremely partisan, quick to denounce visitors for their poor sportsmanship and conduct while excusing the home team, if they mentioned the home team's cheating at all. So if McGraw held on to runners at home, it might never get into a paper, even if he did it every few games. It makes sense, then, to pay more attention to incidents related in biographies or in complaints outside game stories.

We do know that when spiking was seen as intentional, it led to retaliation and, from that, feuds and fights. All of which are far less common in primary sources than you'd expect if intentional spiking were common.

Furthermore, in an atmosphere where collisions on the basepaths were frequent and players were all trying to find ways to trick their opponents, it's likely that only the most egregious actions would ever have drawn notice.

On the belt thing: I was unable to find a contemporary source for this in the years that McGraw might have crossed paths with Browning. However, it does appear in a 1934 *Liberty* article, supposedly from McGraw himself, and in Graham's *McGraw of the Giants*. But while Graham knew McGraw from covering him, it's still not a first-person source. I wish I'd been able to turn up something from the time, but the Graham write-up in particular was convincing enough that I decided to use it.

I originally saw the cutoff claim in the *Sporting News*, May 29, 1957, 3.

Heckling

Early heckling cites came from the *New York Times*, the *Sporting News*, and *Baseball Magazine*. O'Toole and Adelis came from the *Sporting News*. I first found O'Toole's song in *Peanuts and Crackerjack*, by David Cataneo.

Ten-Cent Beer Night has more versions floating around than any other incident in this book. Was it one person or several who charged Burroughs? How many people got on the field beforehand? Was security really doubled, or were they really not prepared? When did the riot police get there, and if they were already on their way when things went wrong, when did they get called? The number of people arrested varied from five to eight, either of which is an extremely small number.

I tried to rely as much as possible on stories written in the immediate aftermath, discounting later ones.

A complete list of items that were allegedly thrown during Ten-Cent Beer Night, arranged alphabetically:

Batteries
Beer bottles

Beer cans
Beer cups
Chair parts
Chairs, folding
Chairs, torn up from fastenings
Firecrackers
Golf balls
Hot dogs
Popcorn (containers, both full and empty)
Rocks
Smoke bombs
Thunderbird fortified wine bottle (thrown at Mike Hargrove)

Doctoring the ball

I leaned heavily on newspaper articles for this chapter. It's interesting to pursue Tommy John's cutting in this way, because mentions crop up every once in a while, often in passing (a Peter Gammons column will describe saved balls, each cut in the same spot), but few accusations are tied to specific games. Following many of their starts, the game stories would include accusations of ball doctoring by the other team, and the does-he-or-doesn't-he story would be written each time they came to town

Gaylord Perry's autobiography, *Me and the Spitter*, should be required reading for serious baseball fans. Its only real flaw is the lack of a good index, which I'm thinking of writing and putting on the Web as a public service. It's shocking that Perry hasn't returned to write a longer book that covers his entire career. It's also interesting, in reading the coverage of Perry through the years, to see some writers, most famously Peter Gammons, turn on Perry when he attacked the umpires.

McGraw's quote was from the *World* (New York), February 26, 1918.

Gil Hodges's quote comes from "Majors start speed-up, clean-up campaign," *Sporting News*, December 9, 1967, 33.

The Wickersham quotes are from *Sporting News*, June 17, 1967, 29.

The Black Sox

The standard 1919 White Sox book remains Eliot Asinof's *Eight Men Out*. I also recommend *Shoeless: The Life and Times of Joe Jackson*, by David Fleitz, as an excellent biography that covers the story in detail. Gene Carney's *Burying the Black Sox: How Baseball's Cover-Up of the 1919 World Series Almost Succeeded* pointed me to the 1935 article by Fullerton and is worth reading itself. What if we never knew that a World Series had been thrown, and what if the rumors that earlier World Series titles might be tainted are true, the difference being that those scandals were better concealed?

The year remains controversial. There's some dispute about whether Comiskey cut back on laundry, but the "Black Sox" dirt thing is in contemporary sources. It's commonly alleged that Cicotte asked for his $10,000 up front in part because that was the amount Comiskey had promised Cicotte as a bonus if he won 30 games in 1917, only to sabotage his quest to reach that number. It's a claim not at all supported by what we know about Cicotte's 1917 season, and there's no evidence that supports the claim that there was a bonus.

One of the more interesting areas I didn't get into is the number of fixes. We know of two, described here, but there are also accounts that other gamblers, seeing the odds on the White Sox tilt so far, tried to force the Reds to lose, most notably by getting their players too drunk to compete. The more we learn about the circumstances around the Series, the more likely it seems that there were even more conspiracies at work.

Also, who was pulling the strings in 1920? If the same group of White Sox conspirators were intentionally throwing games a season later, was that Rothstein, who had managed to cover up the 1919 scandal, or even Attell, to whom much of the disappearing evidence had swum?

McMullin's role as advance scout is noted in Warren Brown's 1952 book *The Chicago White Sox*, a pointer I picked up from *Rob Neyer's Big Book of Baseball Blunders*.

Billy Martin

There isn't a really good Martin biography yet. Martin's autobiography is amusing to read but frustrating to a serious reader, as it contains almost as many lies (self-justifying or otherwise) as sentences. *Last Yankee* by David Falkner, *Wild, High, and Tight* by Peter Golenbock, and *Damn Yankee* by Maury Allen are all decent enough biographies. What I really wanted, though, was a book in the vein of Steven Goldman's excellent biography of Casey Stengel (*Forging Genius*), which focused on Martin's development as a player and manager and his unique place in baseball history more than on his relationship with his various wives. Goldman has so far ignored my pleas to write that book.

The allegation that Martin tried to have Dale Scott rubbed out is in the Golenbock book and has jarred some readers, but I'd seen enough material on Martin that it didn't strike me as implausible.

The "Billy Martin's All-Time All-Horrible Lineup" was surprisingly difficult to put together. For one, there were so many candidates. You could, unfortunately, put together team after team of people who led or participated in massacres. Whether Hirohito belongs here rather than, say, Tojo is up for debate, but since Martin named him, in he goes. I put Genghis Khan in because I imagine that Martin would admire his hell-bent thirst for conquest even if he wasn't a contemporary. If you don't think LeMay belongs here, you haven't read enough history books.

Also, it's hard to figure out where to play them. I tried to assign positions using standard baseball logic (you want smaller, faster guys up the middle, for instance), but in the end it's probably not ideal, and Martin would certainly adjust it after seeing his players and watching them go through drills.

Steroids

The story of Steve Wilstein, the AP writer who saw the andro in McGwire's locker (which it now seems as if it may have been a decoy to distract from McGwire's use of illegal steroids) and was the object of Tony LaRussa's wrath is told in several places, but Howard Bryant's *Juicing the Game* does a good job putting it within the larger history of steroids. Bryant's book is a good overview of the growth of steroids in the game, though imperfect and perhaps overly friendly to "the Crusaders."

There are many sources for stories about teams supplying amphetamines to their players, particularly in the form of "leaded" and "unleaded" coffee.

For information on Canseco, there was his error-ridden and, unfortunately, truth-bearing 2005 book, *Juiced: Wild Times, Rampant 'Roids, Smash Hits, and How Baseball Got Big,* and his many media appearances.

The number of players who tested positive (or refused tests, which counted as a positive) has been rumored in recent BALCO-related coverage to be as high as 100, which would still mean there were an average of only three positive tests or refusals per team in a year when there was no reason not to continue using.

For information on MLB's drug policy before it became part of the collective bargaining agreement, I read MLB's memos on the SABR Business of Baseball Web site, and read Marvin Miller's *A Whole Different Ball Game: The Sport and Business of Baseball* and all the commissioner biographies from Kuhn to Selig. Also, many articles offered information on baseball's drug policy when Ueberroth tried to impose mandatory testing in 1986.

I'm entirely serious when I write that Ueberroth botched an opportunity. At the time, though the public concern was centered on cocaine, working out a strong drug policy that included testing would have provided a framework that could have been expanded over time to cope with steroids and other threats. It's worth noting that while firm numbers aren't available, contemporary sources indicate that a majority of players signed contracts with their clubs that included drug-testing clauses. The clauses were thrown out, since drug testing had to be bargained collectively, but it's fair to say that even in the mid-'80s, a large contingent of players were willing to submit to testing.

Had Ueberroth handled the situation better, baseball could have forged a cooperative relationship with the union and built a drug policy for the future — and we might have avoided the strikes and lockouts of the next two decades to boot. What a missed opportunity.

Jeff Shaw is a real Fulbright scholar. That's not part of the joke or anything.

Index

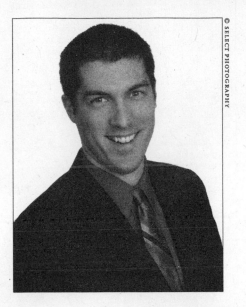

Derek Zumsteg is the coauthor of five editions of the best-selling *Baseball Prospectus* annual and runs the most popular baseball Web site ever, U.S.S. Mariner. He won the title of World's Smartest Human in 2004, was named the 101st most beautiful person for three consecutive years by *People* magazine, and climbed Mount Everest twice in one year to show Jon Krakauer what's up. He also contributes to ESPN.com and cheats at baseball, football, basketball, golf, poker, and his author bio.